THE

STORY

SWALLOWTAIL PUBLISHING

The Authors

Keith and Monika Domone have had an unhealthy interest in music in general, and Barclay James Harvest in particular, for a combined total of over fifty years. Most of their spare time is spent in running the band's fan club, web site, mail-order business and other assorted BJH-related activities. Taking their cue from football fanzines, they've represented the fans' viewpoint, and in the process annoyed managers, agents and players alike. They even met each other through Barclay James Harvest, but insist that they don't hold it against the band. They claim to have a life outside BJH, citing in their defence Keith's career as an Air Traffic Controller and Monika's as an Export Supervisor, followed by the full-time job of looking after their two children, Ian and Stephanie. They live in Hampshire with a cat called Scruffy (whose mother just happened to belong to John and Olwen Lees). The prosecution rests its case.

Special Thanks

Woolly Wolstenholme; John Lees; Les Holroyd; Mel Pritchard - much missed; Madge Liles; Kev Goodman; Lindsay Brown; David Walker; David and Ditas Rohl; Edna Krischer; Olwen Lees; Sue Foulston; David Taylor; Peter Kendall; Martin Lawrence; Ian Southerington; Martyn Ford; Rodney Matthews; Lawrence Moore; Jill Wolstenholme; Mark and Vicky Powell, Alex Rose; Tim Chacksfield; Joe Black; Alan Freeman; John Peel; Kevin McAlea; Colin Browne; Craig Fletcher; Kevin Whitehead; Jeff Leach; Kim Turner; Steve Broomhead; Mike Byron-Hehir; Ian Wilson; Steve Butler; Roy Martin; Chris Jago; Trevor Worman; Nigel and Dawn Banks; Paul Cox.

First edition published in 2005 by Swallowtail Publishing,
Hamble Reach, Oslands Lane, Lower Swanwick, Southampton, SO31 7EG

Contents

Introduction

In the glamorous but shallow alternative reality which is the world of popular music, Barclay James Harvest have always been unlikely contenders. Quiet and unassuming, they have never been a part of the mainstream, but have nevertheless survived as a band for over a quarter of a century, whilst many better-known or more fashionable contemporaries have fallen by the wayside. Their name is not even widely known in their own country, yet they have sold millions of records worldwide and command the kind of fiercely devoted following of which most artists can only dream. Critical reactions have rarely been favourable, with some going so far as to berate the band's audience for enjoying their music.

Faced with such hostility, aficionados of the band have a choice - keep their heads down and pretend to go along with the received wisdom that all seventies rock music was pompous, self-indulgent nonsense, or ignore fashion and follow the music which means something to them, much as the band themselves have done. The sensible decision was obviously to stay in the closet, so we sat down to write this book. In the process we have conducted numerous interviews with the band members and other key players in the story, attended dozens of concerts and collected a vast archive of records, press cuttings and memorabilia from four decades.

In addition to including much background information which has not appeared in previous accounts of the band, the book will, we hope, also throw some light on the reasons for Barclay James Harvest's longevity and enduring popularity. Anyone who is curious about the workings of the music business may find it of interest, but primarily it is aimed at those like ourselves who have experienced that inspirational moment whilst listening to an album or a live performance, that spark of genius which changed them in an instant from cool, detached observers into dedicated Barclay James Harvest fans.

Keith and Monika Domone, August 2005

1

Where It All Began

Even music lovers born and bred in southern England have to concede that the north-west of our country seems to have produced more than its fair share of fine music, from The Beatles, who for many started it all, in an unbroken line through to heroes of more recent times like The Stone Roses and Oasis. For young lads growing up in Oldham, noted chiefly as the centre of Britain's cotton industry, and becoming teenagers before the sixties began to swing, the chances of finding fame and fortune must have seemed slim indeed. Within a few years, everything had changed: The Beatles were the catalyst, of course, partly because their music inspired a generation of would-be musicians, but, probably more importantly, because they proved that a bunch of working-class lads with broad northern accents and little in the way of formal qualifications could, given talent, self-belief and not a little luck, escape from the daily grind and have the world at their feet. Small wonder, then, that many were determined to follow where they led.

One such was John Lees, born on January 13th, 1947 in Bargap Road in Oldham. Fred and Martha Lees' youngest child, John followed his sister Edna to Beever Street Junior School, where she was two years ahead of him, having been born on Christmas Eve 1944.

Passionate about music from a very early age, John Lees took up guitar at the age of fourteen, strumming a cheap acoustic instrument in his bedroom, before moving on to

Edna Lees in the Junior 4 school photo, together with her classmate John ("Jack") Crowther, who will also have an important part to play in this story ...

his first solid electric guitar, a plastic-bodied Futurama 3. Some of his classmates at Beever Street Junior School were also learning to play musical instruments, and John lost no time in forming a band. Bassist Dave Taylor takes up the story:

"John and I were at junior school together and we lived a few hundred yards apart in Oldham. John had this plastic Futurama guitar, I had nothing but a very basic understanding of music from lessons at school. I decided a bass guitar was going to be easier than one of those proper guitars with all them there strings on them and I found a Bill Wyman-style Framus in a junk shop. At the same time, Norman Clark, another Beever Street boy living in the same area, turned up with a plastic bass, probably a Futurama, and there was a view that two basses in a band might be quite novel. I didn't have much say in the matter as I was still learning to play the Framus from sheet music. At the same time another Beever Street boy, Pete Dombavand, acquired a set of drums. I say a set; it was a random assortment of percussion including a bass drum that was probably about four feet in diameter and had probably accompanied many a marching brass band, very dented cymbals that I guess may have been quite good, I also seem to remember some skulls. So you now have the original line up of a band with no name: John Lees, David Taylor, Norman Clark and Pete Dombavand."

Junior 1 at Beever Street School.
Top row, left - John Lees
Bottom row, right - Pete Dombavand

The band's speciality at this stage was rock and roll of the Eddie Cochran variety. John, having moved on to Breeze Hill Secondary Modern school, remained the prime mover musically, as well as instigating most of the personnel changes. The next addition was a distant relative of his, Duncan Watt, who had a guitar and actually knew his chords, and at around the same

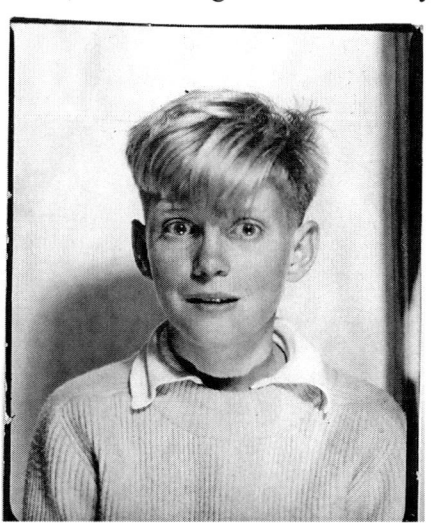

time it was decided that two basses in a band wasn't actually such a great idea. Dave Taylor had now acquired a Burns solid bass and a degree of competence, so Norman Cook was ejected from the band with no name. It was Dave who came up with the name The Sorcerers, suggesting that they start each session with *The Sorcerer's Apprentice*. Although that never happened, the name stuck.

John pictured whilst on holiday on the Isle of Man at about the age of 10

Times had been hard for most people in England between the wars, and Fred and Martha Lees were keen for their children to enjoy the education which they had had to forfeit at a time when only the well-heeled could afford to go to grammar schools or college. They were therefore delighted to find that John had an artistic bent, and provided support and encouragement when he wanted to go on from Breeze Hill to further his studies. Quiet and sometimes moody, John was idealistic and possessed of a self-belief which would stand him in good stead in the years to come. Whilst he was, by his own admission, not a model pupil, he did excel at art (but not music!), and was duly accepted for a course in commercial art by Oldham School Of Art.

There John found Ray Murphy, who owned a drum kit that looked like a drum kit, whilst Ray looked like Charlie Watts, was good fun and did a great impersonation of Mick Jagger. Pete Dombavand found himself redundant and the Sorcerers became John Lees, David Taylor, Duncan Watt and Ray Murphy. Also at Art School, John met Stuart "Woolly" Wolstenholme (born in the Boundary Park area of Oldham on 15th April, 1947) and the pair quickly became friends. Woolly, in his own words, "got roped in as a sort of tambourinist and 'singist'" with The Sorcerers. Woolly shared John's idealism, and his quickfire wit and more extrovert personality made him a natural frontman, leaving John free to concentrate on his guitar playing. By now the blues was the thing to play, so the band changed their name to reflect what they fondly imagined was their pure blues music, and became The Blues Keepers. There was another band around at the time called The Undertakers who eventually became The Takers and The Blues Keepers name was likewise abbreviated to The Keepers.

On 15th November, 1964, The Keepers played their biggest gig to date - a talent show ("Beat Contest") at the Oldham Empire Theatre. The judges were DJ Jimmy Savile, actors John Alderton and Jill Browne from the TV hospital drama series *Emergency Ward 10* and Ray Jones (guitarist with Billy J. Kramer

— ON STAGE —

EMPIRE THEATRE - OLDHAM

SUNDAY, 15th NOVEMBER, 1964 AT 7 p.m.

OLDHAM
'BEAT' CONTEST

Proceeds to the Mayor of Oldham's Appeal in aid of the
"President Kennedy Memorial Appeal" organised by the
Oldham Round Table

Featuring

THE DIABLOS - THE T.K. 5 - THE KEEPERS
THE MISSING LINKS - THE BLUE ANGELS
T.N.T. AND THE DYNAMITES
THE VOODOOS - THE MODROXS
THE HEADLINERS - THE EXILES '3'

PROGRAMME SIXPENCE

4. THE KEEPERS
STEWART WOLSTENHOLME — Vocals
DAVE TAYLOR — Bass Guitar
RAY MURPHY — Drums
JOHN LEES — Lead Guitar
DUNCAN WATT — Rhythm Guitar

and The Dakotas). Backstage, the band found some hats lying around from a previous production, and were clowning around trying them on when the compere came in. Then it was their turn to perform, and they were introduced as "the band with the funny hats", but Dave Taylor was in difficulties:

"We were set up behind the curtain, Jimmy Saddle (my daughter's name for him) comes along, shakes our hands (one hand each that is) and then the light goes out on my amp. I try a note. Nothing. Shit. Panic. Someone grabs my amp mains plug and jiggles it. The light comes back on. I have sound. One of the songs we did was 'Da Do Ron Ron' (Met her on a Monday and my heart stood still, Da do ron ron, da do ron ron etc. etc.). I sang the harmony. In those days our equipment was really basic. We had no monitor speakers. We could not hear what we were creating. All the time we were on stage, the audience were throwing old pennies at us. Jeeeeez but they hurt. And they didn't half chip the varnish on the guitars. John was okay; his was plastic. At the end Fred Lees, John's dad, reckoned it was crap and it was all my fault. The others agreed. Bastards."

The Keepers were allotted two numbers, the other being another cover version, of "You Can't Judge A Book By The Cover" (originally by Bo Diddley). The judges, like the audience, were insufficiently impressed for them to win the contest. That honour went to Ven Tracey and The Diablos. And where are they now?

The band with the funny hats at the Oldham Empire. From left to right, Woolly Wolstenholme, John Lees and Dave Taylor ham it up whilst Jill Browne autographs Woolly's tambourine.

Undaunted by this temporary setback, The Keepers continued to develop their musical skills at live gigs. Whilst Ray Murphy tended to hit the drums louder and louder as the night went on, and occasionally had problems in keeping time, John was becoming a proficient guitarist, progressing from his

Futurama 3 (which Woolly bought from him for six Pounds. "What a rip-off!" - WW) via a Burns Trisonic (later stolen) and a Harmony Stratotone Jupiter to his first Fender Stratocaster, the instrument with which he would have a life-long love affair. Woolly, in the meantime, moved on from tambourine and vocals to harmonica and eventually to guitar and keyboards. Although his initial role in the band was somewhat nebulous, it soon became clear that he had a real creative talent and artistic vision, which would make him a perfect foil for John.

John and Woolly studied not only commercial art, but also the visual arts, poetry, prose and drama. An early joint venture was a stage play entitled "The Crimson Coconut", a comedy spy thriller set in Bradford, starring John as Robert, the doddering waiter in Spaghetti's restaurant, and Woolly as detective Jack Pincher, who eventually gets his man (and the girl). The eponymous coconut is actually a bomb planted by anarchist ruffians Madame Gliserinski and her husband Nitro. Robert mistakes the bomb for a ballcock and eventually defuses it by the simple expedient of dropping it into a bucket of water.

Above: "The Crimson Coconut", starring Stuart Wolstenholme (second from right) and John Lees (fourth from right, in waistcoat).

"What do you mean, I've failed the audition for The Byrds?" (Woolly around the age of seventeen).

The Keepers continued for a while after John and Woolly left college and went to work (both as commercial artists), playing cover versions of their favourite songs of the day. The Keepers were going nowhere, though, and when it was discovered that the hapless Ray Murphy couldn't reproduce the drum part for "You Really Got Me", it was the beginning of the end. It's a cruel world, rock and roll...

Lacking a drum front for The Blues Keepers, Woolly recalls finding a piece of card in the street, printed with "Johnson's Steel Wire Lattice". This was pressed into service, but led to some confusion about the name of the band, culminating in them being advertised at one gig as Bob Johnson's Blues Seekers!

Meanwhile, two other lads from Oldham were also showing early promise, though not always of the musical kind. Les Holroyd (Richard Leslie Holroyd, born March 12th, 1948) and Mel Pritchard (Melvyn Paul Pritchard, born January 20th, 1948), both attended Derker School in Oldham. Mel showed a flair for sports like football and cricket, but also demonstrated his musical leanings at an early age when he borrowed his father's ukulele-banjo. Unimpressed with the sounds it made, he removed the strings and hit it instead, producing a much more satisfying noise. Les, on the other hand, excelled in

A school production of HMS Pinafore, with Les Holroyd second from right.
Below: the Derker Junior school cricket team of 1959, including Mel Pritchard (top row, second from right).

Art, and also taught himself music, starting with Spanish guitar when he was ten years of age. Les and Mel became firm friends, and their shared interest in music continued after school and led to them playing in a band, Heart And Soul And The Wickeds, who began to gain a reputation locally as a live act. Like The Keepers, Heart and Soul and The Wickeds performed on a semi-professional basis whilst working at full-time jobs in the daytime, Les initially as a shop assistant at Harry Fenton's Menswear then at a carpet shop called Lees Higginbottom and Mel as a central heating engineer.

In 1966, The Wickeds' lead guitarist left the band in order to study, eventually going on to become a teacher. Les and Mel were left high and dry. However, having seen John Lees performing with The Keepers, Les and Mel realised that he would fit the bill perfectly, and turned up on his doorstep one evening to approach him to fill the gap.

Coincidentally, he and Woolly had just fallen out with the other members of their own band, but John was unwilling to go on his own without Woolly, so he said, "Yes, I'll do it, but you have to have him as well."! So it was that in September 1966 they decided to amalgamate the remnants of The Keepers and Heart and Soul and The Wickeds to form a new six-piece group. As they were into playing the r'n'b music now becoming fashionable, they adopted The Blues Keepers name again. Covering material from the likes of Jimmy Reid and old Louisiana rag blues, they were the most authentic blues band in Oldham. It was, said Les wryly in a 1975 interview, "really earthy, depressing stuff" - that would have made a romantic backdrop for a number of weddings which were amongst their early gigs! Ray Murphy, Duncan Watt and Dave Taylor carried on for a while on their own, playing local gigs at clubs like the Human Jungle, or Image as it later became, and Dave even remembers standing in for Les once at that venue after the split.

In the spring of 1967 Edna's old classmate, John Crowther, who had by now gone into business and owned a clothes boutique, saw the new line-up of The Blues Keepers play live at a private party in Greenfield. He was interested in bringing together the worlds of fashion and pop music, and liked the band's music enough firstly to book them to play a number of gigs, and secondly to become their manager. By this stage, the group had been reduced to five members: Les, Mel, John, Woolly and singer Rod Buckley (Rodney James Buckley) from the Wickeds. Rod's stage name was Rod Graham, and at one time the band was billed for live shows as "Rod Graham's Blues Keepers". Crowther, sometimes known affectionately as "Joe Crow", had just bought a dilapidated eighteenth century farmhouse

John's sister Edna designed and hand-painted the paisley shop front, business stationery and logo (opposite) for GO Boutique as early as October 1966, before John Crowther got involved with the group.

Dave Taylor
spins the discs
at the Image
club shortly
after the break
up of the
original
Keepers

called Preston House, which had been converted from an old coaching inn just off the route that is now the main A62 road between Oldham and Huddersfield. He had intended to renovate it and live there with his wife, Christine, but he saw the potential in The Blues Keepers and one evening he invited them round for a meeting at his "Go Boutique" in a converted terraced house in Oldham. Here he outlined his vision of the band's future, with financial backing and equipment including musical instruments and a small blue van provided by himself. In return, he expected the members of the band to turn professional and leave their homes to live and rehearse in Preston House, whilst he and his wife stayed with his parents.

After (not!) much agonising, the band accepted his offer and made the decision to leave their day jobs and turn fully professional. The decision was not universally popular: shortly

17

John at his parents' new home in Greenside Avenue, Oldham, shortly before leaving for Preston House in June 1967

afterwards, John's father Fred said, with masterly understatement:- "I thought they were puddled, I thought they wanted their 'eads feelin'. Their mother was a bit perturbed, too, but once they've got it into their 'eads, there's nothing you can do about it, really." John's parents were in fact more than "a bit perturbed" - his father, a rather short-tempered and impulsive man, told John that if he left home then he wasn't to come back! His mother, on the other hand, always the diplomat, told him that he would be welcome back at any time if things didn't work out.

So it was that in June 1967 the band and their furniture arrived bit by bit at Preston House, Lower Standedge in Diggle, high up on the windswept moors at Saddleworth. One room was designated as a rehearsal area, and the largest room became a kind of dormitory, with five beds laid out in line. Les was given the bed under the window, furthest from the door, as he had a reputation for sleeping a lot. Next was John, with Mel in the middle, then Woolly and finally Rod by the door. Rod was a keen cook, so he was quickly placed in charge of the culinary arrangements. They lost no time in investigating the local pubs, and soon became familiar faces in "The Horse And Jockey", "The Hanging Gate", "The Diggle Hotel" and "The Navigation" (from which they were once barred for being rowdy!). None of the band could drive at the time; Pete Young was briefly engaged by John Crowther for the purpose, but was soon replaced by Jim Tetlow, who became their driver, roadie and general minder. The two vital qualities which got him the job were firstly, that he was free to travel with the band, even to very early gigs abroad, for example in Spain, and, secondly, that he lived two hundred yards from Preston House.

Les wrote his first ever original song around this time; "I'm The One Who's Loving You", composed on a 'cello, was, says Les, "a sort of McCartney-type ballad".

```
            I'M  THE  ONE  WHO'S  LOVING  YOU
            ***********************************

    Your mind is filled with sweet ideas,
    You ought to look.
    I read your thoughts my dear, as
    As though they're an opened book.
    You aren't satisfied, to live on your own,
    Your going to change them all, and turn yourself to stone.
    You can't leave me behind,
    I'm the one who's loving you.

    Your eyes are filled with gentleness,
    I ought to know,
    I see them in their tenderness,
    Oh, please don't go.
    You should be kind to me, as I am to you,
    My dear can't you see you can't say we're through,
    You can't leave me behind,
    I'm the one who's loving you.

    I see the day when you'll appear,
    With tears aflood,
    You'll turn to me and cry,
    My dear, I'm misunderstood,
    You won't realize, that your world has gone,
    You can't live again, in this other one,
    I won't leave you behind,
    I'm the  one who's loving you.
```

The original typewritten lyrics for Les's first song.

As they rehearsed, the band decided that they wanted to perform more of their own original compositions as well as the cover versions that had been staples of their live performances to date, and therefore that a new band name would be appropriate. They admired the music and the 'flowery' names of the American west-coast psychedelic bands like Buffalo Springfield, Quicksilver Messenger Service and Jefferson Airplane, and they wanted an exotic-sounding soubriquet to get away from the more mundane English group names like The Who, The Move, The Kinks etc. Here's John's version of how the name came about, from an interview with a Dutch radio station in 1984: "We decided to write down everybody's ideas on bits of paper and fold them up and pull 'em out, and we were going "Oh, no, we can't have that!" and throwing them on the fire, and they were the last three and the guy said, "That's it, whatever comes out now we're having." The first one that came out was 'James' and it was the name of a guy that was at the time singing with the group, and he did actually get elbowed, and he was called Rodney James and he'd put his name in which was the 'James'. Somebody had written - it might have been either me or Woolly - 'Harvest' because of the farmhouse, and I'd definitely written 'Barclays' because of Barclays Bank, expecting to make some money! It sort of got arranged until it sounded right: Barclay James Harvest." Mel said later that at the time he thought, "Oh well, that'll last for a month at the most."

Amongst the suggestions in the hat that didn't make it were "Barney McCooey" and "Great Western" (the name of another local pub).

As John said, there was a price to pay; Crowther felt that the group, already reduced to five members, would be better off without Rod Buckley, who duly received his marching orders. Such high-handed interference from managers was common in those times - there is an obvious parallel with Pete Best and The Beatles - and, whilst the surviving members of the band allowed him to act thus in their names, they were probably too relieved that it wasn't them to voice any protest. His cooking duties were taken over in part by Norma Tetlow, Jim's wife.

So Barclay James Harvest was born in September 1967, and made its public debut under the new name at Middleton Baths in North Manchester. Life at Preston House was no romantic rural idyll: John Crowther described the place as "a dump", whilst, according to Mel in a 1972 interview with Zig Zag magazine, "all we did was sit around, get stoned and do nothing. We used to

Woolly puts his artistic talent to good use, designing the band's first business cards

rehearse in the barn, but it was hardly the period of creative seclusion that you hear about from other groups. We used to put all our gig money into a kitty and it always went on food - there was never enough over to buy clothes with or anything like that." There was little in the way of heating or home comforts, and privacy was a problem, as well, since the rooms were divided up with draped sheets! The members of the band received 12/6d (about 52p) per week "pocket money" and didn't go out much, but generally returned to their parents' homes in Oldham at weekends. With no TV or radio, they wrote and rehearsed in complete isolation and played local club gigs for around twelve to fifteen pounds a time. Their repertoire still incorporated cover versions such as a number of songs from Love's classic *Forever Changes* album (a great favourite at Preston House), Tim Hardin's "Lady Came From Baltimore" and "Black Sheep Boy", "Dangling Conversation" by Paul Simon, The Incredible String

Preston House, Diggle, in more recent times (completely renovated!)

Band's "Painting Box" and The Moody Blues' "Nights In White Satin", a song which appears frequently in this story. However, the covers were increasingly making way for their own songs such as "Mr. Sunshine", "Brother Thrush", "Eden Unobtainable" and "Dark Now My Sky". Their stage act was enlivened with strange costumes and practical jokes: on one occasion, it was announced over the P.A. that the band were unable to appear, but had arranged for a replacement group of old fogeys who arrived on stage in flat caps and overcoats to play some "17th Century Musik". Just as the audience was getting ready to leave, the 'old men' whipped off their jackets and disguises to reveal BJH in their more recognisable T-shirts! They would occasionally dress in mediaeval gear and incorporated cello, oboe, French horn, recorder and glockenspiel into their act - instruments not generally associated with rock music.

John Crowther's persuasive skills are evidenced by the fact that he managed to convince the local secretarial college to get their students to type out all of the band's song lyrics for nothing - just for the practice! He also facilitated the first Barclay James Harvest recordings - Woolly takes up the story:

"The Keepers had previously made some tapes on John Lees' father's Grundig

Bath time at Preston House - 'Ee, by gum, I know times were 'ard, but four in a bath?'

tape machine, but when we arrived at Preston House we had no means of committing our work to posterity. John Crowther produced a Uher Report L recorder (mono, a bit of a poor man's Nagra) and almost as though we were paralleling the history of recorded music we set up the (one) mike and clustered around - if you were too loud in the soundscape you'd move back; too quiet, forward - and although it was useful to hear ourselves it was no more than an aid to songwriting. The next step - get thee to a studio! Eroica Studios (named after the Beethoven Symphony) were run in a semi-grand house in Cheshire (?) by a gentleman who must have been nonplussed by these "oiks" polluting his world. There were many asides during recording:-

Bloke: "Do you sing?"

Mel: "No."

Bloke: "Good. I don't like drummers who sing."

Bloke (re. "The Poet"'s bowed Epiphone bass): "That sounds like an Elizabethan viol."

Les: "It may sound vile to you, but it's our bread and butter!"

At the end of the session we asked for the tapes, but the man said we couldn't have them! A big kerfuffle ensued until he said we'd get an acetate disc instead. It could have been very nasty!" The studio owner liked the music, though, saying that it was "Not a (Beethoven's) 4th sound - but a star!"

At these sessions the band recorded eight songs for what became known, not unreasonably, as *The Eroica Album* (or *Fourth Star* after the comment above). The recordings are primitive, as you would expect, and the songs themselves are often naive and derivative, but they have a period charm as well as (with the benefit of hindsight, admittedly) hinting at original talent and the glorious music to come. The first side kicks off with John's "Is That OK?", the one surviving song from the earliest days of writing. It's a very lightweight song in an almost vaudeville style (no trace of the blues here); "Someday" and "Absent Friends" are rather melancholy slower songs from Les and are followed by an early incarnation of "The Poet". The trademark BJH harmonies are already beginning to appear, and John is featured on recorder. Side 2 opens with a piano-based instrumental by Les called, er, "Joanna", then there's "1923", a jolly little Woolly piece wherein he suggests that, "It would be so nice" to go back in time and "see the things that Mum and Dad once knew". "In The Rain" could be The Hollies in depressed mood, whilst "What A Fool" is a rockier Woolly lament for a lost love. Most of the songs were written with particular artists in mind, and were thus rather derivative; the band had yet to develop their own style at this formative stage.

Very early compositions which were lost (perhaps fortunately) included "How Bill Won The Race", "Mobile Shop" (?!), "The London Psychofrenzic", a song about an orchestra and "Freda, The Singing Dame" ...

Their first break came along almost immediately, when they provided some music for *This England: Living For A Change*, a short film made for Granada TV. The subject was the changing face of Oldham as seen through the eyes of young millworkers, and the film included a clip of the band playing live in John Crowther's *Go* boutique. Director Lawrence Moore explains how it came about:

"The film was my first for TV after leaving the Royal College of Art. The executive producer, one Denis Mitchell, had met John Crowther on the London train. He told me about this and said it would make a good film, as he was starting a boutique and wanted to make Oldham the Carnaby Street of the North. So I met this rather bumptious, but likeable character at his Dad's

First publicity shot with something even bigger than a Mellotron (and Jasper the dog ...)

butcher's shop. We then went round the corner to where he was kitting out his boutique with all the latest Mary Quant-style minis and striped blouses. Great, I thought. I'll have a dancing sequence set here, and also around the mills (which were still standing in those days). "You'll need some music then.." was the instant reply. "Music? Well, guess I will." I said somewhat hesitantly. "I've got a group, just come together...why not come and hear them?"

"Uh, well, I DO have my own music notions, John...."

"Ah - but this is a genuine NORTHERN group, not your pansy southern stuff." The thing about John was that it was impossible to refuse him - must be that Oldham doggedness or something. So with Merete, my researcher, I set out for the upper reaches of the Yorkshire moors, but due to six foot high snow drifts, we had to abandon our car a few hundred yards from the farmhouse where we were to meet the Lads, as John called them. We crunched through the drifts wishing we'd stayed in the nice warm studio, and staggered towards the granite-grey farmhouse. There seemed no sign of life. We looked at each other. The wrong place? We clambered over more drifts blocking a barn door, and pushed our way in. As we did this a blast of sound erupted from within. "Bloody HELL!" I swore to Merete - "where'd they get the power?"

We turned a stone corner, and there, arranged around a stack of amps and speakers were these four characters done up to the nines in what looked like Regency costumes completely ignoring us and powering away with a great bit of music. They finished and we applauded in a tasteful sort of way, and I remember that Woolly took the lead - "OK, we'll let you know - now next time, we'll expect more of you..." Cheeky bugger! Well, of course, the music and their humour won the day. That and touring several Mancunian micro studios to record a piece for the film. "Mr Sunshine" I think it was!! Apt given the weather. There was great debate about the name of the group. Several were bandied about - we were privy to some of the process. Woolly said - "How about Barclay James Harvest?"

"What??!!" I exclaimed, then guffawed. "You'll NEVER get anywhere with a handle like that!!" Just goes to show that I would never have made a promoter.."

Moore was sufficiently impressed to make a second short film with BJH, this time with the spotlight firmly on the band and their lifestyle. Transmitted on 16th April, 1968 on an evening magazine programme, *Scene: Early Morning* had no commentary, allowing the black and white footage of Preston House and recordings of three songs, "Early Morning", "Washing Up Dishes" (a jokey vaudeville-style number) and "Mr. Sunshine" to speak for themselves. To record the music for the film, the band hired a Mellotron, a huge, unwieldy keyboard instrument which used spools of tape to reproduce sounds such as an orchestra. At the time, very few bands were using Mellotrons, the most notable exponents being The Beatles (e.g. "Strawberry Fields") and The Moody Blues.

Another business card

The Birmingham dealer from whom they had hired the instrument was surprised when they were the first customers who wanted to tune it, and asked if they'd like to buy it - they got not only a good deal, but also a very distinctive sound which would rapidly become the band's trademark. Fans regard the instrument with huge affection even today, although those who had to stop them going out of tune, to play them and to transport an instrument which literally weighed a ton don't have quite such rose-tinted memories!

Although none of the band members had affluent backgrounds, having a wealthy sponsor sometimes misled people into thinking that they were rich kids playing at rock and roll, an image a million miles away from the reality of their spartan lifestyle.

However, John Crowther's patronage also gave them a taste of another world, as Les recalls:

"I can remember playing a gig in Londerzeel with the Nice, so that must be '68 or something like that. Our manager at the time had a Ferrari, and I remember driving from Ostend to Londerzeel in this Ferrari doing about 150 miles an hour -a Ferrari "Superfast" - and it was!". The misapprehension also opened unexpected doors for them: "It did get us some cool gigs. We did the Oxford University May Ball. Great fun!"

The world was a larger place in the late sixties, and there were cultural differences to trap the unwary, even within Europe. BJH were delighted to be invited to play in Scandinavia, and launched into their opening number with gusto. Finishing with a flourish, they were somewhat unnerved to receive no response whatsoever - total silence. Undeterred, they played on, working even harder to win over this new audience. Rows of impassive faces and folded arms greeted their efforts, no matter how well they played. Somehow they managed to make it through to the end of the set and with a furious "F*** you!" stormed off stage. Thunderous applause.

"What the ...?"

Light dawned as the promoter explained that in his country it was considered very rude to applaud between songs, until the performance was over, and that rapt attention - in silence - was how one showed appreciation.

"Ah. Er ... guess we'd better do an encore, then".

Several encores later the cultural divide was finally bridged to everybody's satisfaction ...

After just a few months at Preston House, John met his future wife, Olwen Margaret Rider. In 1981, he told German magazine *Bravo* how it came about: "I got to know my wife Olwen near our home village. At the time she enjoyed horse riding in her spare time. One day she risked a jump over a fence; the horse stumbled, and she fell out of the saddle. By chance I was nearby, and helped her to catch the horse." Serendipity, indeed. When John and Olwen first started to go out, they frequently went as a threesome with Olwen's friend Christine Roberts. They introduced Christine and Les to each other, and soon they, too, were a couple. As John and Olwen's relationship developed, the lack of privacy and comfort at the farmhouse became more of a problem, but Olwen's parents came to the rescue by inviting him to go and live at the nearby family home, Sherbrooke Hall. For John, it marked one of his most creative periods; "Mocking Bird", "Pools Of Blue" and "Galadriel" were all written whilst he was living with the Riders, and John first played "Mocking Bird" to Olwen as early as April or May 1968. After her A-levels, Olwen went to work for John Crowther, learning the fashion business and starting to design clothes.

By the beginning of 1968 the members of the band had written around thirty original songs, and John Crowther had negotiated a publishing deal with Ardmore and Beechwood Ltd., who boasted The Beatles and, er, Rolf Harris amongst their other artists. A demonstration "LP" was put together, the idea being for the publishers to 'tout' an LP of the Barclays' songs around record companies, hoping to get established artists to record them. The tracks were mainly recorded above Nield and Hardy's music shop in Stockport, at Peter Tattersall's Inter-City Studios (later to become the first incarnation of Strawberry Studios). The

Inter-City Studios circa 1967

sessions were supervised by the man from Ardmore and Beechwood, Jonathan Peel. The latter, according to Woolly, "was immensely tall, and it always took too long for the rhythm of a piece to reach his feet - he would have made a great drummer."! The resulting vinyl LP, known as *The Ardmore and Beechwood Album,* comprised eleven original compositions, (plus, bizarrely, a completely unrelated instrumental called "Monday Mood", by jazzman Ray Davies) and saw Woolly dominating the writing credits on a set of songs which sound much more assured and fresh. Woolly's "Come Back To Me" gets proceedings underway in energetic fashion and an early version of "Mr. Sunshine" is very similar to the released version. "Am I Right" is more of a throwback, a jaunty Woolly song including lots of "fa-la-las" in the chorus and a lyric which can't, in all honesty, be described as amongst his best. There's also a number of false endings with some very uncertain percussion which may or may not have been intended as a joke... On the plus side, it's very short! By way of contrast, "State Of Mind" is classic Woolly: sounding like one of Tim Hardin's more introspective moments, it's a fine song about loneliness set off by some beautiful cello and recorder. "The Fool" opens with an idiosyncratic rhythm and some unusual electric guitar, before a melodic chorus concerned with Woolly's regular preoccupation of star-crossed love. John's guitar solo at the end is a trifle tentative, but there is definitely a touch of that style and slightly distorted sound that would make his playing instantly recognisable in the seventies. For "I'll Be Back" it's heads down, no nonsense boogie time, with Woolly's vocal backed up by some scorching guitar rifts which are very like those on "Taking Some Time On" and "Too Much On Your Plate". Shades of Clapton in his days with Cream. Side 2 of the LP kicks off with "For The Loving Of", a guitar-led rocker from John, with Woolly handling the lead vocal. The song extols the virtues of living a loving life, and the overall feel is very late-sixties psychedelia, but the harmonies in the chorus are pure BJH. On "It's Better If I Don't See You" Les's voice is instantly recognisable on a bitter-sweet tale of love thwarted by what the singer sees as an insurmountable age gap. Happily, it ends on a positive note with him vowing to wait for her. On "Up With The Sun" it's back to Woolly for a very up-tempo rocker powered by riffing guitar and a thunderous rhythm section. At this stage of the band's development, they could easily have become a heavy rock outfit if these early

The fabulously rare Ardmore and Beechwood LP

glimpses are anything to go by. However, it's the strength of the songs and melodies which really stands out. "Sarah" is a lovely ballad from Woolly, underpinned by Les's 'cello. The song was one of a number of compositions written by the group members for a concept called *The Birds Of Britain*, based around girls whom the band had known (though not necessarily in the Biblical sense!). Finally, "Senses" is a joint composition with a lot of input from Mel. Woolly takes lead vocals, but John and Les are clearly audible on the harmonies which are now becoming a regular feature. There's a definite Beatles influence at work here, with the main melody having something in common with "A Day In The Life".

Woolly's artwork for an imaginary debut single of "Come Back To Me" backed with John's composition, "For The Loving Of"

John Crowther began to make the first approaches to record companies on behalf of the band: Decca were interested, and paid for a recording session where the band performed "Death Of A City", "The Poet" and "For The Loving Of". Decca's in-house producer, Wayne Bickerton, was very keen on the band, and although Decca eventually missed out in the race to sign them, Bickerton would still have a part to play later in the band's story. One annoying side effect of this interest from the band's viewpoint at the time, though, was that they temporarily lost the rights to issue the songs recorded for Decca - "For The Loving Of" never officially reappeared, "The Poet" was shelved for three years and, in the case of "Death Of A City" it would be another thirteen years before it was released! It was also around this time that the group made their first attempt at recording "Pools Of Blue", one of John's favourite compositions which, sadly, the band never managed to capture to his own satisfaction. Crowther also arranged for them to record some demos for John Burgess at EMI, comprising "Words And The Way" (a Les song with some fine Beatles-style harmonies), "Early Morning", "Mr. Sunshine" and "Sarah". EMI were sufficiently impressed to offer a one-off deal for a single, so on Valentine's Day, 1968, Barclay James Harvest went into Chappell Studios in London's Bond Street and recorded "Early Morning" and "Mr. Sunshine". Under the "lease-tape" contract, EMI released the single, but the band did not sign to the company, and had to pay their own recording costs. "Early Morning" was the song selected as the A-side: a genuine group effort in the writing, Woolly admits that it was a conscious attempt to capture the 'feel' of Procol Harum's influential "A Whiter Shade Of Pale", but it has a simple charm about it even today. For the B-side, they used the backing track of the Granada film recording of Woolly's "Mr. Sunshine", recorded at Strawberry Studios in Stockport, with new vocals and recorder part overdubbed at Chappell.

Advert from the New Musical Express, April 1968

"Early Morning" was issued on 26th April, 1968, accompanied by a press release penned by one Max Clifford, better known these days as a publicist for more controversial causes. Whilst the single wasn't a hit, the response was encouraging and the reviews good. At the same time, BJH also signed a formal contract with John Crowther, which stated that "with the approval of their parents", they would "authorise the manager to sign and make agreements on their behalf". The immediate result was that an "in house" agreement for further recordings was made on 1st May, 1968 between EMI and John Crowther on behalf of the band. This agreement assigned copyright

in the band's recordings to EMI, in return for a royalty rate of 9% (of the price charged by EMI to dealers) on UK sales and 4.5% elsewhere, except for the U.S.A., where the rate was a paltry 3.4%. These royalty rates, whilst not exactly generous, were standard for new artists at the time, but it's clear that, when divided between the four of them, would require a large volume of sales to provide a reasonable living. The contract was for a year, but also gave EMI, but not the band, the option to extend it for up to three more years.

The band were amazed to hear "Early Morning" played before release on Radio 1 by the station's most "hip" DJ, John Peel, who was sufficiently taken with their sound to invite them in to record a session for his *Top Gear* programme. At the time, any band recording for the BBC had to pass an

31

audition; they were given just three quarters of an hour to set up their gear and record up to three numbers. The tapes, which were not marked with the name of the artists, were then vetted by a panel of Light Entertainment producers called the Talent Selection Group. Having been given a "unanimous if unenthusiastic pass", BJH were allowed to record their first BBC session on 23rd April, 1968. Apart from both sides of the single, they played "So Tomorrow", "Eden Unobtainable" and "I Can't Go On Without You". The last two belatedly received an official release when EMI's *The Harvest Years* retrospective appeared twenty-two years on.

A second Peel session, featuring "Night", "Pools Of Blue", "Small Time Town" and "Need You Oh So Bad" was recorded shortly afterwards and broadcast at the beginning of August. There were plans for "Pools Of Blue" to become BJH's second single, but although a number of attempts were made to record it, the band was never happy with the finished result, and the song remained in limbo until the EMI compilation *The Harvest Years* came out in 1990, whilst the other BBC recordings had to wait a third of a century before finally being unleashed on an unsuspecting public.

The independent way of operating was expensive: by July 1968 John Crowther had already spent £5,000 on the band - a small fortune in those days. For live bookings, the band signed to Blackhill Enterprises, an agency formed by Pink Floyd's early managers, Pete Jenner and Andy King. Another significant event took place on December 7th, when the Barclays supported Gun, then in the singles chart with "Race With The Devil", at a gig at the Roundhouse in London's Chalk Farm. After this gig they were approached by one Robert John Godfrey, who was very interested in the band's stage act, particularly the dramatic presentation and classical "feel" of songs like "Dark Now My Sky". Robert was a larger than life character who had studied at both the Royal College and the Royal Academy of Music, training as a concert pianist and being drawn into what he later described as "a kind of middle-aged famous composers' gay circle" with the likes of Sir Michael Tippett and Benjamin Britten. He had became disillusioned, though, and in classic sixties style, "dropped out" to join the burgeoning underground movement.

Robert and the band got talking, and he went back with them to their hotel. As a result of this meeting, Godfrey later arrived at Preston House and the band agreed that he would become their "musical director". Les's part of the

A glamorous personal appearance in June 1968 at the Honresfeld Gala in Royton Park, Lancashire, didn't quite go according to plan - during the procession their car broke down, and they ended up having to push it. They still found the energy to take part in an autograph-signing session, though...

main living area was curtained off to afford more privacy and after John had moved out of Preston House, Godfrey moved into the vacant space and shared the remainder of the "dormitory" with Mel and Woolly. He brought with him a taste for flowing gowns and classical music, introducing Woolly to the delights of Gustav Mahler and other classical composers, and eventually persuading the band that they should work with a real orchestra. This was a decision that, with the benefit of hindsight, could be regarded as one of the best, or the worst, that they ever made.

2

Our Harvest Home

For a time it seemed that the relationship between John Crowther and Barclay James Harvest would be a great success; John opened a second shop, called *Crowther's,* in Manchester's King Street South, and this would be followed by further branches in Birmingham and London. Both the rag trade and underground music were the epitome of cool, and both profited from the association. The band promoted John's clothing and spent their spare time helping to decorate his shops and transporting his clothes around the country. For his part, Crowther paid their bills, got them live bookings, arranged numerous recording sessions at local studios and even found them extra work to defray some of the costs, such as running a stall on Stockport market selling "end of lines" from his shop.

The door at Preston House was always open, and at times the place resembled a commune. The natives were friendly, though, as Mike Tobin, agent for the band Steamhammer, discovered - Al Read, author and friend of Mike's, takes up the story:

"Mike was sent up ahead of the band to check out the situation at a rock festival on the Yorkshire moors. Rumours were filtering back to London that it was a potential disaster. It was! Bands were pulling out, the promoter had vanished with the money and the site condition was so bad that ambulances couldn't get through to rescue the fans who were suffering from hypothermia due to the appalling weather. Barclay James Harvest lived in a remote farmhouse nearby and were there as the 'standby band' to fill in for missing artists. When Mike met up with BJH he was soaked through, freezing cold, penniless and verging on delirium. They hauled him back to their farmhouse where he was steadily returned to a well state over a couple of days. When the weather had improved they drove him to Leeds and loaned him the cash for the train fare back to London. Nice guys."

The local police were not quite so impressed when they stopped John and Woolly, who were riding two up on a scooter (belonging to Olwen). Neither of our heroes had passed a test to carry passengers, and consequently both found themselves with penalty points on their (provisional) licenses!

Musically, the band continued to pen new material, whilst still incorporating some cover versions into live shows. One of Mel's party pieces was to sing the old standard, "She's Funny That Way", then mimic a trombone solo with his voice whilst holding a real trombone up to the microphone. Gradually, though, the band's versions of songs like "Yesterday", "Turn, Turn, Turn", "Reason To Believe", "Tuesday Afternoon" and "She Said, She Said" made way for their own compositions such as "White Sails", "Brother Thrush", "Too Far Away", "Taking Some Time On", "Cream In My Coffee", "Mocking Bird", "She's So Fine" and "The Elephant Song" (?!). Live dates saw them rubbing shoulders with other luminaries on the underground circuit as they shared bills with The Pink Floyd, The Pretty Things and Fairport Convention, amongst others.

Earliest on-stage shot, circa 1969

Photo session in a snowy Hyde Park, including a rare shot of John Crowther, right

The significance of the changing face of popular music was not lost on EMI: a number of labels operated under the EMI umbrella, including Columbia, specialising in pop music, and Parlophone, which featured rather more adventurous groups such as The Beatles, and which had released BJH's first single. By the end of the sixties, however, it was apparent that a new label was required to exploit the burgeoning "progressive" movement, and in December 1968 Malcolm Jones, an economics graduate from Manchester University, was given the job of launching it. Nine of his signings in the first year were represented by the Blackhill agency, and among them were Barclay James Harvest, who signed a new one year recording agreement dated 25th April, 1969, extendable by EMI for up to three more years. A name had yet to be found for the new label, and a minor controversy has arisen in recent years over whether the label was named after BJH. Until recently the official histories of the label put it down to coincidence, but Woolly recalled in a 1973 interview

*Another shot from the same session in Hyde Park,
with the band looking decidedly chilly*

that they had discussed the label name with Malcolm Jones: "We flippantly suggested that they use Harvest and we all laughed about it. A month or so later we found out that someone from above had suggested Harvest". Decades later the *Harvest Festival* five CD and book set put the record straight, with archivist Brian Hogg and Pink Floyd manager Peter Jenner agreeing that the label was, indeed, named after Barclay James Harvest. A new publishing contract was also signed, this time with Initial Music, which would run until February 1970, and treated all BJH songs as joint compositions of a four member Partnership.

The Harvest label was launched in June, 1969, and amongst the first releases was BJH's second single, "Brother Thrush", backed by "Poor Wages", both recorded on 4-track tape at the famous Abbey Road studios in London between May 11th and 15th, under the tutelage of producer Norman Smith. Smith had engineered The Beatles and had production experience with Pink Floyd and The Pretty Things, both of whom were subsequently to join the Harvest label. Robert Godfrey also joined them for the session, and provided organ and backing vocals for "Brother Thrush". The single didn't get anywhere, and the band felt rather frustrated that their name wasn't even mentioned on the publicity for the launch of the Harvest label. Mel blamed it on the fact that the band had nobody working for them in London, where most of the music industry was (and still is) based, and that John Crowther was still involved in other business apart from managing the band. In fact, "Brother Thrush", with its green message of nature's eventual triumph over the works of man, may not have been the most radio-friendly choice, and the group's career might have been better served by releasing the more dynamic "Poor Wages" (originally entitled "Being Satisfied") as the A-side.

It could have been the start of a beautiful friendship: on April 27th the group performed a concert for the Stockport Schools Union at the Poco a Poco club in downtown Stockport. Also on the bill was one David Bowie; the Thin White Duke had scored a hit with "Space Oddity" six months earlier, but had yet to really make his mark, and was still short of cash. He and John got chatting, and he bummed a cigarette off John. However, when Bowie pushed his luck by asking if he could crash at John's, he was told to go forth and multiply, only in not so many words ...

In 1969 Mel was paid a big compliment when he was approached by Fairport Convention to audition for the drum seat made vacant by the death of Martin Lamble in a road accident. Mel turned down the opportunity, though, as he later explained in typically modest fashion:

"First of all I think my ego was given a good massage by them asking me. To be perfectly fair I don't think I came up to the standard they were looking for, being absolutely honest. Certainly Fairport were getting the better gigs, the

better money. At the time Fairport were a big band and a damn good band as well, and it was just this thing that permeates all the way through BJH, this kind of loyalty. You can't put a price on it."

November 8th saw BJH back at Abbey Road with Norman Smith, this time to begin work on their debut album. Not for the first time, The Beatles cast a long shadow over the Barclays' career, for during the entire recording sessions, the number one album in Britain and America was The Beatles' *Abbey Road*. Robert Godfrey was there, too, together with a number of music students from the Royal College of Music and the Royal Academy, whom he assembled to form the rather grandly-titled "Barclay James Harvest Symphony Orchestra". The experience of recording with an inexperienced band and a motley crew of under-rehearsed classical music students must have been a nightmare. The band and orchestra recorded their contributions separately, but there were problems from the start with the orchestra: "Dark Now My Sky" went well, but the other recordings were unusable, so a second session was arranged using more experienced musicians, former members of the New Symphonia under the leadership of Martyn Ford. Norman Smith managed, astonishingly, to get the whole thing recorded in about eighty hours, using only two eight-track recorders. Mel explained in an interview with *Beat Instrumental*,

"We had drums, bass, Mellotron, piano, organ, double-tracked guitar, orchestra, vocals and effects to go on. It took time to work out how to do it, because we didn't want to lump the bass and drums together, and we also wanted the stereo effect of the guitars, so in the end we used two eight-tracks."

It was an extremely ambitious project for a new act, and the resulting eponymous debut album proved to be something of a flawed gem. The non-orchestral songs have a real freshness and originality about them, evident in "The Iron Maiden" and "Taking Some Time On". However, in numbers like "When The World Was Woken", the unsubtle orchestral arrangement (borrowing a fanfare from Handel's *Water Music*) constantly threatens to overwhelm Les's voice. As he later recalled: "I remember writing all the melody lines for that on a Hammond. The singing was all over the place, but in those days you didn't have the luxury of going back and doing it all again!". The real title of this song, incidentally, is "When The World Has Woken", but a misprint on the album artwork changed it for all time. It could have been worse - the Abbey Road log sheets render it as "When the World Has Broken"! "The Sun Will Never Shine" showcased Woolly's emerging interest in fusing rock and classical music, and John's gothic "Mother Dear", orchestrated by Norman Smith, owes a debt to mediæval poetry such as "True Thomas". Where the true potential of Barclay James Harvest became apparent, though, was in the one song where the fusion of band and orchestra really worked, the magnificent "Dark Now My Sky". Based on the classic ecological text, Rachel Carson's *The Silent Spring*, this epic piece combines cod Shakespearean dramatics, searing guitar and the orchestra at full-tilt to create the first real BJH classic.

Local celebrity Woolly Wolstenholme was invited to attend the Honresfeld Gala in a very special capacity:
"I judged the 'Beautiful Baby Contest'! All was well (plenty of oo-ing and coo-ing - they were all beautiful - to their mothers) and finally I plumped for one, only to discover 'It' was called Wolstenholme ... It all goes black then."

Early on in the recording sessions, it was planned to release the commercial rocker, "Good Love Child", written by John but sung by Les, as a single in the New Year. This plan was dropped when difficulties over the cover design caused the album's release to be delayed until June 1970, even though the first white label test pressings were ready in March, complete with catalogue number. The band was not keen on the Hipgnosis covers used for other Harvest album releases, comparing the designers to dominant producers - "The sleeve was everything with them, and the act didn't really matter", explains Woolly. Instead, the band chose the stained glass butterfly effect designed by Ian Latimer and thus sowed the seeds for one of the band's most enduring images. The delay in the album's release may have also been the reason why a planned visit to the United States in February 1970 - the first of many ill-fated attempts to break into the lucrative American market - never got off the ground.

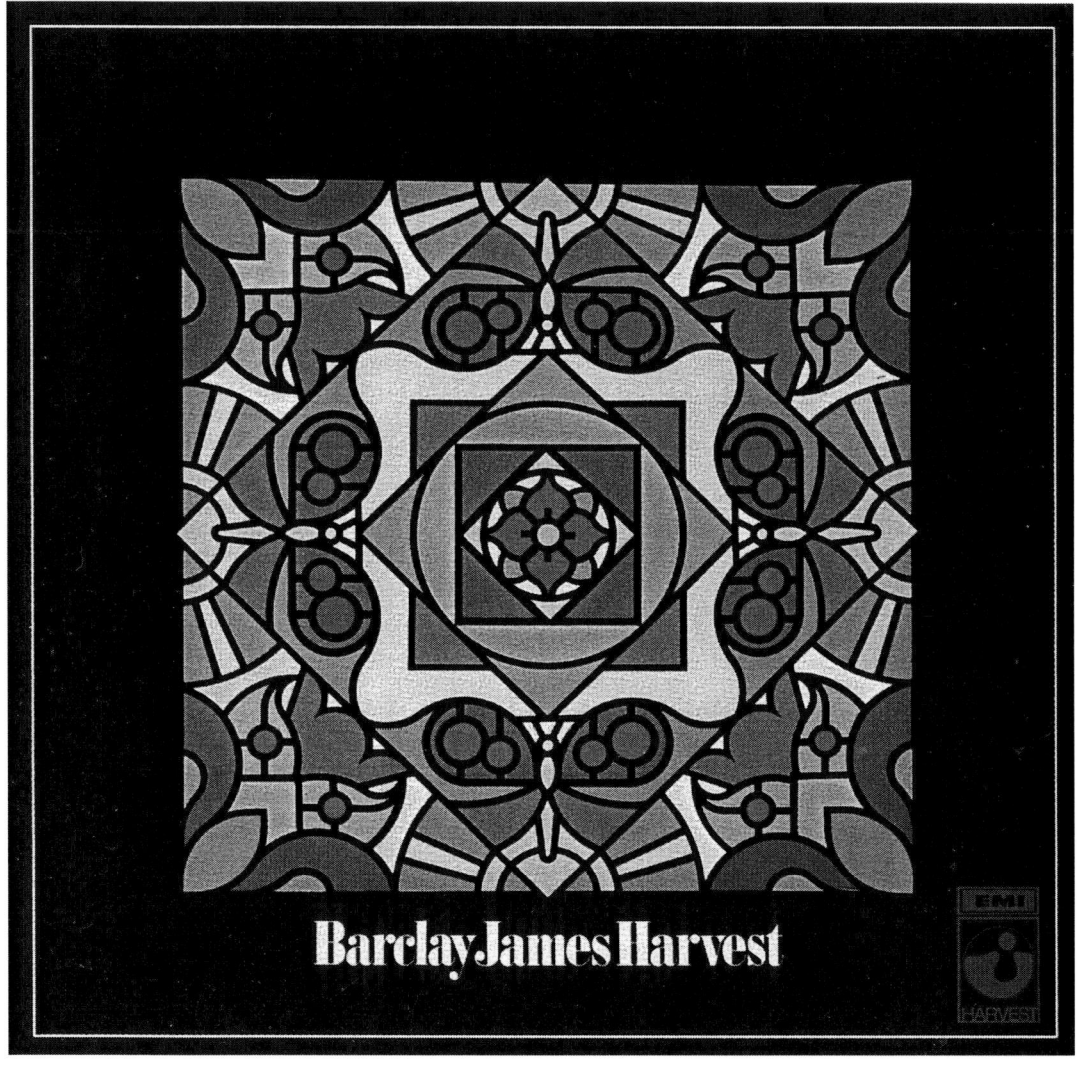

The debut album

The album garnered encouraging reviews and radio support from the likes of John Peel and Alan 'Fluff' Freeman, and some welcome exposure came their own way when "The Iron Maiden" was played on BBC2's *Disco 2*, accompanied by film of Brunel's iron-hulled steamship, SS Great Britain.

The most ambitious promotional undertaking, though, was a "mini-tour" complete with a full orchestra, possibly the first time ever that a rock band had taken an orchestra on the road (as opposed to one-off shows like Deep Purple's *Concerto For Group And Orchestra*). The tour encompassed shows at Manchester's Free Trade Hall, the Royal Albert Hall in London, Birmingham Town Hall and Edinburgh Usher Hall. Even before the first show, John Crowther estimated that they would lose £8,000 on the tour, a very large sum in 1970, but the show went on, and the small crowds were treated to live renditions not only of several of the album tracks, but also unreleased songs such as "White Sails", "Too Much On Your Plate", "Galadriel", "She Said" and the song which was to become the standard by which all their future work would be judged, the timeless "Mocking Bird". Another song which appeared in the programme for the orchestral tour was "Wandering", which was never recorded but part of which was recycled many years later in "Festival!". In the *Harvest Festival* set, Woolly recalled that playing gigs with an orchestral still didn't mean that the band had any delusions of grandeur: "I didn't drive then, and I've done orchestral gigs at the Free Trade Hall in Manchester, and after been on the bus back home with the audience. Always the people's band!"

A break in rehearsals for the 1970 orchestral tour

2. Our Harvest Home

*Original programme
from the orchestral
concerts*

The band were now getting through a prodigious quantity of live work - apart
from the orchestral gigs, their live engagements covered the spectrum from
festivals in Belgium to opening for Led Zeppelin at Edinburgh's Usher Hall.
Even with fame and fortune beckoning, they also found time to get involved in
a charity fund-raising scheme back home in Saddleworth. After local teenagers
raised over £3,000 for a special ambulance, BJH raced home after the Saturday
night show at the Albert Hall in order to play a free "thank you" show the next
day at Buile Hall Park in Salford, billed as the first open-air concert in the
North. Unfortunately, the national publicity which the concert was given
frightened the city's parks committee and local police into
holding an emergency meeting at which it was decided
that the organisers couldn't cope with the expected
crowds, and the show was called off at the eleventh hour.
Despite some hurtful remarks from the local mayor to the
effect that the band were merely seeking self-publicity,
BJH proved their good intentions by going along to the
park anyway to explain to the crowds who had not heard
about the last-minute cancellation. Other charitable
ventures, such as benefit gigs for the Diggle Old People's

Welfare Committee, were more successful. By now the old Mellotron Mark 2 had finally bitten the dust after an unfortunate incident involving a trip down a flight of stairs, and they were not displeased to see the back of it - it was too too big to take on tour, and, besides, the insurance payout meant that they could now afford a new compact 300 model. Les was quoted in an interview as saying that they were having a new one custom-made, which would weigh only (?) about 2½ hundredweight (about 125 kg) and cost £850.00. The original Mark 2, incidentally, went back to the factory where it was repaired and sold on to another owner!

Whilst appearances at prestigious venues like the Albert Hall were becoming more common, the band's bread and butter was still the rather less glamorous touring circuit. Here's an example as told by John to Tim Jones of *Record Collector:*

"We played with The Sweet when they hit. Les and Mel got a bottle of whisky and were drinking five fingers' worth a time. Les decked half and went absolutely rigid. We had to drive home in our Luton van with aircraft seats in it, and Robert Godfrey was with us and decided Les'd taken a turn for the worse. So we got him out of the van to get him to puke over a nearby wall. So I thought, as you do, over the wall for a piss. It was only about a fifteen foot f***in' drop and whumpf, I landed in all these nettles. Then the driver was pulling away near a Nissen hut and hooked the bumper against it, but couldn't be arsed reversing. So he just drove forward and the whole bloody thing collapsed! Of course, we made a swift exit".

As the band's sound and equipment became more complex, they could no longer rehearse within the confined spaces of Preston House, and the "commune" began to drift apart. Robert moved to another house belonging to John Crowther to prepare for the second album, but Crowther had begun to run into financial difficulties (not least because his large investment in BJH had so far shown scant return) and was beginning to lose interest in the band. To Les, Mel and Woolly's dismay, Crowther began to talk about selling Preston House, although he found some difficulty in finding a buyer when visitors were greeted by strange unearthly noises and disgusting smells. The band's resistance crumbled, though, when Crowther threatened to put their affairs into the hands of an accountant, and they fled back to their parental homes. There were also differences of opinion about Robert's role in the band: during the recording sessions for the first album, Woolly, in particular, felt that his position as arranger and keyboard player was threatened by Godfrey's increasing influence. Robert had ambitions to appear with them on stage at all the concerts, not just the orchestral ones, and to be an official member of the band. Godfrey did travel with them to some gigs, and even appeared on stage with them as a temporary replacement for John on a three week visit to Spain when John was too ill to travel, but he was never accepted as a full member of the band by the others.

At the end of August "Taking Some Time On" was rather belatedly launched as the single from the debut album, and then it was time to think about the follow-up LP. The band was given permission by the local council to rehearse for six hours a day on Thursdays and Fridays at the Civic Hall in Uppermill, provided that the noise was kept to a reasonable level! Norman Smith and the orchestra were booked, and work began at Abbey Road on October 9th.

Woolly: "We would start at about 6.00 p.m. We would do the night shift there and stay at The Madison in Sussex Gardens and spend all day walking aimlessly around Paddington."

It seems astonishing now that an album of the complexity and maturity of *Once Again* should have been recorded in a mere six weeks, but the experience of playing a number of the songs on stage with the orchestra must have helped enormously, and the rather uneasy alliance of band and orchestra from the debut was transformed into an inspirational synthesis to produce an album truly worthy of that overused accolade "classic". From the dramatic opening of "She Said", with its startling contrast between delicate Elizabethan-style recorders and crashing guitar chords, through the bleak irony of "Happy Old World" to the fragile Tolkien-inspired "Galadriel", the band hardly put a foot wrong. Norman Smith was fresh from recording with The Beatles, and to the band's delight, brought out John Lennon's blond Epiphone Casino guitar from a cupboard at Abbey Road and let John Lees play it on "Galadriel", thus unwittingly inspiring another Barclay James Harvest song twenty years later.

Then, of course, there was "Mocking Bird". Already becoming a live favourite, the song was actually based on a musical phrase from "Pools Of Blue", and for the album version was augmented by an orchestral arrangement written by Robert Godfrey, which was to be the subject of a bitter dispute many years later. "Mocking Bird" brought together all that was best about the early BJH - a deceptively simple song with a memorable chorus, melded to an inspired arrangement to create a unique fusion of rock and classical music. The somewhat hurried recording meant that band and orchestral parts didn't always

Early 1971 photo shoot on the Thames Embankment

synchronise perfectly, and in fact the orchestra is off the beat for much of the piece, but even that didn't prevent "Mocking Bird" from becoming a true classic - in fact, the song became synonymous with the band for many, an association which threatened to turn the mockingbird into an albatross until the band could prove that they were capable of writing many more classics. "Vanessa Simmons" is an acoustic guitar-led paean to an early girlfriend of John's, whilst at the other extreme, "Song For Dying" showcased the rockier side of the band, borrowing the line about "the dawn's early light" from the American national anthem, "The Star-Spangled Banner". Woolly's anguished "Ball And Chain" showed that he, too, could rock out, and featured a distorted lead vocal, achieved by the simple expedient of singing through a paper cup with the bottom pushed out. The speed with which the album was recorded is underlined by the fact that one verse of "Ball And Chain" was accidentally sung twice, but there was no time to re-record the song, so the verse which had been missed out was lost forever - until now:

> *If I could live my whole life again*
> *I would not be on this prison train*
> *And I'd have no trouble from my ball and chain*

Without the prison reference, the meaning of the song is more obscure, although it still makes a convincing allegory of the human condition.

Amongst those involved in the recording sessions was a tape-operator by the name of Alan Parsons. Parsons, of course, was later to be a legendary figure in his own right, renowned not only as the engineer for Pink Floyd's *Dark Side Of The Moon*, but also for his own Alan Parsons Project. Speaking to the Alan Parsons fanzine *The Avenue* almost twenty-five years later, he recalled being involved in "probably three albums all together. 'Mocking Bird' was the big track. They were absolutely up my street, they were just the kind of music I really liked. I did a bit of engineering, a bit of tape op-ing. I even played the Jaw's harp on a session for them once." The song in question was, of course, "Lady Loves", where the twanging of the children's playground-favourite instrument contrasts oddly but pleasingly with the multi-tracked electric guitar of the coda. It would be another six years before Parsons made his name as a musician with the sublime *Tales Of Mystery And Imagination*, but perhaps that first taste of recording as a performer set him on the way to that ambitious masterpiece! There must have been something in the air at Abbey Road during the recording of *Once Again*, as not one but two of the tape operators in the studio went on to become movers and shakers in the industry; the other was John Leckie, who graduated to engineer albums such as Paul McCartney's *Red Rose Speedway* and, together with Alan Parsons, Pink Floyd's *Dark Side Of the Moon*, before achieving fame as a producer with Simple Minds, Radiohead and many others.

When it was time for the new BJH songs to be assigned to the publishers, John Lees was negotiating a new deal with Initial Music when a disagreement arose within the band about the advisability of continuing to assign the songs as joint compositions. A new contract was therefore drawn up, this time with Mickie Most's RAK Publishing, under which songs were assigned to the individual who had actually written them. The mechanical publishing royalties (the money paid by the record company to the publisher, who then pay the artists their share) continued to be divided equally, although the Performing Rights Society royalties (income from public performance such as radio airplay) now went to the songwriter. This may have been fairer in that John, Les and Woolly received credit where it was due, but it also led to a greater degree of competition between the three writers than was healthy, perhaps.

Once the album was finished, but before it was actually released, the escalating tension between Godfrey and the others came to a head in January 1971 when the band told him that he would no longer be required for live performances at all, and that they would let him know if they wanted any arrangements written. There ensued a row between Godfrey and Crowther, resulting in Godfrey being paid a hundred pounds and dismissed.

When *Once Again* hit the shops in February 1971, it didn't so much set the world on fire as light a torch for a discerning audience to follow, as the band's fan base grew by word of mouth and developed into a loyal cult following. The critics and media received it well, too, but still there was no major commercial breakthrough, although the album did, eventually, garner enough sales to qualify the band for a silver disc. Harvest issued "Mocking Bird" as a single to promote the album, and the band set out on a gruelling schedule of live shows around Britain. These included a few showpiece dates with the orchestra, but mostly it was just the four of them, Woolly recreating the arrangements with the Mellotron.

By now John Crowther was finding it difficult to run both his own, ever-expanding clothes empire, and the band's affairs, so a booking agency was engaged to look after the band's concert schedule. The White Agency was run by Ian Cassie (former social secretary at the Manchester College of Commerce) and Dave Crowe, but much of the donkey work was done by local lad Ian Southerington. Ian not only booked the whole of the *Once Again* tour, but was also the band's driver. His life changed dramatically on 12th February, 1971, the day that he had booked BJH to play two shows in one evening. The show at Didsbury College of Education went off without problems, but by the time the gear was set up at the *Way In* in Kendal's store on Manchester's Deansgate for the second performance, the band's sound man decided that he'd had enough, and quit on the spot. The band was aghast, and rounded on the man who had booked the shows:

"You got us into this f***ing mess, now you get us out of it!"
It was Woolly who suggested that Ian take over as sound man himself.

"But I don't have a clue about mixing!"

"It's easy - just make sure the vocals are louder than everything else, and if you get feedback, turn everything down."

"What's feedback?"

Ian winged it, and to everyone's surprise, not least his own, it worked. He turned out to have a natural ear and feel for the band's music, which was just as well, because a week after his debut he was mixing a concert at the Maidstone College Of Art complete with forty-piece symphony orchestra. An interesting challenge for a man who began his working life as a chef, but one which he rose to meet many times in the ensuing years. Soon Ian Southerington became a familiar name at gigs, to the point where he was described as "the fifth member of the band".

One rather strange concert in May saw them playing the Berne Ice Stadium in Switzerland, accompanied by a rather uninterested and under-rehearsed Berne Symphony Orchestra, with Martyn Ford now in the conductor's role, valiantly trying to prevent the whole thing from falling apart at the seams. In spite of a recalcitrant Mellotron and some difficulties in keeping band and orchestra together, the audience of over six thousand approved and gave the band a foretaste of playing in front of enthusiastic stadium crowds.

3

The Storm Clouds Gather

In May 1971 the band were, according to a contemporary interview with Woolly, "planning a double album of one LP featuring the group on its own and the other with the group augmented by a full orchestra. We might also have them available for sale separately." An article in *Melody Maker* towards the end of the same month claimed that "Barclay James Harvest are to record an album with the Boston Pops Orchestra in New York next month. The band already have a fair amount of material ready and will be working flat out on new numbers before the two day recording session."

In the midst of this frenetic writing activity, the band somehow found time to record another BBC session, this time for "Whispering" Bob Harris, on June 29th. The four songs performed show the diversity of the band's repertoire at the time - a powerful take of "She Said" with the Mellotron replacing the orchestral parts, a delicate rendition of "Galadriel" and then two tasters for the forthcoming album, both from Woolly's pen. "Someone There You Know" would sound very similar in its album guise, but "Ursula (The Swansea Song)" was played as a plaintive, piano-led lament with a lovely guitar solo reminiscent of Fleetwood Mac's "Albatross".

Wally Allen

The American adventure never came to fruition, either because of cost or because the bosses at EMI felt that, with the critical acclaim accorded *Once Again*, it was important to capitalise on it and release new material quickly. Consequently the band headed not for Boston but for Kilburn, back to Abbey Road, and the recording sessions were squeezed into a period of less than a month, from July 18th to August 16th, at the end of another tour. They found themselves working with a new producer, in the shape of Wally Allen (a.k.a. Alan Waller). Wally was the bassist with label-mates the Pretty Things, but left the band when Norman Smith invited him to become a staff producer at EMI. The album was recorded with Norman Smith theoretically in attendance as Executive Producer - in practice he was rarely to be found in the studio and Wally was left in sole charge.

In the absence of Robert Godfrey, the mantle of orchestral conductor fell on the capable shoulders of Martyn Ford. Martyn already had considerable experience, having studied horn at the Royal Academy of Music for four years, then in the fourth year formed his own symphony orchestra made up of talented music students from the four London music colleges. The orchestra led a somewhat schizophrenic life, inhabiting both the classical and rock worlds under different names and with different subsets of the musicians as required. The orchestra's first concert was at the Royal Albert Hall, to great critical acclaim, and in the classical world it became known as the New Sinfonia. Many of the same musicians also formed the Barclay James Harvest Orchestra, including Wilf Gibson, later violinist with the Electric Light Orchestra, and Richard Studt, who is credited as orchestra leader on the BJH *BBC In Concert* CD and who later rose to the heights of leader of the London Symphony Orchestra.

Martyn Ford also worked with a host of other artists - amongst the classic songs he arranged or orchestrated were David Bowie's "Space Oddity" and Johnny Nash's "I Can See Clearly Now" (a seven million seller for which Martyn received all of £35!), The Rolling Stones' "Angie" and Led Zeppelin's "Kashmir", not to mention collaborations with artists such as Elton John, Phil Collins, Paul McCartney, Bob Marley and Kate Bush.

Just after wrapping up the recording of the new LP at Abbey Road, the band and orchestra played one of their most memorable concerts - the legendary Weeley Festival, sited in a small village just outside Clacton-on-Sea and attended by over 150,000 fans. Although the festival was marred by trouble with self-appointed bouncers from roaming gangs of Hells Angels, the line-up of classic progressive artists made it one of the most memorable music events of the time. BJH played in the balmy air of the early evening on the Friday, accompanied by a 45-piece orchestra and psychedelic images projected on either side of the stage. Amongst those with fond memories of being mesmerised by a stunning rendition of "Mocking Bird" were Radio 1's John Peel, and Steve Harley, later to form the band Cockney Rebel.

Released in November 1971, *Barclay James Harvest and other short stories* has the makings of a fine album, but lacks the coherence of its predecessor. True, there are some *bona fide* BJH classics like John's menacing "Medicine Man" (inspired by the Ray Bradbury novel *Something Wicked This Way Comes*) and the apocalyptic "The Poet"/"After The Day", the first half of which had been written and recorded back in 1967 for the *Eroica* album. However, the recording was rushed and some of the songs simply weren't finished - "Harry's Song", for instance, was left incomplete, minus piano, an additional guitar part and backing vocals which the band had intended to add. "Harry's Song", incidentally, was written about the death of a much-loved family pet, namely a

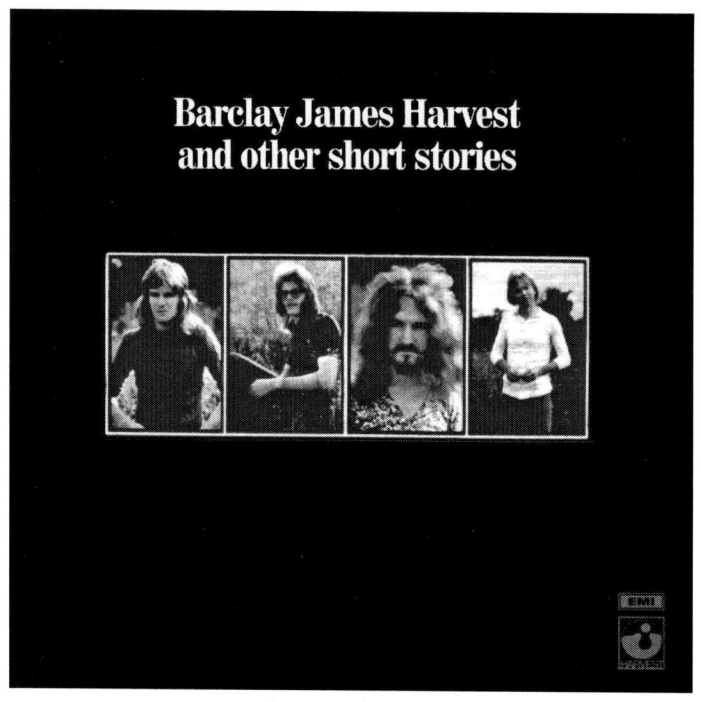

parrot (insert Monty Python jokes here!). "Blue John's Blues", an exasperated dig at the band's management, with its second half dominated by bar-room piano and strained vocals, sits rather uncomfortably on the album, whilst the bittersweet "Ursula (The Swansea Song)" hid behind an inappropriately jolly string arrangement. "Little Lapwing", a rare writing collaboration between John and Les, and Woolly's "Someone There You Know" possessed a great deal of charm, whilst the dreamy "Song With No Meaning", with lyrics from Les, his girlfriend Christine and Mel, evoked a romantic pastoral idyll. However, the overall impression was of an album which didn't quite do the band justice, and won them few new converts. There was no let-up for the group after the album came out, as they hit the road again for a tour which ran almost continuously from November 1971 to August 1972.

Relations with John Crowther had deteriorated as the prospect of instant success receded and he spent less time on the band's affairs. It was a source of irritation to the band that they had nobody working on their behalf in London, where the music business was based, so Crowther appointed Ian Cassie and Dave Crowe, who had previously booked gigs for the band, to represent BJH in a more formal capacity in September 1971. Crowther remained as manager until October 1971, at which point Cassie and Crowe took over all management duties for the band.

If the band expected the change of management to presage happier times, they were soon to be disabused of the notion. The constant touring was bad enough, but then EMI, impatient for results from their investment in the band, began to pressurise the band to come up with a hit single. John's "I'm Over You" was a pleasant enough song, but not what was needed to secure that elusive chart placing. The single's B-side, "Child Of Man", was another John Lees composition, and the first one in which John's Christian beliefs were made explicit. It was around the time of the recording of "I'm Over You",

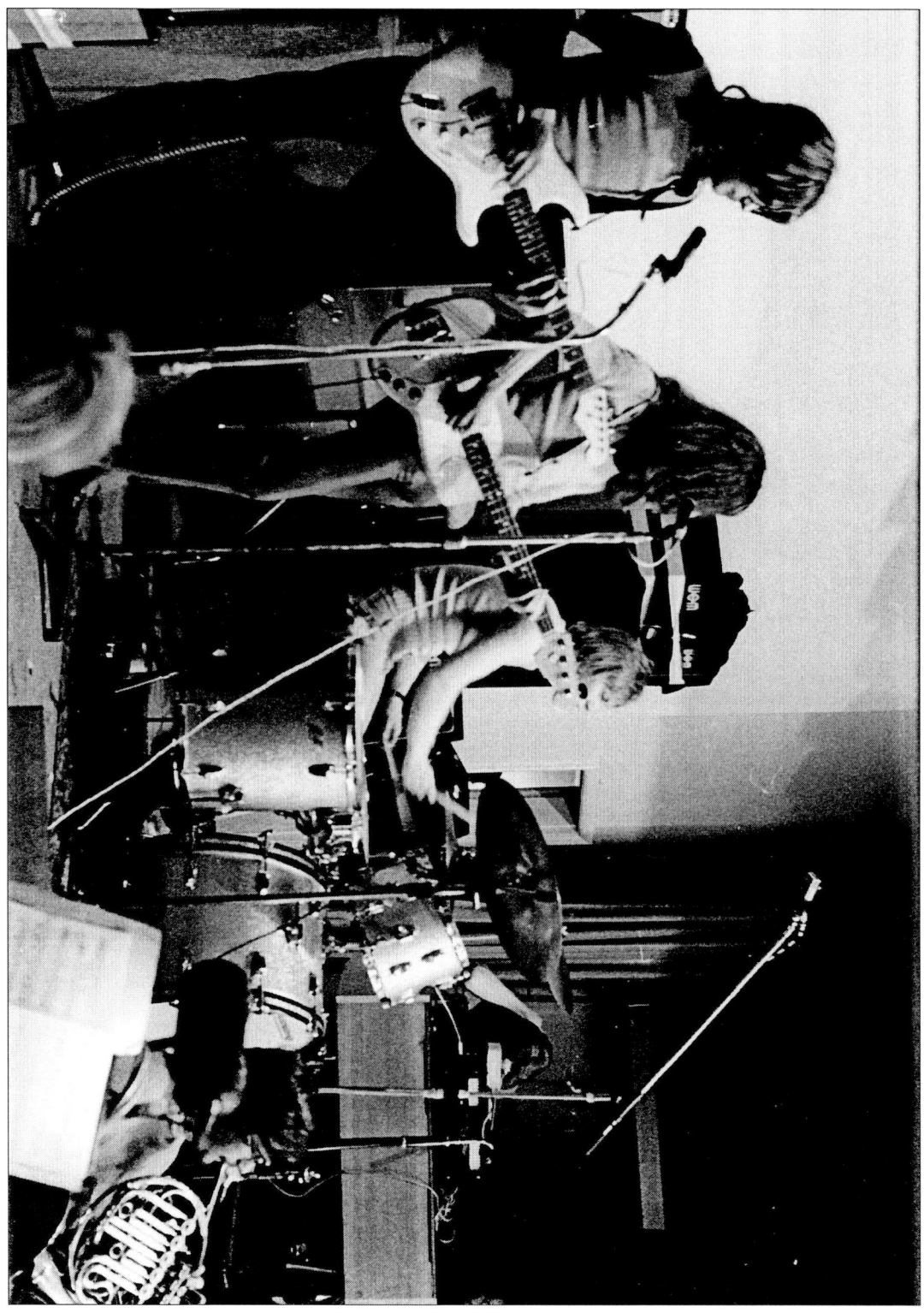

incidentally, that the band made the acquaintance of sound engineer David Rohl, a chance meeting on the train journey home from a recording session which was to lead to a fruitful partnership in the years to come. The failure of the single was not of itself disastrous, but it meant that the record company pressure intensified, and the band were given a mere two weeks in which to produce their fourth studio album.

In the meantime there was no let up in the relentless live schedule. A six-week U.S. tour, including an 18-day concert series with Poco was scheduled for March to May 1972 but then cancelled, but BJH were still playing numerous gigs, including a couple in Switzerland and a prestigious showpiece concert with the orchestra in the (drained!) moat of the Tower of London. Unfortunately the band's performance coincided with the Ceremony of the Keys at the Tower, so a 9:30 p.m. curfew was imposed on the concert. Two of the supporting bands overran their allotted times, and BJH were told with minutes to go that they would only have around half an hour to play! The orchestra opened up with Handel's Water Music, then BJH ripped through "She Said", "Mocking Bird", "Galadriel" and "Medicine Man" before John announced to the disbelieving fans that the next song would be their last. Even that was too long, though, as the ceremony was under way and BJH succeeded

U.S. promotional photo taken from the other short stories session

in interrupting it where two World Wars had failed. Just as the band and orchestra were in full flight on "Dark Now My Sky", a nameless official decided that the concert had to end and the power was cut off, prompting disgruntled fans to set fire to seats and get involved in a fracas with officials. This ignominious end to the night's proceedings ironically gave the band more publicity than they'd ever had before, receiving as much coverage in the national press as reports of the death of Chi Chi the giant panda ...

Suddenly the band found themselves in the studio again, woefully ill-prepared. Grandiose plans for a double album set with the working title *Four Winds*, containing one side each of the individual band members' ideas were rapidly scaled down, as there simply wasn't enough material ready. The bulk of the recording was to be done in Waterloo Road, Stockport, at Strawberry Studios (the successor to Inter City Sound), co-owned by Peter Tattersall and 10cc's Eric Stewart and within a convenient distance of the band's homes. Woolly's "Moonwater" would have the orchestral parts recorded at Abbey Road and the band's contributions at Strawberry. It was bad enough that the band didn't really have enough songs ready for a whole album, but then Woolly, who had been working on the orchestral recordings in London, came back with the tapes only to find that there was a technical incompatibility and that they would have to be recorded again from scratch. He had to leave the rest

Baby James Harvest

of the band to their own devices and return to London, and the time constraints meant that they couldn't wait for him, so they went ahead with recording the remaining five songs without him in an unintentional foretaste of the band's later career. The results were patchy. John's "Summer Soldier", with the coda arranged by Woolly, was an undoubted BJH classic, but whilst Les's "Crazy (Over You)" and "One Hundred Thousand Smiles Out" and John's "Delph Town Morn" had plenty of potential, the

3. The Storm Clouds Gather

finished recordings betrayed the rushed manner in which they were arranged and recorded. "Thank You" was a great riff thrown together with a lyrical credits list, whilst several of the songs seemed stretched more thinly than their natural span - the fade-out at the end of "One Hundred Thousand Smiles Out", for instance, seems to go on forever. Woolly's "Moonwater", whilst a beautiful piece in itself, suffered from a poor arrangement, and bore no musical relation whatever to the rest of the songs. More than one member of the band was subsequently quoted in the music press as saying that *Baby James Harvest* was a "schizophrenic" album, but it wasn't a bad effort, for all that, and certainly not as dire as John believed when he said "we should have wiped the tapes" and described it as "ashtray material"!

No sooner was the recording completed than the band was off on tour again, this time to South Africa. For a band with a strong student following on the college circuit, it was an incomprehensible decision; it was almost certainly naïvety combined with bad advice which led the band to accept an invitation to play in South Africa at a time when there was a Musicians' Union boycott of that country's apartheid regime in force. The band was effectively conned, as they were convinced that they were striking a blow for freedom by performing to multi-racial audiences - what wasn't mentioned in the agreement, of course, was that the audiences would be segregated by the colour of their skin. According to manager Dave Crowe, the band "were saying things on stage which could have got them into trouble - they did in fact get fined". Altogether BJH played around twenty concerts, some with the orchestra, and travelled around the country in an old VW van, accompanied by their support act, blues man Gary Farr. The tour did have its lighter moments - one of the orchestral gigs was in Durban, but there was no orchestra available there to back the band, so the promoters put an advertisement in the newspaper for musicians. The motley crew who turned up for the show included a number of enthusiastic but rather decrepit elderly people who were completely unfamiliar with the music, and were expected to sight-read with little or no rehearsal. John takes up the story:

"On 'Dark Now My Sky' he (Woolly) did the intro, then this woman came in at twice the speed and in the wrong key. I just started creeping behind this riser trying to get lower and lower."

Mel: Woolly did the Laurence Olivier bit, and it came in on moody cellos and everything. God bless her, she did it at double speed. Instead of it being moody and sombre and like impending doom it was like the f***ing Keystone Cops. It was like a f***ing hornpipe.

Woolly: "I was crouched on the floor, hiding behind the Mellotron, crying with laughter!"

John: "I looked over the stage and all I could see were his hands. It was the most appalling racket. And in the local paper it got a great review!"

Shot from the 1972 photo-call for Baby James Harvest

Whilst they were away, EMI and the Harvest label were still pursuing the holy grail of a hit single, this time with a piece of instrumental foolery called "Breathless". For this slice of instantly disposable pop the band hid behind the Tolkien-inspired alias of "Bombadil", whilst the composition was credited to one Terry Bull. The B-side was the give-away, a Wolstenholme song called "When The City Sleeps", on which Woolly played and sang everything, and which purported to be written by Lester Forrest. One of the motorway service stations between Manchester and London which was frequented by the band was Leicester Forest ... Perhaps fortunately, the single didn't trouble the chart compilers and BJH's cover wasn't blown until many years later.

The record company's quest for commercial success now reached its apogee with the release of a compilation album, *Early Morning Onwards* on EMI's budget-price imprint, Starline. On the face of it, this was a good decision - the LP, at the giveaway price of 99p, brought together the non-album single tracks, already much sought after by existing fans, with classics like "Mocking Bird" and "After The Day" to tempt the uninitiated. The album sold well, and served as an introduction to the band for a large number, many of whom still remember the LP fondly today. The problem was the timing of its release - just a couple of weeks before the release of *Baby James Harvest*. Whether the people at Starline didn't consult their colleagues at Harvest, or whether it was a conscious decision, there can be no doubt that the release made a serious dent in the sales of the new studio album, and hastened the deterioration of the relationship between band and label.

"Thank You" was issued as a *bona fide* BJH single when the band returned from South Africa, as a trailer for *Baby James Harvest*, and almost immediately they hit the road again. Predictably, they were greeted by anti-apartheid student demonstrations trying to organise a boycott of the band's concerts. Several gigs were cancelled, including some when Woolly became ill, whilst the remainder were hampered by demonstrations and fake "cancelled" notices. When it became apparent that the forthcoming "Harvestmobile" tour, featuring numerous bands signed to the Harvest label, could also be disrupted, the band was forced into an embarrassing climb-down and issued the following statement to the press:-

"Following the tour of South Africa by Barclay James Harvest, during which they performed largely before segregated

Woolly on the integrity of the press: "John and I were press-ganged into appearing on the panel of a competition run by a music paper to find the next stars of 197?. Most of them were twangy four-piece guitar groups, but one band had a Hammond and just played to a better standard than the rest. In the final decision me and John voted for our favourite but the chairman (a Brummie) said that we were 'blasé' and gave the prize to 'The Twangs'! Just like being in the government, I imagine."

audiences in agreement with South African law, students at Leeds, Liverpool and Portsmouth have protested against performances due to take place at the universities and colleges by this group. We have now joined the Musicians' Union and agreement has been reached with the Union that no further visits to South Africa will be made while the present South African government laws prevail. Agreement has also been reached with the Anti-Apartheid Movement to the effect that, whilst Barclay James Harvest went to South Africa with the intention of helping to bring a new culture to the young people of the country, they now realise that the international cultural boycott is a more effective method of opposing the South African government's abhorrent policies."

For any cynics who might think that the statement was born out of expediency rather than any real change of heart, one glance at the lyrics of 1987's "African" paints a very different picture. The statement didn't bring this sorry episode to a close, though, as the disruptions and demonstrations continued: determined to play on, BJH found themselves on stage at Leeds University whilst bricks crashed through windows and the band was forced to leave the stage after every couple of songs because another bomb threat had been received.

A live performance in November at the BBC's Paris Theatre in London was well received, even though the tiny stage limited the orchestra to 30 players. Their performance was exuberant if not entirely accurate - Woolly later said that it was a case of "Forgive them, for they know not what they do!", but described the end result as "Chaotic and tumultuous, but charming". However, the indifferent response to *Baby James Harvest* and the tour debacle did nothing to endear the band to their record label. The band's managers weren't happy with the EMI deals, as the band was having to work virtually continuously simply in order to make ends meet, and, without even consulting the band, tried to negotiate a better deal with Harvest. Unfortunately, without any major successes they were hardly in a position to make demands, and the talks resulted in a stalemate. Unsurprisingly, morale within the band was also at rock bottom, and there was serious discussion as to whether they should carry on or split up. They arrived instead at the compromise solution of taking time out from the group to work on solo projects. John Lees explained his thinking thus:

"I have reached a stage where I have got to try it just by myself. I am really tied down by the group because when you are playing with an orchestra the part is set and there's no changing it spontaneously. There is nothing left to chance, so you are restricted in experimenting, and I often feel I am not doing my best because of this. Most of the members of the group have changed their musical taste over the last year. Everybody is going their own way, but the group will stay together. Probably when I've done my solo album the others will follow me. I don't feel dissatisfied with the group but everybody has something to say and they want their own recognition besides being a member of a band. Barclay James Harvest isn't going to go on *ad infinitum* and we are at a turning point in this country. We have got to open up somehow or other".

So John went off to record his album at Abbey Road and Strawberry studios. For his solo work, John worked not with the other members of BJH, but with other musicians whom he had met over the years. These included most of 10cc, Rod Argent (formerly of The Zombies, then his own band, Argent), Wally Waller, better known as Wally Allen of the Pretty Things, on bass and production duties (having previously produced *Barclay James Harvest and other short stories*), Skip Allen (born Alan Skipley), also formerly with the Pretty Things, on drums, piano from Gordon Edwards, who later worked with

the likes of John Lennon, Paul Simon, Hall and Oates and The Pretty Things and Graham Preskett, whose CV includes Manfred Mann's Earthband, Gerry Rafferty, Paul Young and A-Ha! The choral effects on "Child Of The Universe" were courtesy of the Mike Sammes Singers. As might be expected, the resulting album, entitled *A Major Fancy*, was very different to BJH - it has a more relaxed, jazzy feel at times, occasionally verging on self-indulgence, but rescued by some very strong songs, notably the first

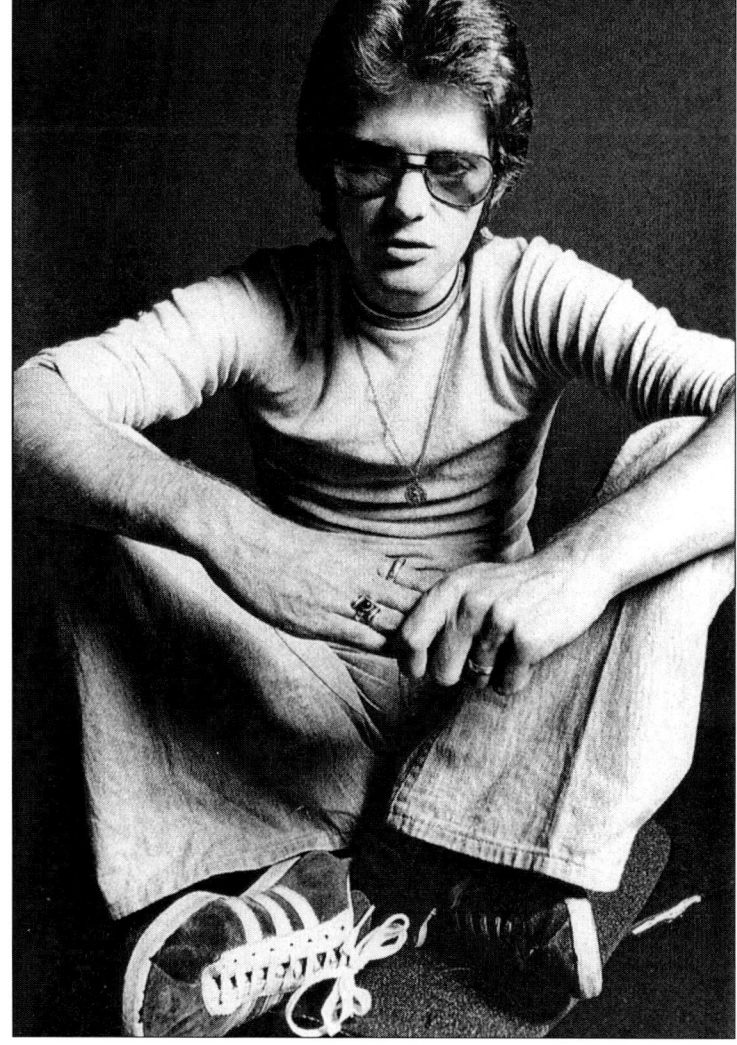

Publicity shot for
A Major Fancy

recording of "Child Of The Universe". However, it would prove to be a very long time before *A Major Fancy* would see the light of day.

If 1972 had been a low point in the band's career, the early part of 1973 showed no signs of improvement; in January the band was involved in two car crashes, forcing the cancellation of four gigs, then in March they set off for what they hoped would be a pleasant change, a short tour of Yugoslavia. Instead it turned into a nightmare - having travelled across Yugoslavia in a crowded coach, the band discovered that the promoter wasn't going to pay them their much-needed cash for the gigs, and they were obliged to accept a guitar and an organ in lieu of payment. On the return journey the road crew became embroiled in a border dispute and all of the band's gear was impounded. The next project was a whistle-stop orchestral tour of Common Market countries, playing gigs in six countries within six days. The tour, taking in Amsterdam, Zurich, Rome, Frankfurt, Copenhagen and London was to be accomplished using a hired jet airliner, seventy people (including a thirty-six piece orchestra) and five tons of equipment. A publicity photo was made, with the band and personnel posed in front of an aircraft [right], but the tour never took place - the record company took one look at the estimated £20,000 cost and promptly pulled the plug.

As a holding operation, EMI re-issued the *Early Morning Onwards* collection, re-packaged in a smart new white sleeve with an orange Barclay James Harvest logo and butterfly. The main reason for the new design was that the original black cover had included multicoloured lettering, which was so difficult to read that it was hard to pick out the name of the band!

Work with the band continued, however, including the occasional showpiece concert with the orchestra. One of these took place on May 18th at the Royal Festival Hall in London, and sold out despite the fact that Pink Floyd were in town on the same night. A contemporary review gives a wonderful insight into the sartorial elegance of the early seventies: "the bright young Barclay James Harvest orchestra all in white with smart BJH T-shirts, Paul Buckmaster simply devastating in glittery green suit and ginormous platforms"! Fortunately the music was rather more tasteful, from orchestra leader Buckmaster's self-composed overture through all the BJH classics right up to the new single "Rock And Roll Woman". The latter was based on a riff which Les had intended to use for his solo album, but the rest of the band picked up on it in the studio and it was developed into a commercial song which they felt would make a good single. By the time it was mixed, though, even Les was unsure of its merits - "Once you start adding and mixing you go through it 40 or 50 times and you come out with a product you don't know. You just don't know how good it is any more." In fact the B-side, a joint Holroyd and Lees composition entitled "The Joker", a plea for man to show compassion and understanding, is much stronger.

The band's approach to their work was, by now, much more professional - the concerts with the orchestra were reserved for special occasions to avoid incurring further debts, and they had their own light show. Rather less successful was an inflatable butterfly, made for the band by a man from the BBC's props department; intended to emerge from a cocoon and take flight majestically over the audience at the climax of the live shows, the butterfly was covered with fluorescent paint and was quite heavy, and unless filled with pure helium, had the flying characteristics of a brick. As Woolly recalled in a later interview, "The cocoon would creak open most nights and then the butterfly would try to launch and always failed. It just sat there through the whole gig like a giant haemorrhoid." Not a pleasant thought ...

The Harvest label's next BJH release was aimed at the more affluent hi-fi buffs who were prepared to shell out for four speakers and a special decoder in order to enjoy the wonders of "quadraphonic sound". The system encoded four tracks onto a standard LP, which were then unscrambled by the decoder to produce an early incarnation of surround sound. One of the early releases in this format was *Once Again*. Regrettably, the band were not consulted, and the engineers simply used parts of the original multi-track which had been discarded at the time of mixing the stereo LP (usually for very good reasons!)

to create a new surround sound mix. Whilst this approach led to some interesting spatial effects and improvements such as the extra lead guitar overdubs on "Ball And Chain", it also allowed the reappearance of some out-of-tune backing vocals (on "Vanessa Simmons"), and Woolly's jokey aside, "as we travel through space", which was never meant to be included on the finished track, on "Happy Old World". The offending backing vocals on "Vanessa Simmons" were corrected for a later pressing of the disc, but by then the whole quadraphonic system had proved such a commercial failure that the improved version only appeared on a rare pressing from Brazil!

Martyn Ford conducts the Barclay James Harvest Orchestra at London's Rainbow Theatre

There were further disasters in the live arena: appearing at the Great Western Express open-air festival in London's White City Stadium in July, the band were greeted by torrential rain, which collected in the canvas canopy over the stage. Ten minutes into the set, the canopy collapsed, flooding the stage and nearly electrocuting John - band and orchestra were forced to flee! More happily, John and Olwen were married in April that year, and Mel, too, found time to wed his long-time girlfriend, Janet, a few months later. By August, though, the band hit rock bottom, when negotiations with EMI turned so sour that EMI opted not to renew the band's contract, and Barclay James Harvest were staggered to find themselves without a record deal. A sympathetic letter to the band from Harvest label manager Nick Mobbs makes it clear that he and others within Harvest had fought the band's corner, but without success - Mobbs even added a P.S. saying "I still think Mockingbird's a hit!". The resulting shouting match, followed by legal proceedings, between the band and Cassie and Crowe left BJH without management or agent, either, and they were right back where they started.

4

A Helping Hand

At the time that EMI dropped Barclay James Harvest, the band still seemed intent on pursuing solo projects. John's *A Major Fancy* had been delayed from its original release date of June 1st, and was now on hold whilst the contractual ramifications of the split with Harvest rumbled on, but Woolly was writing songs for his album and Les was reportedly ready to begin recording. In truth, the band would probably have folded after their brief but glorious Harvest years if it weren't for the fact that they were by now deep in debt. Not for the last time in their careers, the musicians discovered that the name "Barclay James Harvest" was a marketable commodity, and that without it they would struggle as individuals to make any impact in the cut-throat music business. Such luxuries as solo albums would have to wait until the more important matter of securing a new contract as a band was settled.

For advice, John turned to Eric Stewart of 10cc, with whom he'd formed a good relationship whilst working on BJH and solo material at Eric's Strawberry Studios. Stewart recommended Harvey Lisberg's Kennedy Street Enterprises in Manchester. Initially the band were reluctant, as Kennedy Street had tried to sign the band in their formative days and BJH had not been impressed, but Stewart spoke very highly of them, so they went in to ask for some general advice. Harvey Lisberg was from the old "Tin Pan Alley" school of pop star managers, used to manufacturing an image for his acts, but was interested in getting away from the Herman's Hermits style into rock acts, so Kennedy Street offered to help the band out, even though they couldn't sign any contract with them until the legal situation was resolved.

The negotiations for a new contract were complex. Polydor were very interested in signing the band, not least because Wayne Bickerton, who had been very keen on the band when he was an in-house producer at Decca, was now Head of A&R at Polydor.

Wayne Bickerton

The Liverpudlian's musical career had begun as a member of the Pete Best Three after Pete was relieved of his duties in The Beatles, and would go on to encompass writing hits (with his partner Tony Waddington), including "Sugar Baby Love" and "Juke Box Jive" for The Rubettes. His listening tastes were somewhat different, fortunately!

The main obstacle to any new deal was that EMI were owed a great deal of money by now (in the order of £80,000, a not inconsiderable amount at the time), and were understandably keen to recoup it. Lisberg acted as intermediary, and in December 1973 a deal was finally struck: Polydor got BJH as recording artists, and gave them a "signing on" advance, but the band had to pay £30,000 of this back to EMI as part payment of their debts. In return, EMI agreed not to release any BJH LPs for three years, and allowed Polydor to issue live recordings of songs from the Harvest label albums. Whilst this was undoubtedly a satisfactory deal for the band, it had its drawbacks - firstly, they still had large debts, only now to Polydor, which would have to be paid off if they ever achieved a commercial breakthrough, and secondly, John's solo album was covered by the embargo on EMI BJH releases, and could not be released for a further three years. Lisberg's reward for his hard work was a management contract with Barclay James Harvest, and, later, a publishing deal with Kennedy Street's sister company, St. Annes Music.

Fired up with enthusiasm at this fresh start, BJH immediately set to work recording a new album. The band still had an open invitation to work with the Boston Pops, but crippling costs meant that gigs with the orchestra had already become few and far between, with the band in general, and Woolly in particular, becoming adept at reproducing the orchestral textures on stage. It was a logical step, then, on both artistic and financial grounds, to record an album without orchestral backing. The producer brought in to do the job at Olympic Studios in London was Rodger Bain, best known for his hard rock productions for bands like Black Sabbath and Budgie - not the most obvious choice for the more melodious music of a band like Barclay James Harvest. Indeed, there were occasional problems, with band and producer unable to capture the subtleties of a group version of "Child Of The Universe" to everyone's satisfaction. Woolly was disappointed, too, that his *magnum opus*, "Mæstoso - A Hymn In The Roof Of The World" was seen as too much at odds with the style of the rest of the album, and was unceremoniously discarded.

In spite of these difficulties, the end result of the band's labours was a very strong album, which is still rated by many aficionados as one of their best ever. *Everyone Is Everybody Else* was a big change in direction for the band, with the lush orchestrations of the Harvest-label albums replaced by a harder, sparser sound which allowed the strength of the songs to shine through. What songs, too, with "Child Of The Universe", "Crazy City", "Poor Boy Blues" and "For No

One" demanding admittance to the pantheon of BJH classics from the word go, and not a weak track to be found on the album. This was the sound of a band setting out its stall and showing unequivocally that Barclay James Harvest was a long-term force to be reckoned with. "Child Of The Universe" was rescued from the ignominy of being rejected for previous BJH albums by John's decision to record the song for his solo album; when the rest of the band heard it, they realised its potential, and of course Harvest couldn't release their recording of it, so the way was clear for a BJH interpretation. Mel's contribution to the album was a revelation - not only did his rock-solid drumming form an essential part of the new band sound, but for the first time his talents as a lyricist were also centre stage. "Negative Earth" was based on the near-disastrous Apollo 13 space mission in April 1970, when an explosion forced the astronauts to use the lunar module Aquarius as a "liferaft" to return to Earth, whilst "Paper Wings" was inspired by a visit to the Eiffel Tower. In an interview for the fan club magazine, Mel explained:

"I wrote all the lyrics to 'Paper Wings'. On 'Negative Earth' Les had got this thing that I couldn't get out of my head, and I wrote everything except 'For fifty-five days'. It struck a chord with me, and I like the alliteration of 'here in syncopated time, while my tangled web of rhyme ...'. I just thought about the isolation of this guy. With 'Paper Wings' I was up the Eiffel Tower and I'm not gifted with a head for heights, so I got to the first stage. The rest of the guys went up and I came down, and there's a plaque at the bottom and this dent in the floor – it's like 'Suicide?', was he pushed or did he jump? It was basically that he was 'a broken man without a dream' because if he jumped and he couldn't fly it was a broken dream, or if somebody pushed him then it's still a vision that finished up as a bump in the floor. I'd like to do more. I like lyrics, but with such good lyricists as we've got it's very hard."

"The Great 1974 Mining Disaster" was a deconstruction of The Bee Gees' 1967 hit, "New York Mining Disaster 1941". John changed the melody and then completely re-wrote the lyrics as a comment on the 1974 UK miners' strike that finally brought down the Conservative government. Subtle alterations to the original lyrics such as changing "don't go talking too loud, you'll cause a landslide" to "all you have to do is smile to cause a landslide" were combined with contemporary political and musical references to people such as "a sailor oh so gay" (Prime Minister Ted Heath), "Mister Groan" (miners' leader Joe Gormley) and songs by David Bowie ("The Man Who Sold The World" and "Space Oddity"). Les's "Crazy City", one of the finest songs which he ever penned for BJH, introduced a harder edge to his writing along with some Crosby, Stills, Nash and Young-inspired harmonies, and "See Me, See You" is a reflective John Lees song which includes a cheeky "Hey Jude" quote at the end of the chorus.

EVERYONE IS EVERYBODY ELSE
BARCLAY JAMES HARVEST

The Everyone Is Everybody Else LP (above) and German picture sleeve single of "Poor Boy Blues"

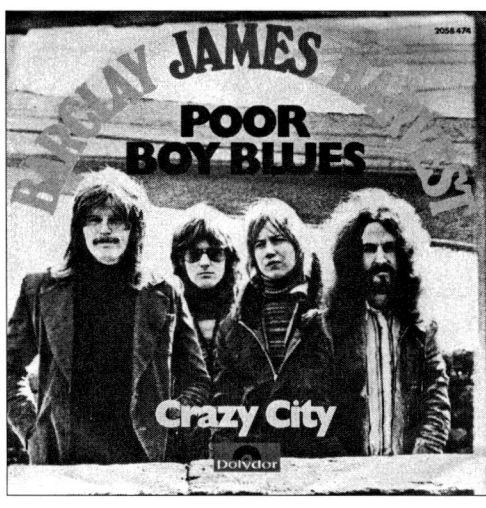

For many, the highlight of the album was the trilogy of songs with which the second side closed. It begins with Les's lilting "Poor Boy Blues", a snapshot of the life and loves of working-class man which was chosen as the single from the album in the UK. "Poor Boy Blues" is interwoven (each supplying the middle eight for the other) with the next song, "Mill Boys", John's observations of work in the major local industries, namely coal mining and the cotton mills. The *pièce de resistance*, though, is the finale, when a brief reprise of "Poor Boy Blues" gives way to the thunderous opening chords of John's anti-war masterpiece, "For No One", with its masterful Mellotron and wah-wah guitar solo. It's one of those albums where the fade-out of the final song leaves you wanting more.

The critics, not for the first or last time, disagreed with the fans, the reviews being at best lukewarm and at worst downright hostile; John Peel was not among them, though, and rated the album very highly. At one point he described on air how, when he first played any new album, he would mark the tracks which he thought were good enough to play on his show, and found that, when he'd reached the end of *Everyone Is Everybody Else*, he'd marked every single song! Ironically, in the light of the band's overall dissatisfaction with the recording of "Child Of The Universe", that song was picked up by radio stations, particularly Radio Caroline, where it still receives regular airplay today. The album gained valuable publicity, too, when Polydor put "Negative Earth" on a promotional flexi-disc which was given away on the front cover of the weekly music paper, *Sounds*. The disc was backed by "Diamonds" by labelmates Rare Bird, who were the Barclays' special guests on the UK tour to promote both bands' new albums.

At about this time reports began to appear that BJH were to be involved in a film project, not only writing the soundtrack music, but also appearing in it. The film was to be called *Windsong*, and was about a group touring the world, although the hero would not be the band themselves, but a roadie! Gliding was another theme of the film, to be set in exotic locations such as Argentina, The Grand Canyon and Switzerland. Mel told music paper *Disc* that the band were hoping that their music would replace dialogue in parts of the film, in a similar way to Neil Diamond's soundtrack for the film of *Jonathan Livingston Seagull*. Plans for a tour of the U.S.A. had to be shelved again because of BJH's commitment to the film.

John must have been in workaholic mode at the time, for, not content with a new Barclays album and tour plus the prospect of appearing in a film, he also found time to record solo again. Using spare time at Olympic Studios, he worked with Les plus two outside musicians, namely B.J. Cole and Mike Moran, to record a couple of songs which weren't considered suitable for Barclay James Harvest. "Best Of My Love" was a straightforward cover version of The Eagles' song, unknown in England at the time, and which John felt deserved more

Birmingham Town Hall, June 1974 [photo: Martin Smith]

The Theatre Royal, Drury Lane

exposure. At the same time they recorded one of John's songs, "You Can't Get It", about The Beatles and The Rolling Stones, and another cover version, this time of Charles Scott Boyer's "Please Be With Me", best known from Eric Clapton's rendition on *461 Ocean Boulevard.* "Best Of My Love" was released as a single in September 1974, with "You Can't Get It", now credited to "Rider" (the maiden name of John's wife Olwen), on the B-side. The single began to pick up airplay, with Anne Nightingale in particular raving about it. At that point the powers-that-were at Polydor, who had apparently been unaware of the project, decided that there was a danger of their new investment fragmenting if such solo ventures were successful, and promptly withdrew the single. The end result was one less hit and one more collectors' item which became a much sought-after and expensive rarity. Spare a thought for one fan who stumbled across a copy in a bargain bin for 50p; being unaware of the release he assumed that the name of the artist was a coincidence and left it there, a decision he rues to this day! John's version of "Please Be With Me" languished on the shelf for another quarter of a century, when it, plus both sides of the single, were added to the CD release of *A Major Fancy.*

The tour to promote *Everyone Is Everybody Else*, by contrast, was a great success. The tour schedule demonstrated the band's steady rise in popularity, with less emphasis on the college circuit where their following had traditionally been largest, and more concerts in bigger halls and theatres, plus appearances on BBC Radio One's *In Concert* programme (an experimental quadraphonic broadcast!) and at the Reading Festival. The tour culminated in two shows at the Liverpool Stadium and The Theatre Royal in London's Drury Lane, which were to be filmed and recorded by Polydor for promotional use and for the band's first live album. Unfortunately, the best-laid plans never seem to go smoothly, especially where BJH are concerned! Roadies trying to trace the source of a loud hum on the guitar amps at the Liverpool Stadium were horrified to discover that it was due to the fact that there was a short in the mains cable, which had no fuses! The concert had to be cancelled and rescheduled for a later date. Then Woolly's Mellotron 300, an unpredictable beast at the best of times, chose the night of the London concert to go haywire, drifting in and out of tune alarmingly all night. Woolly explained his normal technique in an interview for the *New Musical Express*: "My way of solving the tuning problem is to get a 2kW electric fire and place it by the Mellotron, then take the cover boards off and blow the warm air into it for about two hours. Also, you have to switch the Mellotron on about an hour beforehand; it takes a long time to warm up". Sadly, on this occasion, even Woolly's tender ministrations were of no avail, and the recordings were occasionally graced by what might well have been the sound of a lovesick whale. In the end it was decided to mix the offending Mellotron down as far as possible, and to overdub the minimum of new parts to cover it up.

The resulting double album, *Barclay James Harvest Live*, sounds remarkably good, considering its inauspicious beginnings. True, the sound quality is a little rough around the edges, and those with headphones and acute hearing will still be able to make out the unscheduled Mellotronic key-changes, but more importantly, the album captures the live feeling and magic of a fine band at their peak. The rawness of the recordings is a more faithful reflection of the true sound of the band than many live albums which are extensively overdubbed and re-recorded. Many of the performances add a great deal of power and impact to their (already impressive) studio counterparts, and "For No One", in particular, benefits from a superb, chiming finale in place of the anti-climactic fade of the original. The set included many of the band's Harvest-era live favourites, which were used on the record with the permission of EMI, so the album represented a neat way of encapsulating their career to date whilst drawing a line under the

past. Some useful exposure for the album was garnered when parts of the Drury Lane film were shown by Bob Harris on BBC2's *Old Grey Whistle Test* programme. Better still, the band's growing popularity (and the reasonable selling price of £2.94) meant that the album edged its way into the charts at number 40 - at last, after six years of hard work, their first chart record!

Everyone Is Everybody Else received a U.S. release towards the end of the year, and Polydor executives, looking for a single to promote the album, settled on "Child Of The Universe". Given the band's discontent with the original version, the decision was made to re-record the song, so on January 5th, 1975, they went into Polydor Studios with Rodger Bain. The result still wasn't to everyone's satisfaction, so another attempt was made at Advision Studios on January 13th, and yet another at Advision on February 13th. Ironically, Rodger Bain chose the first take, described by John as "terrible", for the American (and French) single and, despite John's misgivings, it became a local AOR radio hit in Los Angeles and was played on regular rotation on L.A. FM rock stations KMET and KLOS. The other January take lay in the vaults unreleased for over a quarter century until it appeared on the *Time Honoured Ghosts* remastered CD in 2003, whilst the February cut appeared on the *Endless Dream* compilation CD in 1996, together with the Barclays' version of Woolly's "Mæstoso".

Whilst EMI were unable to capitalise on BJH's growing success by issuing any new albums, their contract with Polydor did not cover singles, so in March 1975 a single of "Mocking Bird" backed with "Galadriel" appeared on the Harvest label and suffered the same fate as all the other singles. Almost unnoticed at the time, the Bombadil "Breathless" single was also reissued with a new catalogue number, but even the BJH faithful were unaware of the true identity of the artists behind it, and it vanished without trace for a second time.

The band were quick to capitalise on the success of the live album, setting out on yet another UK tour at the beginning of 1975, supported by Julian Brook. Once again there were few college gigs, although one of them was to have a lasting impact on at least one member of the band - at the Brunel University show in Uxbridge on Valentines Day, Woolly met a young fan called Jill Clarke, who would become not only his wife, but also at various times the founder and guiding light behind the band's first official fan club and Woolly's tour manager! The tour was also significant for the fact that after the British concerts the band ventured into other European countries. These were by no means the first shows that they had given outside the UK, but they did mark the first concerted effort to break out of their home territory, and with some success. The European dates were planned as a double-header with the Electric Light Orchestra, who had also just completed a UK tour, promoting their latest album, *Eldorado*. ELO, with a great deal of American success and a Europe-wide hit single in "Roll Over Beethoven" already under their belts, would be the headliners, with BJH adding value as the guest artists. On paper it was a sensible pairing, as musically the two bands had something in common and would be likely to appeal to a similar audience. Unfortunately for the headliners, the fans in The Netherlands and Germany decided that they preferred Barclay James Harvest, and were still shouting for encores from them when ELO were on stage. ELO's manager was Don Arden, a man with a fearsome reputation within the music business as a man who knew what he wanted and wasn't too fussy about how he got it. He was unamused by the situation in which his charges found themselves, and let it be known to the Barclays' entourage that he would quite understand if they wished to bow out of the remaining dates of the tour. BJH and tour manager Lindsay Brown refused to be intimidated and carried on regardless, with the result that it was ELO who ended up on an early flight home, leaving the Barclays as headliners for the rest of the tour. It wouldn't be the last time that big-name acts were bemused to find themselves playing second fiddle to Barclay James Harvest in Europe.

5

London to L.A.

Plans to record a new studio album at the end of 1974 or in the early weeks of 1975 had to be revised because of the success of the live album and the band's continuing tour commitments, whilst the "Windsong" project fizzled out completely. After their not entirely satisfactory experience with Rodger Bain, the band were looking for a new producer, and happily the timing coincided with the availability of a famous American producer who had already expressed an interest in the band. Elliot Mazer, known principally for his work with Neil Young on classics such as *Harvest*, had seen the Barclays performing at the Royal Festival Hall in 1973, and felt that "good songs make good records, and the skills of Barclay James Harvest match up to any of the great artists." He was less than impressed with their previous productions and arrangements, though: "I get very pissed off with wasted talent. Often if a record's a piece of shit it's only because it's been produced badly. I'd seen the band overpowered by an orchestra and working these terrible arrangements at the Festival Hall, but I basically didn't produce them then because of a four-month overrun on Neil Young's *Time Fades Away* album." Not a man to mince his words, Mr. Mazer, but as John Lees put it at the time, "He has a very strong personality, and if there's one thing this band lacks it's anyone with a strong personality." John, was, perhaps, being a little harsh on himself and his fellow band members, but it's undeniable that several times in the band's career they have allowed themselves to be driven by stronger wills than their own, frequently with disastrous results.

The association with Mazer proved to be a fruitful one. The band flew out to San Francisco at the end of April to begin work at Mazer's *His Master's Wheels* studio, taking wives and girlfriends with them for their first trip to the States. Although the sunshine and affluence of California were light years from the band's origins in Saddleworth, both John and Les were fans of bands like The Eagles and Poco who hailed from the area. Whilst some songs, as might be expected, took on a slight American flavour, the band's sound retained at least some of its quintessential Englishness, although the producer and local engineers didn't know quite what to make of Woolly's Mahlerian influences, leaving him feeling somewhat sidelined. As he later put it:

"Some of the band thought it might be some kind of extra injection of energy or whatever if we went over to the States and made an album there. So we did that, and I wasn't really happy with it. Neil Young-type laid back and spaced out was the order of the day, and you felt a bit like that, I must confess, but we weren't producing English music, so it seemed a bit of a waste of having a natural resource and then trying to do something else with it."

On the other side of the cultural divide, the more innocent members of the English contingent were puzzled that so many of the American crew seemed to have runny noses and head colds in the middle of summer …

Lancaster University, 31st October, 1975
[photo: David Bradbury]

When *Time Honoured Ghosts* appeared in October 1975, it was apparent from the first song that Barclay James Harvest had moved on again; "In My Life" (no relation to the Beatles song) set off at a cracking pace, then changed tack with some choral strangeness in the middle eight before John's guitar wound the whole thing back up to speed for the finale. The variety and inventiveness shown throughout the album are astonishing - from Les's haunting, almost *a capella* "Sweet Jesus", through Woolly's inspired but distinctly unusual "Beyond The Grave" to John's world-weary "One Night", by way of classics such as "Jonathan", "Song For You" and the exquisite "Moongirl", there's never a dull moment. "Jonathan" was a survivor from the shelved *Windsong* project, with its "like the windsong on the breeze" refrain. A recurring story in the band's lengthy career has been that of songs which were discarded for one reason or another when written being resurrected later and becoming favourites with the fans! "Jonathan" was inspired by the novel *Jonathan Livingston Seagull* by Richard Bach. The book, first published in Britain in 1972, was a modern-day fable about self-imposed limitations, and used the allegory of a seagull breaking free from physical constraints to make its point. Regrettably, for the film of the book, the soundtrack was commissioned not from Les but from Neil Diamond!

Predictably, the single which was subsequently pulled from the album was the least original song: "Titles" was a collage of Beatles song titles and musical excerpts, cleverly pieced together by John to illustrate the falling out of Lennon and McCartney. Seen in some quarters as a gimmick or attempted cash-in, the single nevertheless received considerable airplay, and made the Top 10 in The Netherlands. Woolly always believed that the American studio and producer didn't do justice to his sole composition on the album, "Beyond The Grave", as it wasn't "rawk and roll" as they knew it! The lyrics were completed on the 'plane on the way over to the States, and the title came from an old horror comic. The original recording went on much longer, but, rather than have a fade-out at the end of the album side, the rather abrupt ending was achieved by the simple expedient of stopping the tape!

The recording of Les's "Song For You" caused some raised tempers in the studio: in a bid to capture the band's sound faithfully, a deliberate decision was made to record as much of the album as possible "live" in the studio. However, this method had its disadvantages, particularly for this song, where the strident opening gives way to an almost elegiac main theme. For the gentler second half of this song, Woolly turned around to switch from organ to piano, whilst John had to put down his electric guitar very carefully, tiptoe across the studio, and pick up the acoustic without making any extraneous noises. After many frustrated attempts, John finally got there in silence. At which point Woolly played a bum note and ruined the take! John exploded with anger: "You c**t!" It was a couple of hours before Woolly was forgiven ...

John described "Hymn For The Children" in a contemporary interview with *Sounds* music paper as "like a follow up to 'Child Of The Universe' which is a follow-on from 'Summer Soldier' which is a follow-on from 'Dark Now My Sky' - there's always one statement-type song on each album." This song is an attack on racism and discrimination; a plea for equal treatment for all mankind, regardless of colour or creed, and features some particularly fine percussion from Mel. "Moongirl" still has a timeless romantic feel to it, despite Woolly's typically irreverent on-stage introduction of it as being "about groupies - you know, the sort of women who wander around in see-through negligées"! Les was not amused, but, perhaps fortunately, the joke was rather lost on the audience, as the band were playing in Heidelberg at the time! "One Night" closes the album by tackling the unusual subject of prostitution from the point of view of a customer. John takes a non-judgemental approach, leaving listeners to adopt their own moral stance.

Time Honoured Ghosts showed the band's status growing apace. With its beautiful album artwork by Bill Dare (inspired by the painting "Harvest", from Maxfield Parrish, shown opposite) and an intriguing title, a quote (but from where nobody can recall!) suggested by the wife of manager Harvey Lisberg,

not to mention the fine music within, the album bettered the sales of its predecessor, charting at No. 32 in the UK and going silver within six weeks. In Switzerland, though, the response put Britain in the shade, with the album reaching No.1. Even the reviews, whilst not all favourable, were considerably better than the band had received for some years. The publishing credits on *Ghosts* reflected the new deal with Harvey Lisberg's St. Annes Music. In previous contracts, mechanical royalties were divided equally between the four band members irrespective of the credited writer.

Now, though, fifty per cent of both mechanical and PRS royalties went direct to the songwriter, leading inevitably to competition between the band members to get more of their own songs onto each album. It was a publishing deal which moved the band further away from the co-operative principles and equal remuneration of the original partnership, a move which had begun with the RAK deal some four years earlier.

The album launch was timed to coincide with the band's autumn tour of the UK, and BJH packed them in at larger theatres and halls up and down the country. Their other European fans were not forgotten, either, as the tour went on to visit Denmark, Sweden, Germany, The Netherlands, Belgium and France. After the largely retrospective concerts in 1974, the band were obviously determined to make a fresh start with *Time Honoured Ghosts*, performing no less than eight of the new songs, plus a sprinkling from *Everyone Is Everybody Else* and finishing with the sole survivor from the Harvest days, "Mockingbird". Continuing another old Barclays' tradition, the support act which goes on to become famous, their guests on the tour were a new band called Café Society, protégés of The Kinks' Ray Davies, who featured Tom Robinson in their line-up.

Lancaster University [photo: David Bradbury]

Café Society's live act featured a drum machine, which the band would solemnly introduce as a band member. After thirty shows, this mildly amusing stunt had worn rather thin for the Barclays' entourage, who planned a little surprise for the last night of the UK tour, at Sheffield University. As Tom Robinson did the introductions, the spotlight shone on the drum seat, now occupied by Charlie Kidd, a very large, and very naked, member of the BJH road crew, waving happily to the cheering students ...

Barclay James Harvest's star was in the ascendant, and the band was beginning to be taken seriously. Mel's wife, Janet, even closed down her successful business, The Buttery in Lydgate, so that she could accompany Mel on tour - and maybe keep an eye on him! 1976 dawned brightly for the band, with a prestigious appearance at the Great British Music Festival at Earls Court in London on New Year's Day, followed a couple of months later by the band's first ever American Tour. After numerous attempts at booking tours across the Atlantic, they'd finally made it. The plan was to kill two birds with one stone by recording a second studio album with Elliot Mazer and playing a series of club gigs across the whole of the States from New York to Los Angeles. The gigs, where the band was supported by acts as diverse as the Sutherland Brothers and Quiver and sci-fi novelist Ray Bradbury reading his own work, were successful, the putative album sessions less so. Mazer was still working on another project by the time that BJH arrived in San Francisco, and the band were left kicking their heels, waiting for the mæstro to turn up. They killed some time by providing some backing vocals for a deep and meaningful David Soul song called "Black Bean Soup", for which they didn't even receive a credit! The devil soon found work for the BJH entourage's idle hands: having met David Soul, they emulated his performance in *Starsky And Hutch* by jumping out of the hotel windows straight onto their rented car. Ian Southerington went one better when, exasperated by the hotel staff's insistence on valet parking the car and expecting a tip every time, drove it up the stairs and straight through the glass doors into the lobby. He then got out and left the car where it was, shouting at the stunned staff, "Now park that, you bastards!" Idle observations that the hotel lifts were as big as a normal bedroom also gave the band an idea: they got to work and shortly afterwards hotel guests entering the lift found themselves in a fully furnished room. To the band's delight, the in-house musicians joined in the joke, and lift passengers were serenaded by a dinner-jacketed string quartet as they ascended together in splendour!

After several wasted weeks the band had to return home to England, as their visas were only valid for a limited period. They decided to produce the album themselves in the more familiar, if prosaic, surroundings of Strawberry Studios North in Stockport.

For ten weeks in the summer of 1976 the band members travelled backwards and forwards to the studio in a battered Austin Maxi every afternoon, working up until midnight. The budget for the album was around £20,000, a fairly modest amount by the standards of the day. John, Les, Mel and Woolly had plenty of experience of recording, if not production, and were ably assisted by an old friend, David Rohl, on the engineering side. The recording process followed a now-familiar pattern for BJH: the basic tracks were laid down with all of the band members present, then piano and drums were added, followed by other

keyboards. Next it was the turn of the lead guitar and vocal parts, then the harmony vocals and extra percussion, before the final process of mixing and overdubbing.

It was Les who came up with a title for the LP. It would be their eighth album, excluding compilations, and was planned for release in October, so why not call it *Octoberon*? The sleeve was another superb piece of artwork - embossed on the front was a painting of Oberon (Shakespeare's King of the Fairies from *A Midsummer*

Night's Dream) rendered as an androgynous figure holding an orb and sceptre. The picture, artist unknown, was half of a pair, and the companion piece representing Titania is believed to be owned by Sir Paul McCartney. Musically, the American influence is still discernible, but variety is again to the fore. "The World Goes On", a fine ballad overlaid with some great guitar work and soaring strings arranged by Ritchie Close, is followed by "May Day", a jaundiced view of totalitarian politics, whether from left or right, which ends in a choral mélange of traditional songs of the *Brave New World* variety. The title refers, of course, to the traditional communist country parades on May 1st, and there are allusions to "the State" and "a party

man", but elsewhere the words attack simplistic black and white notions of right and wrong. The song can also be read as a description of personal confusion and uncertainty. The coda to the song offers no further clues, consisting as it does of a choir singing excerpts from six songs (all at the same time) ranging from traditional English pieces such as Elgar's paean to patriotism, "Land Of Hope And Glory" to the socialist anthem "The Red Flag"! The other songs included are "It's A Long Way To Tipperary", "We'll Meet Again", "There'll Always Be An England" and "The White Cliffs Of Dover". The 'Capriol Singers' included Martin Lawrence and David Rohl. Regrettably, the choir's enthusiasm outstrips their ability in places, with some decidedly dubious harmonies creeping in, and the whole coda smacks somewhat of self-indulgence, tending to spoil an otherwise excellent song. As John told *Beat Instrumental* the following year :

"I wondered what the reaction of the British people would be to a takeover by a totalitarian regime, and I had a funny idea that everyone reverted to the wartime songs. Instead of doing the arrangements myself, I let someone else do it, and they did this really big choir thing and it got totally out of hand. If I had the experience of self-production then which we have now I would have nipped it in the bud."

The "Red Side" closes with Woolly's superb anthem "Ra". Ra was the Ancient Egyptian sun god, and Woolly was inspired by the long hot English summer of 1976 to write one his most dramatic pieces. Doubtless David Rohl, with his lifelong interest in Egyptology, approved of the theme and helped to achieve the semi-classical feel of the recording. Woolly cheerfully admits to having borrowed the first four notes from Mahler's Symphony No.1, although, as he says, it's hardly a major musical theme in the song. The delicate verses lead to some suitably languid guitar work from John, before a reprise of the opening section builds up to the extremely powerful ending.

The "Blue Side" (to be honest, there doesn't seem to be a great deal of meaning behind the colour "themes" of the two sides) opens with Les's song about the trials of making it in the music business, "Rock 'N' Roll Star". There's an obvious reference here to The Byrds' "So You Wanna Be A Rock 'N' Roll Star", and Les's song carries a similar view of the pitfalls of seeking stardom, although musically it is completely different. A more obvious comparison is to

The Eagles' "One Of These Nights", particularly the guitar solo, which bears more than a passing resemblance, but in spite of that, (or perhaps because of it!), the song has become an enduring part of the BJH repertoire. "Polk Street Rag" definitely merits the "blue" tag, being a rare X-rated BJH song! The inspiration for this jokey rocker was the controversial film *Deep Throat*, starring Linda Lovelace. The film had pretensions to artistic content, but was basically a soft-porn movie about a woman with the unusual anatomical feature of having sexual organs in her throat! Polk Street is in San Francisco's red light district, and the band being underemployed in San Francisco at the time of the film's release, presumably decided to pass the time by finding out what the fuss was about! "Believe In Me", Les's delicate love song, has some beautiful vocal harmonies, which have been compared with the style of Steve Stills and Manassas, an early influence on his writing, but it was the album's closer which caused the most controversy and became the fans' favourite. "Suicide?" (the question mark, often missed, is vital) features graphic sound effects of somebody climbing onto the roof of a building and then jumping, or being pushed, to their death. It's a magnificent, thought-provoking song, with John's black humour to the fore in the line, "Don't jump, please for God's sake, let me move my car!"

The chilling special effects don't lose much of their impact, if you'll pardon the expression, even when you know that they were achieved by throwing a dummy, complete with binaural microphones in a specially-designed pair of headphones, off the top of the Holiday Inn in Manchester! The preceding footsteps and lift sound effects were courtesy of Woolly, wearing a pair of traditional Lancastrian clogs, going up in the service lift at Strawberry, but apparently he refused for some reason to wear the headphones for the finale. Legend also has it that the sound effects of the club's bar had to be re-recorded when Ian Southerington, playing the bouncer, said not "Are you a member, Sir?", as we hear on the album, but, "Can I see your member, Sir?"…

The now-traditional autumn tour of the UK coincided with the release of *Octoberon*, and the record company publicity highlighted the fact that the band was celebrating its tenth anniversary with an unchanged line-up. The trek, with

newcomers Easy Street as support, got off to the best possible start when the album entered the UK chart at number 19, becoming their first ever Top 20 record, and continuing the upward trend started when they joined Polydor. The live set endeavoured to strike more of a balance between new and old, featuring four of the songs from the new album, two of which would become fixtures in the act: "Rock 'N' Roll Star" was a popular inclusion for three decades, and "Suicide?" would become one of the fans' all-time favourites; in a later fan club interview John related how, "On that last verse you could hear a pin drop - I was always really impressed with that, people were really listening to it." Full houses around the UK were a further indication of the band's growing popularity, and increasing interest from other European countries, especially Germany, convinced the record company and promoters to extend the tour onto the Continent. Not everything in the garden was rosy, though: the press reviews for *Octoberon* and the tour were almost uniformly bad, with the band being accused of everything from pomposity to plagiarism. John was so incensed by one review, penned by Andy Gill for *New Musical Express*, that he launched a tirade against the music press from the stage at the Hammersmith Odeon show and the band cancelled all interviews

During the seventies, Dave Rohl called on various members of BJH to record jingles for a Manchester ad agency. Clients included National Tyre Services, Asda and Lancaster Carpets, whose slogan featured the words, "Look for the butterfly". Ribald speculation about how they might advertise a well-known brand of condoms resulted in a rather different version, with new words sung by Woolly in a Nöel Coward voice, and Ian Southerington's Dennis Healey impression giving a "One bang guarantee against leaks and inflation", which ended with the immortal lines:

*" ... that isn't too short or too tight,
F*** with a Fetherlite"*

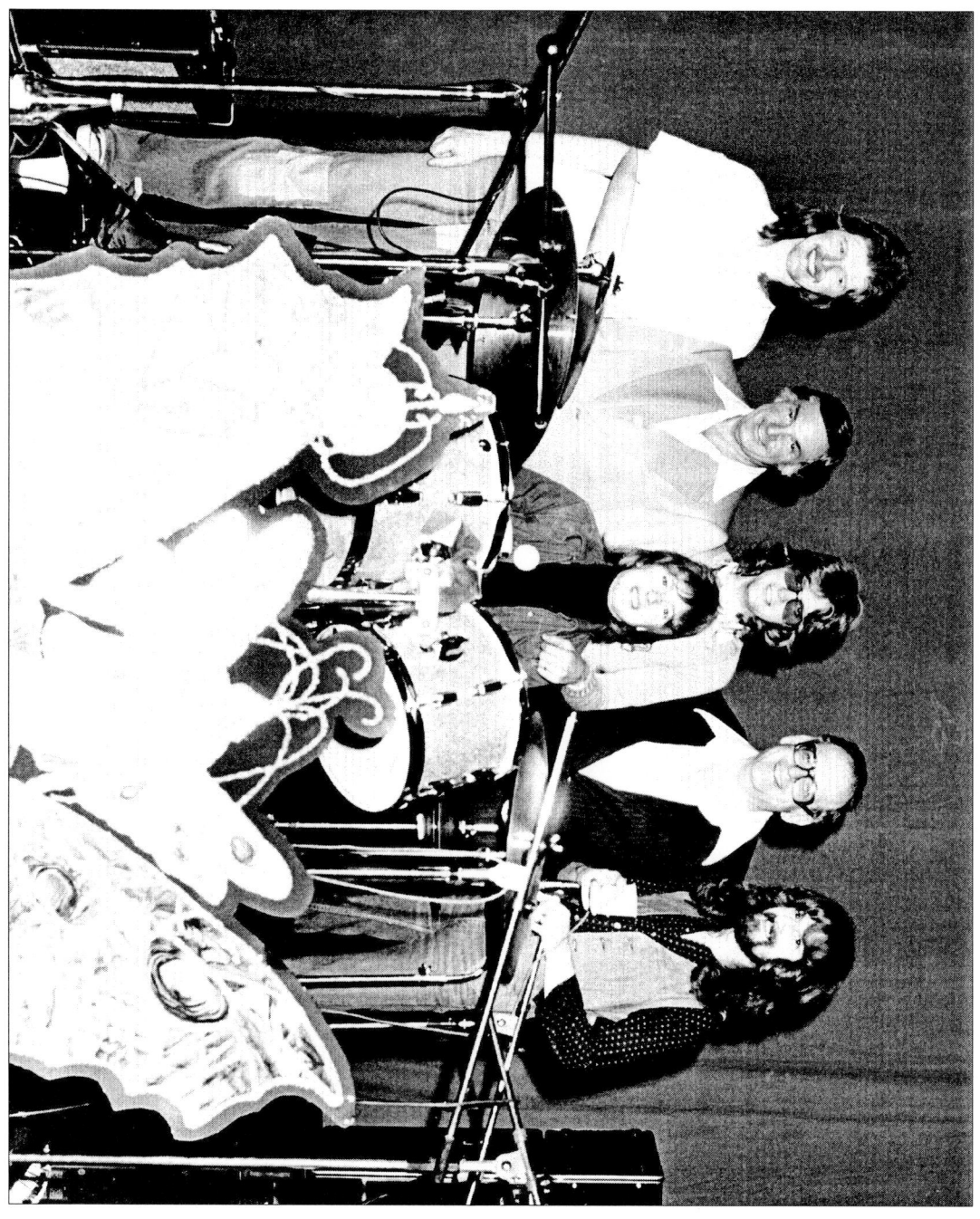

Publicity shot for the 1976 tour, with unnamed representatives of the German record company

for the remainder of the tour. The exception was an interview with Norman McDonald in *Sounds*, where John admitted that the *NME*'s Sheffield City Hall review had shocked the band and left them completely demoralised.

Worse followed when John became ill and the European leg of the tour had to be cancelled. The itinerary was to have included ten shows in Germany, concerts in Scandinavia and Holland and the possibility of visiting Belgium, France and Switzerland, but by the end of the UK leg, John had collapsed and was described as "suffering from physical exhaustion". The media backlash may well have been a factor in John's condition, which was almost certainly as much to do with mental exhaustion as with his physical state.

January 1977 saw the release of *The Best Of Barclay James Harvest*, a mid-price compilation of the band's Harvest label material. Under the terms of the deal made between EMI and Polydor when the band switched labels, three years had elapsed and so EMI were now free to exploit the band's earlier material. Some confusion was caused by the fact that EMI let it be known that they planned to re-package and reissue the long-deleted and by then much sought-after *Early Morning Onwards*. What appeared was actually a new selection which, whilst including some undoubted classics, missed out many of the band's rare single-only tracks, and disappointed the fans.

In April the band's first proper fan club was launched to deal with the growing volume of mail and the demand for more information about their activities. *Friends Of Barclay James Harvest* had impeccable credentials, being run by Jill Clarke, who, as a long time fan of BJH and Woolly's girlfriend, had both an empathy with the band's most loyal followers and the inside information required to make a success of the club.

A number of concerts on the previous year's autumn tour of the UK had been recorded with a view to producing a live album for the American market. In order to bridge the gap between albums, Polydor UK issued a live EP at the

Radio Caroline DJ Andy Archer recalls inadvertently delaying a 70s BJH gig:
"I interviewed Woolly on several occasions. I have one particular memory of when they were playing in Ipswich. Woolly and I went out for a drink before the concert (which was a sell out) and we sat talking for ages when we suddenly realised it was 8.15 and the Barclays were due on stage at 8.00. We rushed from the pub only to arrive at The Gaumont to 1500 people slow hand clapping!! We went in the front entrance as the stage door meant quite a diversion, and walked the length of the theatre with Woolly looking away from the audience and following me so that he wouldn't be recognised! Woolly's Mellotron needed some time to warm up which delayed the start even longer. They didn't get on stage until well after half past eight, but it was a great concert!"

beginning of March, comprising "Rock 'N' Roll Star" and "Medicine Man" from these recordings. The fine live performances were not best served by the sound quality of the EP, since the long running time (totalling over seventeen minutes) meant that the record had to play at 33 r.p.m. Nostalgia for the heyday of vinyl sometimes blinds us to just how bad singles could sound in those times before 12" or CD singles! Worse still, "Medicine Man" was split between the two sides of the record, fading out after a few minutes of the song and fading back in at the beginning of the second side. Heresy! Carping aside, the EP was well presented in a full colour sleeve (rare at the time for singles) and widely advertised, with the result that "Live" became the band's first single to trouble the UK chart compilers, reaching the giddy heights of number 49 for two weeks! This was enough to earn them an appearance on that institution of the BBC, *Top Of The Pops*, where "Rock 'N' Roll Star" was introduced by Tony Blackburn, housewives' favourite and the butt of many jokes from the likes of John Peel as a man entirely devoid of musical taste. "I think it's one of the best numbers out at the moment", enthused Tony, as ten years of hard-earned "serious albums band" credibility went down the pan. The EP dropped out of the charts the following week …

6

Taking Me Higher

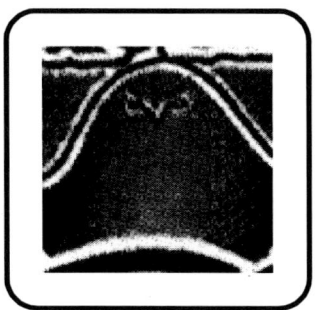

Undeterred, the band began work at the end of March 1977 at Strawberry on the next studio album, with David Rohl elevated from engineer to co-producer with the band. Determined to avoid the mistakes which they felt had been made with Octoberon, they opted for more and shorter songs and less grandiose arrangements. The first results of their work appeared in July, with the single "Hymn". Starting gently with acoustic guitars, the song builds steadily to an inspirational peak, augmented by massed twelve-string guitars, organ and horns. The religious symbolism of the lyrics led many listeners to assume that the song was a Christian anthem or even a Christmas song, but, as with many of John's songs, the surface meaning is only half the story. "Hymn" is actually an anti-drug song, drawing unfavourable comparisons between chemically induced "highs" and those of a spiritual nature. As John explained in a *Daily Mirror* interview ,

"I'm not a religious freak and I don't go to church, but I do believe in God and I also believe that He is preferable to cocaine. Part of my lyrics say 'don't try to fly, you know you might not come down', in other words you might take an overdose and die."

The song which was to become synonymous with Barclay James Harvest actually had an inauspicious start: it dated back to 1971, when it was presented in demo form for possible inclusion on the *other short stories* album, but rejected! During the 1977 recording sessions it had the working title "Hymn For A White Lady", white ladies being a popular recreational barbiturate tablet at the time. However, it was felt that this more explicit title could be misinterpreted as advocating the use of drugs, so it was shortened to "Hymn". The single was issued with a picture sleeve and the non-album track, "Our Kid's Kid", as an incentive to existing fans on the B-side. This is another Lees composition, a personal song about his sister, Edna, and her daughter Ruth. "Hymn" received a moderate amount of airplay, but the BBC considered it "too Christmassy", and so the sales push was postponed until later in the year. In Germany the response was much more positive, and the song became a "turntable hit", getting a lot of airplay but not quite breaking into the charts.

At about the same time, BJH were announced as special guests at a Beach Boys concert at Manchester's Belle Vue on July 24th, but the festival was cancelled when the Beach Boys pulled out because of illness. Another non-event was the Bremen Festival, where the band had been booked to play in the summer - when the German army was called in to quell rioting and the stage was set on fire, BJH were advised not to travel. The history books don't reveal the cause of the rioting, although it's probably safe to assume that it wasn't because the good burghers of Bremen were outraged at the prospect of crazed BJH fans wrecking the town ...

EMI chose this time to give John's "lost" solo album, *A Major Fancy*, a belated release, trailing it with an edited single of "Child Of The Universe". The album was included in their Harvest Heritage mid-price series, and unfortunately the packaging reflected this. The originally planned gatefold sleeve featuring a kestrel painted by a well-known wildlife artist had apparently been lost, and for reasons which we've never been able to discover, the track titles were quite different from those advertised in 1973 - the actual recordings and running order were the same (and the original catalogue number can be seen in the LP's run out groove, suggesting that stampers made for the original release were used to press the 1977 version), but all of the "Untitled" track titles were changed: "Untitled No.6 - Allergy" became "Untitled No.1 - Heritage", "Untitled No.8 (A Lost Affair)" became "Untitled No.2", "Untitled No.2 - Sweet Faced Jane" lost the untitled bit of its title, "Untitled No.1 - Heritage" turned into "Long Ships", and "Untitled No.4 - Hands Across The Water" mutated into "Untitled No.3"! Given that the original artwork was lost, it's possible that the track titles, too, had gone missing, and that someone retitled them incorrectly from memory. The LP didn't include lyrics, and the sleeve notes were not only unflattering and inaccurate, but also failed to mention the fact that the recording was four years old. The album didn't sell well, and was quickly deleted, becoming highly collectable in the process.

Sketch for the original artwork of A Major Fancy (left) and the 1977 LP issue (right)

Gone To Earth was released in the September, and featured a beautiful cutaway sleeve designed by Maldwyn Reece Tootill. Mal explains how it came about:

"In 1977 I was working as a freelance illustrator in London and still had close ties with the band, who'd always shown interest in my work. I had become very involved in developing my work in the field of natural history with a keen interest in painting birds of prey. Mel Pritchard purchased and commissioned several works around this time so I guess I had a reasonable currency with the band. I came across a very specialist book entitled *Gone To Earth*, a publication on Australian owls. After securing a vote of confidence from the band I set about developing some ideas. I used to meet the band in *The*

Hanging Gate pub on a regular basis when I came up from London and this was where much of the business was done! Several titles were kicked about and I proposed *Gone To Earth* which was evocative of the owl striking its prey as it descends to earth. After seeing my ideas and turning the project over and over, it was decided that the band would support my ideas of using the owl coming in to land and utilise the title *Gone To Earth*. I can't fully recall how the cutaway cover emerged, but I do recall feeling quite pleased with myself at innovating the concept of using the inner sleeve or bag as a fundamental part of the illustration, and one which carried an alternative image on the reverse side, showing a dawn scene in contrast to the dusk image which formed the main concept image. Being a young and inexperienced illustrator at the time I was blissfully unaware of the production problems inherent in producing the cover in this way, and to this day I'm eternally grateful for the band's support throughout the project in the face of some initial shock-horror responses from Joe Mirowski, the art director at Polydor."

On the back of the cover was a montage created by David Rohl and the band from photographs taken by Les's brother-in-law, Christopher B. Roberts. The album opened strongly with the recent single, "Hymn", followed by another Lees song, the romantic ballad "Love Is Like A Violin". Curiously, the verse beginning "Love was like a summer breeze", which is printed on the inner sleeve, does not appear on the recording. Memories differ as to whether it was actually recorded, but the full version has never come to light, so it seems likely that it was truncated before the recording was completed. Les's up-tempo, country-tinged "Friend Of Mine" (featuring a rare example of his banjo-playing!), was followed by the oddly-titled "Poor Man's Moody Blues". John, speaking to *Beat Instrumental* magazine, explained the genesis of the song thus:

"We've always been accused of being like the Moodies; we started off at a similar time, had the Mellotron around the same time and perhaps we did progress on parallel lines although we weren't aware of it. But last year in the press someone actually called us a 'poor man's Moody Blues' and I got a bit aggro-ed about this. I wondered how I could answer it back, and decided to do it musically, and I've written a song entitled 'Poor Man's Moody Blues'. I took the skeleton structure of 'Nights In White Satin' - just that drum beat, put a new melody to it - you listen to it and you think you're listening to 'Nights In White Satin', with the same breaks and everything, but the moment you try singing that melody you'll find it doesn't work at all. OK, a lot of people may be upset by it, but we were also upset at that kind of accusation."

Ironically, the song rapidly became one of the most popular in their repertoire, and not just amongst Moodies fans! Les's funkier "Hard Hearted Woman" is a tale of being bewitched by an unfeeling siren and contrasts nicely with Woolly's symphonic "Sea Of Tranquility", which whilst ostensibly about the futility of the space race in the 1960s and 1970s, can also have a meaning which is somewhat closer to home. Returning to a regular Barclays theme of environmental concern which can be traced right through from "Dark Now My Sky" to "Stand Up", the delicate "Spirit On The Water" takes a swipe at the exploitation of animals in general and the fur industry's slaughter of pup seals in particular. John's rocker, "Leper's Song", was inspired by two novels: Graham Greene's *A Burnt Out Case*, which deals with the so-called burn-out syndrome, and Joseph Conrad's *An Outcast Of The Islands*, which has a similar theme of one man's alienation from the society in which he finds himself. Finally, "Taking Me Higher" closes the album on an simple but uplifting note.

One more song was recorded at the *Gone To Earth* sessions, but was left off the album in the final accounting, probably because of the time limitations peculiar to vinyl LPs: "Lied", also known as "Please Give Me One More Chance", was a John Lees song with a twist about a relationship in difficulties, and bears all the hallmarks of the BJH sound of the time. Abandoned at the time, it was rediscovered in the vaults in the next century and took its rightful place again on the remastered version of the *Gone To Earth* CD. Even without "Lied", though, *Gone To Earth* was a well-balanced album showcasing three writers working at their peak. As Woolly later put it, "a lot of good things came together on *Gone To Earth* - some of John's best, like 'Poor Man's Moody Blues' and 'Hymn', and Les's 'Spirit On The Water'. There was a nice balance, the artwork was good and somehow everything happened at the right time."

Predictably, the contemporary reviews of the LP in the UK press were dismal, not least because the British music press had by now caught on to punk rock and leapt aboard the bandwagon, dismissing established bands as dinosaurs who were no longer relevant. To be fair, the self-indulgence and preposterous excesses of some of the "progressive" rock bands invited a backlash, and punk and new wave were probably necessary in order to prick the bubble of egotism gone mad and to get music back to its rebellious roots. However, to tar BJH with this particular brush was to do them a great injustice; this was a band which, whilst possibly guilty of the occasional over-elaborate arrangement, had never inflicted a concept album on an unsuspecting public, had never performed with pointless pyrotechnics or dancing dwarves in their stage show and, best of all, eschewed the almost obligatory tedious drum solo so beloved of their contemporaries. For that alone we should be prepared to overlook the occasional Tolkien reference or dodgy haircut ...

The annual UK tour was arranged to coincide with the issue of *Gone To Earth*, plus a more extensive European schedule to make up for the previous year's cancelled shows. The band took a chance by concluding the show with the untested "Hymn", and the gamble paid off handsomely, with the song becoming an instant classic. Interestingly, the live reviews were significantly better than those garnered by the LP, which reached a slightly disappointing chart peak of number 30 in the UK. By the time the band got to Germany, they were a little worried that the enforced gap since they had last appeared there would have affected their popularity, a concern doubtless intensified by the fact that they had a camera crew in tow, making a documentary about the band. In fact, their fears were unfounded: radio support for "Hymn" had been redoubled with the release of *Gone To Earth*, whilst programmers had also been much taken with "Poor Man's Moody Blues". The cancellation of the previous year's concerts had led to greater interest in the current tour, and the band was amazed to find that extra concerts had to be added in many of the major cities to cope with the overwhelming demand for tickets. Concerts sold out in Holland, Germany and Switzerland, while *Gone To Earth* reached the Swiss Top 10 and became a fixture in the German album chart. Although it only peaked at number 10, the album refused to go away, and went on to spend almost three years on the chart, putting the band right up there with acts like Pink Floyd and Supertramp. At last Barclay James Harvest were beginning to reap the rewards that their talents, not to mention ten years of hard work, deserved.

"Meet the press" meal on the Gone To Earth tour in 1977 [Photos: Ueli Frey]

Whilst the successes which were finally coming their way were undoubtedly welcome, the downside was that the band was caught on a treadmill of constant recording and touring, leaving them no time for projects outside of the group line-up. Woolly was particularly frustrated that although John had been given the opportunity to record a solo album, not only was Woolly unable to do so but he was also increasingly having to fight to get any of his own songs included on BJH albums. The decision made back in 1971 to credit individual writers rather than assign songwriting credits to the band as a whole was coming home to roost, as the inevitable rivalry it engendered created rifts within the band. Hindsight is a wonderful thing, but with the benefit of it, there were some cracks to be seen in the facade. Woolly, already disappointed that "Mæstoso" had been dropped from *Everyone Is Everybody Else*, was not happy with the way that BJH's music was progressing. He resisted what he saw as the increasing Americanisation of their music, and had been against recording in San Francisco. As already touched upon, the lyrics of "Sea Of Tranquility" speak of dissatisfaction with the band. Lines like:

Our hopes ever high that the songs we sing
and the words we bring should never die!

speak of a "star-struck" optimism, whilst

We sold our souls for senseless gain
and brought our harvest home in vain

reflect a bitter disillusionment. In the meantime, though, everyone was kept busy trying to capitalise on the success of the *Gone To Earth* album and tour.

The live album destined for the American market was now scheduled for the UK, too, before Christmas 1977, with the following track-listing:-

Crazy City; Medicine Man; Rock 'N' Roll Star; The World Goes On; Child Of The Universe; Polk Street Rag; Mockingbird; For No One; Hymn For The Children; One Night; Jonathan; Suicide?

The plan had to be changed again, though, when the proposed deal to release the album in America fell through. Since Europe would now be the only market for the LP, and the 1974 live album was still available there, it was decided to avoid too much duplication of tracks by using more recent material recorded for the documentary film in Germany on the 1977 tour and making it another double LP. "The World Goes On" and "Hymn For The Children" were therefore dropped, and four *Gone To Earth* songs, namely "Poor Man's Moody Blues", "Hard Hearted Woman", "Taking Me Higher" and "Hymn", added. It's

Winterthur Eulachhalle, 27th October, 1978 [Photo: Ueli Frey]

not known exactly where each song was recorded, but the 1976 songs were taped at the Liverpool Empire (October 14th), Hammersmith Odeon (19th) and Croydon Fairfield Halls (24th), whilst some of the 1977 tracks were recorded in the UK and some in Hamburg. The one hour documentary film and the live album were scheduled to come out in April, with the film being shown on Belgian and Swiss TV and in German and British cinemas. The LP, though, was delayed when the band was unhappy with the quality of printing on the sleeve, which was largely designed by themselves. Another factor was the proposed title - *Caught Live*. A fan club member, Chris Naylor, pointed out that the Moody Blues had recently released a double live album with the title *Caught Live - Plus Five*, so for BJH to release a very similarly titled album including the song "Poor Man's Moody Blues" would have given the critics a field day. The band had, apparently, been unaware of the similarity, and acted quickly to change the album title to *Live Tapes*, although the film, in a more advanced state of production, retained the original title.

In order to bridge the gap whilst the live album was finished, Polydor released "Friend Of Mine", remixed to pull the vocals up and give the song a more AM radio-friendly sound, as a single in March, backed with the forthcoming *Live Tapes* version of "Suicide?". At about the same time, *Gone To Earth* qualified for a silver disc in the UK, having sold over £150,000 worth. This was the sixth time they had gone silver in Britain, the previous ones being *Once Again, Everyone Is Everybody Else, Barclay James Harvest Live, Time Honoured Ghosts* and *Octoberon*. March 1978 also saw the band meeting to review new material for the next studio album. Of twenty-five new songs presented, three (one each of John's, Les's and Woolly's) were chosen to be worked on immediately, with more to be selected later.

In May of that year an interesting "side project" made its appearance; for over two years producer David Rohl had been using all his spare time in writing and recording an ambitious concept album, using many of the musicians with whom he had worked at Strawberry, including all four members of Barclay James Harvest, plus Justin Hayward, Maddy Prior, Sad Café and many more. The members of Sad Café, with the exception of singer Paul Young, had previously been in an outfit called Mandalaband, whose eponymous album had been largely written by Rohl. The same band name was retained for the new album, entitled *The Eye Of Wendor - Prophecies,* which appeared on the Chrysalis label. The concept encompassed a fantasy storyline with the guest singers performing individual character roles which were further developed on the lavish illustrated fold-out story included with the LP. BJH didn't sing on the album, but all four members made musical contributions, most notably Woolly, who appeared on almost every track and helped to provide musical continuity.

Whilst working on *The Eye Of Wendor*, Woolly got to know many of the other musicians, among whom were guitarist Steve Broomhead and drummer Kim Turner.

The release of the Mandalaband album came at a singularly inappropriate time for BJH, as by now they were back in Strawberry Studios with engineer and co-producer - David Rohl. There was friction from the outset between Rohl and some members of the band, as they felt that he was too involved in the promotion of his own album to do justice to his work with them. On the other hand, David complained that he was frequently at work early in the morning with Mel and Woolly, and that Les and John didn't turn up for work until the afternoon. There were frequent interruptions from Chrysalis about the Mandalaband project, but the final straw came when BJH realised that his album included the taped rototom introduction to their own stage show, to

which they thought they had exclusive rights. Rohl's subsequent stormy departure left the recording sessions in limbo, with no trained engineer - Strawberry's manager, Peter Tattersall, stepped in temporarily until a replacement was found in Martin Lawrence, best-known for his work on Godley and Creme's *Consequences* set.

David Rohl and Les take a break during the Mandalaband sessions at Strawberry (above).

John, vocalist Fiona Parker, technician Trevor Worman and David relax at the studio (below).

Recording of the new album was well under way by the time that *Live Tapes* finally appeared in June. The album still hangs together well as a record of a band close to their artistic and commercial peak, even though the recordings are taken from two different tours and many different concerts. However, many UK fans felt that a second double live album, coming less than four years after their first, was pushing things, and despite extensive advertising, the album failed to crack the UK chart at all. In Germany, where the first live album had not been released, the response was more encouraging, with the LP reaching the Top 20.

Events were moving quickly now, and the dust had barely settled on *Live Tapes* before the new studio album was ready (one contemporary German magazine article described the band as being "as fertile as rabbits"!). The departure of David Rohl as co-producer didn't have a significant effect on the final sound, since much of the work had been completed before he and the band parted company. The main difference in comparison with *Gone To Earth* was that the band chose to go for a more "live" sound in the studio, in an attempt to get a less clinical, more energetic result. It was said in the *Friends Of Barclay James Harvest* newsletter that this method was promoting more interaction between the band members and producing a constant flow of ideas.

The unimaginatively titled *XII* (so-called because it marked the band's twelfth anniversary together, as well as for the more obvious reason that it was their twelfth album if *Early Morning Onwards* is included in the tally) was released on September 15th, 1978. If *Gone To Earth* was a hard act to follow, then *XII* was a very creditable attempt, and indeed some prefer the diversities of *XII* to its more commercial predecessor. The album runs the gamut of styles from the word go, with two very different BJH classics: John's musical homage to Free's guitarist Paul Kossoff in the stomping "Loving Is Easy", and Les's magnificent piano-led "Berlin", inspired by the plight of the city which, at the time the song was written, was still divided by that relic of the Cold War, the infamous Wall separating East and West. In the punning Dickensian title "A Tale Of Two Sixties" John takes an affectionate look back at some of his early inspirations: including *Easy Rider* (the film whose soundtrack included The Byrds), Bob Dylan's *Rolling Thunder Revue* and Arthur Lee of the band Love, whose timeless *Forever Changes* album contains "Andmoreagain". "Chairman Young", whose thoughts were said to have inspired the song, was Pete Young,

who worked with John Crowther and introduced BJH to the music of bands like Love. "Turning In Circles" carries on where "Hard Hearted Woman" left off, and John courted controversy again in "The Closed Shop" (about the then-prevalent practice in some professions of having an agreement between union and management that nobody would be allowed to hold a particular job unless they were a member of the union). John Peel grumbled on air about the latter that it was impossible to tell whether

John was pro or anti; in a later interview John denied that he had been union-bashing, but explained the song thus:

"I wasn't against the working class, I wasn't against the unions - I was against the closed shop. I thought it was a destructive force, and I still do. If you look back through all the songs I've written in that kind of vein, they're all pro-working class, because that's what I am, and you can't change where you come from. I'm not really political, I've got a social conscience."

Woolly described "In Search Of England" as being "about youth and principles on one hand and the voice of experience on the other, a kind of father and son thing." "Sip Of Wine" was a cautionary tale of the perils of being seduced by groupies and loving it! Les's tongue-in-cheek song also includes the wonderful piece of wordplay, "I held her breath and she was holding mine!". We were shocked ... Woolly's "Harbour" was written about "coming home on a 'plane from some monstrous tour or from America." At one stage it was considered as a single and was recorded really fast, then slowed down for use as an album track, losing some attack in the process. The Morse code at the beginning of "Nova Lepidoptera" spells out "U.F.O.", and the lyrics are made up from cut-up titles and phrases from John's collection of science-fiction novels; in spite of this rather mechanistic approach to songwriting, the lyrics work well, and the twin guitars turn it into a standout track. "Giving It Up" is another atmospheric love song with massed choirs courtesy of Les and John, multi-tracked, and the album bows out with "The Streets Of San Francisco", based on the American film and TV series of the same name starring Karl

Malden. The song namechecks the neighbourhood of Haight(-Ashbury) and the Golden Gate bridge across "Frisco Bay", and showcases Woolly's evocative harmonica playing. Woolly's retrospective view was that, "Things seem to have happened in twos; I felt that *Other Short Stories* was overshadowed by *Once Again*, and *XII* was overshadowed by the success of *Gone To Earth*, although sonically they are more of a pair. I personally think that some of the songs on *XII* are better."

The album could have looked very different, as at one point it had the working title *High*, and the sleeve as envisaged would have been based on a photograph of a sunset taken by Woolly from an aircraft when flying to a promotional engagement. The proposed title was deemed too open to interpretation as a reference to illicit drugs, though, and changed to *XII*. The picture being no longer relevant, the butterfly artwork incorporating drawings of the band's faces, conceived by Mal Tootill and executed by Chris Clover, was commissioned instead. Woolly's photo wasn't wasted, however, as it later graced his solo album, *Mæstoso*. UK copies of XII also included a large fold-out poster with the cover design on one side and lyrics and credits on the back, although this was accidentally omitted from the whole of the first batch.

One curious feature of this album is the listing of John's songs with categorisations befitting a library - "Science Fiction: Nova Lepidoptera", "Fantasy: Loving Is Easy" etc. Had the scheme been followed through the whole album, it would have been an interesting concept, but there was no agreement within the band, so John's idea was applied only to his own songs, much to the puzzlement of fans.

The widening gap between the band's popularity at home and in Germany meant that whilst *XII* made only a fleeting appearance in the UK album chart at number 31, it stayed in the German chart for months. In spite of peaking at a relatively low number 18, *XII* sold 250,000 copies in its first year, becoming the band's second German gold disc only six months after *Gone To Earth* achieved the same sales figure.

The choice of single from the album became the cause of some controversy, verging on farce. "Loving Is Easy" seemed an obvious choice, a commercial rocker with a sing-along chorus, but when it was previewed to the BBC for inclusion on the Radio One playlist, there was a problem: they loved the song, but felt that lyrics such as "I shoot all my love into you/into your fire" were a shade too risqué for daytime radio's squeaky-clean image. This is the same station which had been happy to give great exposure, so to speak, to songs such as The Kinks' "Lola", a song about a young man's relationship with a transvestite - presumably the subtleties of lines like "I'm a man, I'm a man and so is Lola" were lost on the censors. In any case, the band agreed to re-record the vocals of "Loving Is Easy", substituting the more innocuous, "I send all my love out to you" and "I burn all my love in your fire", and were rewarded with an invitation to record the song for *Top Of The Pops*. Having done that, they looked forward to heavy airplay and TV coverage giving them their first major hit single, only to discover that the BBC had banned the song

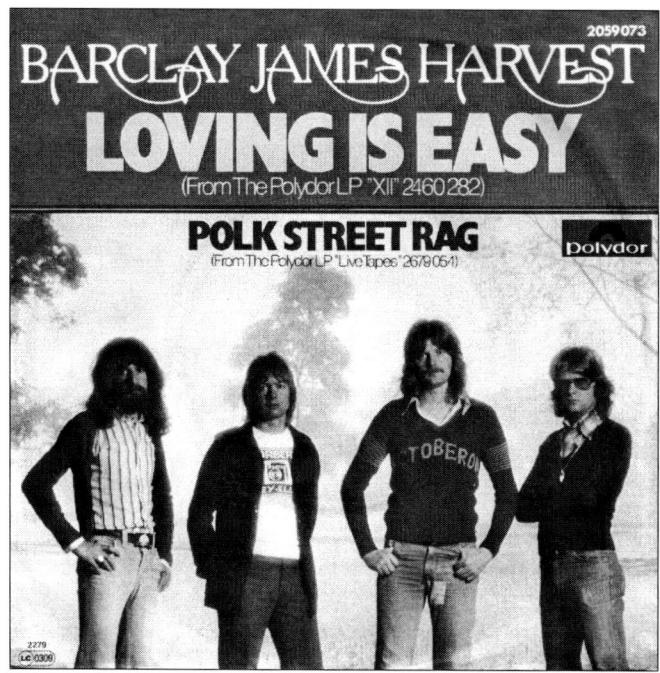

German picture sleeve for the "Loving Is Easy" single

121

anyway! The reason - another line in the song, which goes "Just get a hold and watch how it grows"!! Had things turned out differently, BJH's staid image could have been banished forever. As it was, the limited edition of 20,000 in blue vinyl pressed in France for the UK market barely sold out, with the result that the second "unlimited" pressing on black vinyl has become a much sought-after collector's item ...

Within a fortnight of the album's release the band was on the road again for the traditional autumn tour, taking in sixteen shows in the UK, followed by a similar number in continental Europe. The second half of the tour understandably concentrated on Germany, but also included concerts in Switzerland, France and, after an absence of many years, Denmark. Concerts in Portugal and Spain were also planned, but the business deals fell through. This proved to be a blessing in disguise, though, as the demand for tickets in Germany exceeded expectations by a wide margin, and the Iberian cancellations enabled the promoters to slot in five extra shows. "Hymn" was the showstopper again; in Düsseldorf John dedicated "Hymn" to rock stars who had fallen victim to drugs, saying "let's hear it for Jimi Hendrix ... Paul Kossoff ... Janis Joplin ..." etc. The fans responded with a roar of approval, thus starting the tradition of audience participation in "Hymn", with John and the fans trading shouts of "Yeah!" at live shows over the next couple of decades.

Although the band's relationship with David Rohl had ended somewhat acrimoniously, this didn't prevent Woolly from continuing to work with Rohl on a series of soundtracks for TV projects. The first of these was *The Talking Parcel*, a children's feature-length cartoon based on a story by Gerald Durrell and animated by Brian Cosgrove and Mark Hall. Most of the music was written by Rohl, with additional contributions from Woolly, and there were plans for a soundtrack album of extended and modified musical themes from the film to be released by Phonogram, although this never materialised. The film was premiered by ITV on Boxing Day, 1978, and subsequently released on video. Woolly and David Rohl went to work again on another Cosgrove Hall film, this time a puppet animation of the *Cinderella* tale with no dialogue, with the whole story told only by the music and sound effects. The film won awards and was shown on TV in the UK and Germany (the latter under the title *Aschenputtel*).

Early 1979 saw the release of a second volume in EMI's *The Best Of Barclay James Harvest* series, and it seemed that EMI had listened to the criticisms of the first LP, because the new one included several non-album rarities, notably the debut single, "Early Morning"/"Mr. Sunshine", in the original mono versions, plus both sides of the fabled (if not fabulous) Bombadil single.

On March 23rd, 1979, the band signed a new management contract with London-based Handle Artists, leaving Harvey Lisberg, although the change

wasn't as drastic as it first appeared. Lisberg worked closely with Danny Betesh's booking agency, Kennedy Street Enterprises, and their London booker was Lindsay Brown, a former college Social Secretary. Lindsay had become a close friend of the band over the years, and left Kennedy Street to become a director of Rockbray Ltd., a new company jointly owned by David Walker and himself. David Walker was, perhaps, best known for his work with Mud and The Sweet, as well as coming up with the 1966 football World Cup mascot, World Cup Willie! David and Handle Artists would later represent Status Quo, too, and his primary function in the new set up was to put the band's financial affairs onto a firm footing and to deal with business contracts, with Lindsay Brown concentrating on day to day organisation.

Harvey Lisberg had never really come to terms with the seventies rock scene, having cut his teeth with sixties pop stars who performed other people's songs and were told how to dress and behave. Those fresh-faced, malleable young men in suits must have seemed light years away from these long-haired youths in jeans who wrote their own music and saw themselves as serious artists who wouldn't dream of compromising their ideals for crass commercialism. Lisberg didn't see the sharp distinction that the rest of the music business and, more importantly, the fans, drew between superficial pop "singles bands" and serious "albums bands". There was a long-running battle over singles - whilst the band saw them as a necessary evil to promote a new album, Lisberg had a vision of the band as a pop act with a string of hit singles. When John, Les, Woolly and Mel presented him with the tapes of their latest opus, he would listen carefully and then pronounce of one song or another, "That's the hit single!", to a chorus of groans. It must be said that BJH were probably not the easiest band with whom Lisberg had to deal. All four members could be obstinate in their refusal to compromise, but Lisberg's later description of the band as, "an absolute quagmire of personality problems" (in Johnny Rogan's book *Starmakers And Svengalis*) seems somewhat overstated! Lisberg was also quoted in the same book as saying, "I've never had an act that can deliver on stage. With all the success I've had I can never look back to a great performance". With that he dismissed not only Barclay James Harvest, but also 10cc and Sad Café, fellow Mancunians who, like BJH, were a superb live act whose reputation was built on the quality of their stage performances. Little wonder, then, that BJH were keen to sign to a management company which showed more belief in them. The Kennedy Street links were not broken completely, though, as the band's tours continued to be promoted by Danny Betesh of Kennedy Street, and sister company St. Annes Music retained the rights to all the band's publishing for the three years for which BJH had been signed to them.

Gone To Earth passed the magic 250,000 German sales mark in March 1979 and qualified for a gold disc. Encouraged by the burgeoning sales of the band's most recent albums in Germany, Polydor GmbH launched a big campaign in March to promote BJH's back catalogue. *Barclay James Harvest Live,* previously available only as an import, was released for the first time in Germany, as was a special limited edition (of 20,000) maxi-single of "Sip Of Wine", backed with "Hymn". As part of the push, it was decided that instead of the usual autumn tour, the band would play four massive gigs in Germany in June, delaying a full tour until early 1980. In the meantime, new material was previewed and eight songs chosen for the next studio album, namely John's "Capricorn", "Sperratus" and "Skin Flicks", "Play To The World" , "Rock 'N' Roll Lady" and "The Song (They Love To Sing)" from Les and "Lives On The Line" and "A Prospect Of Whitby" by Woolly (although "American Excess" was rejected as "too pretentious"!). The plan was to begin recording in July after the German concerts, then to write the material for a second studio album before setting out on the next tour. The plan was destined not to come to fruition. As Woolly put it in a later interview,

"We went into rehearsals and we started to trot through 'Capricorn' or something, and it just ... the bottom went out of it all, it felt so pointless. It had been something that I'd been running up to for a while, and my heart just wasn't in it any more. I just didn't want to go on."

To the consternation of the rest of the BJH camp, Woolly walked out. His wife Jill knew that Woolly was prone to depression, and persuaded him to go back and talk to the others again before making a rash decision. He agreed, and a tense meeting took place at the studio to discuss the future of the band. Woolly's own position in the band was not his only cause for complaint; since Jill had been running the *Friends Of Barclay James Harvest* fan club, he felt that she had not received enough support and encouragement from the other members of the band, leaving Woolly as the only one contributing to the club newsletters. On being asked what kind of support he envisaged, Woolly replied, "You could at least give her some feedback." At that point, in an ill-advised attempt to lighten the atmosphere, John turned up his guitar in front of the speakers, producing a loud squeal, joking, "There's some feedback for you!" Woolly exploded with rage and stormed out of the studio again. Part One of the Barclay James Harvest story was over.

7

Tonight Lives On For Years

At a series of crisis meetings with the band's management, several agreements were hammered out: Woolly would honour the band's live commitments for the four German concerts, and nothing would be said about his departure until an agreed point later in the year. He would continue to be represented by Handle, who would negotiate a solo recording contract for him, but he would be restricted in the use of the Barclay James Harvest name for promotional purposes - the agreement was so detailed that it even specified what size of print and proportion of the total area Woolly could use for the BJH name on album sleeves, advertising etc. Barclay James Harvest would continue as a trio. To their credit, the remaining three members decided not to introduce a permanent replacement for Woolly on the grounds that he was irreplaceable, and to use guest musicians where required instead, a policy to which they adhered right through the next two decades.

The atmosphere during the rehearsals at Oldham's Queen Elizabeth Hall must have been awkward, but ironically the four German concerts were a huge success. *Gone To Earth*, after eighty weeks on the chart, was still at number 15, and *XII* was rapidly heading for gold status, too, so tickets went like hot cakes. 76,000 people came to see BJH headlining over acts of the calibre of Talking Heads, The Police and Dire Straits, blissfully unaware that they were witnessing the end of an era. The first show took place in the spectacularly beautiful open-air setting of Loreley, high above the Rhine, where the mythological siren was said to have lured sailors to their doom. John watched the twinkling lights of matches and lighters of fans who had climbed up into the

trees around the fringes of the amphitheatre with tears streaming down his face, and tried to persuade Woolly that he couldn't walk away from this kind of magic, just as the band was beginning to reap the rewards for thirteen years of hard work and adversity. Woolly was not a man to change his mind, though, and on 1st July, 1979, BJH played their last show as a quartet to 28,000 fans packed into the Olympisches Reitstadium Rein in Munich - ironically, it was the largest audience to which the group had ever performed as headliners.

Back in England in the cold light of day, Barclay James Harvest was still alive, but only just. Could the band survive without one of its founder members? It must have been with some trepidation that the remaining trio considered their next move and the prospect of recording an album without Woolly. The reaction of the band members was markedly different: John put a brave face on it at the time, telling German magazine *Pop/Melody Maker* in November 1979 that

"At first the split affected me a lot. Woolly and I had been best friends from very early on. For thirteen years we worked very hard, got into debt together and shared our last penny. But then, when the big breakthrough was about to happen, Woolly didn't want to be part of it any more. I couldn't believe it. More and more often we had musical differences - Les, Mel and I wanted to widen the musical horizon of the band, but Woolly wanted to stick to the old BJH sound and go even further into the classical direction. We just about persuaded him to do the festivals in Berlin, Munich, Dortmund and Loreley. Secretly I hoped that he would think about it and change his mind, but at the Loreley festival it became clear to all of us that the thing with Woolly was finally over. After the show backstage we both cried a lot. Les and Mel didn't cry any tears after Woolly, but I wanted to throw in the towel. Without Woolly I didn't see any future for the band. Now I've got over the split and see the positive side of it. The eternal arguments with Woolly are finally a thing of the past. When we recorded the new LP, which we did without Woolly, we noticed how much easier it was suddenly. At last it was real fun making music together. Today I'm convinced that Woolly leaving is good for the band, for himself as well. He can finally realise his own musical ideas."

Ten years later, John admitted in an interview for the fan club magazine,

"I've missed him ever since, because he was like a real ally. I write songs, but I'm not terribly up on arranging them, and he used to be of great assistance in that respect. I think he was fed up of the continual touring - it's really hard work - and that combined with a lot of other things, he made his mind up and that was it. We went to do these summer festivals in Germany, which were like a prelude to the Berlin gig; they were enormously successful, and I pleaded with him the whole time. At this place called Loreley there were thousands and thousands of people as far as the eye could see, you just thought there couldn't be any more people, and we were top billing over people like Dire Straits and

The Police. It started to go dusk and we started playing 'Hymn' and there were people sat in all the trees and there were all these lights in the trees! I got backstage afterwards and I said, 'You can't walk away from all this, you can't do it', but anyway he did."

Les's viewpoint was somewhat different. When asked in 1990 how Woolly's departure had affected his role within BJH, he replied:

"Not a lot, to be honest. We'd always all of us played guitars and keyboards, so even in the days when Woolly was there a lot of the keyboard stuff was done by myself and John. From that point of view getting our personal ideas across was much easier. In recording I could take my song in and play it rather than having to say to someone how I wanted it and having to compromise. Not replacing him, not getting a fourth member as such didn't limit us in any way. It didn't matter if it was one, two, three or ten people there so long as the band was still the three of us."

Mel had mixed feelings:

"I think at the beginning there was this terrible shock, and then, we had to go in the studio. I think we were all a little bit petrified about going into the studio, because it's like one of your legs has gone or something. Obviously it left a massive hole, but I think as often happens you tend to close ranks. Woolly used to come up with ideas on other people's songs, he's got a very fertile mind, so it's not just a matter of a missing musician. He was a good ideas man; that side more than any was missed. I think I understood what Woolly was going through, and I think that he felt that his music was relevant to the band and I think that the band was going away from what he regarded as his ideal - on the other hand, and I've got to say this, Woolly, I think that a lot of the way it was going was pretentious and too floral. I'm not saying I'm glad he left, but it then created a more direct way for us to go. I don't think San Francisco helped, he didn't like that at all, because the producer there was very much an American producer, and a lot of Woolly's ideas were just so alien to him musically - you can imagine, a West Coast producer meets Mahler Mark IV!"

The band decided to waste no time but to go ahead with their recording and touring plans, with a tight lid kept on the news that Woolly was no longer in the band. Two additional songs were chosen to replace Woolly's contributions - Les's had been submitted in instrumental form first time round, but now got a second chance with newly written lyrics and title: "Love On The Line", which, presumably by chance, was a remarkably similar title to Woolly's "Lives On The Line". John's "new" song was also an earlier reject in its former guise of "Ride, Cowboy, Ride!". The original tongue-in-cheek lyrics, concerning an encounter with a transvestite in a night club, were, sadly, deemed unacceptable, and were completely re-written to create "Alright Down Get Boogie (Mu Ala Rusic)". Les stood in on keyboards, with occasional assistance provided by guest musicians Kevin McAlea (ex-Bees Make Honey and Kate Bush's touring band) on keyboards on "The Song (They Love To Sing)" and "Sperratus" and Alan Fawkes, who provided the saxophone solo on "Play To The World". Recording began in July 1979 at Eric Stewart's Strawberry Studios North in Stockport, and Martin Lawrence again took on the engineering and re-mixing duties. The work overran the planned schedule, and John, who was booked to go on holiday to Malta immediately after the studio sessions, had to leave as soon as recording was complete in September, leaving Les and Mel to oversee the mixing. Only then did anybody realise that there were no photos of the trio to publicise the album, so it was arranged that Les and Mel would join John and Olwen in Valletta for a three day break and shoot with Swiss photographer Hannes Schmid - the resulting shots were unusually informal for BJH, showing them at play on the beach and in the sea, actually having fun!

The news of Woolly's departure was finally broken in September by the *Friends Of Barclay James Harvest* newsletter, with a personal statement from Woolly:-

Dear Friends,

A hard letter to write, this. How do you inform some of the most devoted followers of B.J.H of your departure, but Munich was my last gig as a member of Barclay James Harvest. After twelve years with B.J.H. it would seem rather pointless to express my regret that I should be finding myself unhappy, not musically satisfied, and not fulfilled within the framework of the band as it stands. B.J.H. will continue, with John, Les and Melve producing the good music you expect of them - meanwhile, I'm off to try something a little different. Perhaps the most enduring memory of my time with B.J.H. will be the loyalty of the public at home and abroad, who have supported the group, and through it, my work, with such quiet and appreciative understanding. It is to you, the 'fans', that I make my promise to try to be as deserving of you in my future endeavours. For a short while, cheerio!

Woolly

Jill announced that she, too, would be standing down from running the fan club. Her job would be taken over by Chrissie McCall, an employee of Kennedy Street who had previously run fan clubs for David Walker's bands like The Sweet and who had recently been drafted in to help Jill. Regarding future plans, Jill said that Woolly was writing and demoing new material for possible use on a solo album. She also mentioned that he was working on the music for a new ITV children's programme - this was *S.W.A.L.K.* (Sealed With A Loving Kiss), a teenage love story for which Woolly wrote several songs and sang one himself, entitled "First Night Nerves". At the same time, to soften the blow, fans were told that BJH would continue, and that a new album and tour were imminent.

Eyes Of The Universe was released at the beginning of November, and showed that Barclay James Harvest was very much alive and kicking. Woolly's presence was missed in terms of the songwriting, which had polarized into the two distinct styles of Les and John, and in his contribution to arrangements, which on earlier work helped to unify the other writers' differing styles. Still, his absence in the latter respect wasn't so immediately apparent, as *Eyes Of The Universe* still showed some of his influence, although his trademark Mellotron sound was, of course, lacking from the proceedings, replaced by more fashionable synthesiser sounds.

*Eyes Of The Universe
early artwork (left) with
old-style BJH "scroll"
and mysterious figure at
lower right, and finished
version (below) with
spaceships/windows and
modernistic lettering.*

Opening the show is Les's synth-looped "Love On The Line", followed by the jokey "Alright Down Get Boogie (Mu Ala Rusic)", one of John's weaker offerings in its re-written form. "The Song (They Love To Sing)" is one of two classic Les Holroyd ballads on the album, with some lines in the verses starting a beat early with the same syllable and note as the end of the preceding line. The first side ends on another light note with "Skin Flicks", a morality tale about the porn industry which cheekily borrows a riff from the Moody Blues' "Question". The flip side leads with John's classic duelling guitar-driven "Sperratus" (an anagram of "superstar"), whose lyrics provided the album title:

> Look in my eyes,
> See the light of the universe

Les's upbeat paean to the music business and its camp followers, "Rock 'N' Roll Lady", is next, with a "Don't Fear The Reaper"-style intro and punning lines about "... bars where the stars drink tequila and wine (whine?)". "Capricorn" fuelled much speculation about the meaning of its portentous lyrics, all dashed when John revealed that they were merely cut up lines from some of his favourite books, a la "Nova Lepidoptera". "Play To The World", another slow Les ballad, sees the album out in fine style. Whilst not, perhaps, a classic BJH album, it was a solid effort under the circumstances in spite of one or two decidedly lightweight efforts. Reaction to the record highlighted the growing disparity between the band's status in the UK and Germany. At home, it was the band's first album in five years to fail to make the charts at all, whilst in Germany it reached number 3 and went gold within three months, selling over 300,000 copies.

"Love On The Line" backed with "Alright Down Get Boogie (Mu Ala Rusic)" was the band's first release of the eighties, and did creep into the UK singles chart at #63. The number of UK dates on the 1980 tour to promote *Eyes Of The Universe* was noticeably fewer than in previous years, but across the water the size of venues was increasing dramatically as BJH became a *bona fide* stadium band in both Germany and Switzerland. As the band rehearsed at Shepperton, they would have been delighted with the news that all of the German shows had sold out within days. A film of them performing "The Song (They Love To Sing)" at Shepperton was later introduced by Anne Nightingale on BBC2's *Old Grey Whistle Test*. The touring band was completed by Kevin McAlea on keyboards and sax, plus new boy Colin Browne on guitars, bass, keyboards and backing vocals. Colin's CV included playing bass under the pseudonym "Stoner" in proto-punk band the Doctors Of Madness and brief spells with The Adverts and TV Smith's Explorers.

Rehearsals complete, BJH set off in a luxury tour bus owned by The Who, which had also seen service with Boston, Leonard Cohen and many others. Starting with eight UK shows, including two nights each in London and Manchester, BJH played 53 concerts in all to a total audience across Europe of more than a quarter of a million people, breaking German attendance records previously held by Pink Floyd and Supertramp. *Gone To Earth*, still in the

Right: Les is spotted by a fan at an open-air festival in Germany

Left: John in full flight at the Hammersmith Odeon, 1980

chart after more than two years, doubled its sales tally to reach half a million copies sold in Germany, and the band received a platinum disc for this and a gold one for *Eyes Of The Universe* at a presentation following a concert in Düsseldorf on February 13th *[photo over page]*.

Polydor GmbH's campaign had paid dividends, with the band's German sales now standing at over one and a half million units, a million of which had been sold in the previous twelve months. Swiss reactions, too, although obviously on a smaller scale, were in many ways even more impressive. BJH sold out a concert at the 10,000 seater Hallenstadion in Zürich - not bad going in a country with a population of 6.3 million. *Gone To Earth*, *XII* and *Eyes Of The Universe* all went gold in Switzerland with sales of more than 25,000 each.

Exciting though all of this was, John had other things on his mind: he had long wanted to have children, and now, after seven years of marriage, Olwen was expecting their first child. Finally, on 28th July, 1980, Esther Jane Lees was born and John experienced the joys of fatherhood for the first time.

Meanwhile, Woolly had not been idle, and had teamed up once more with producer David Rohl at Strawberry Studios North to record his own album between January and April 1980. Working with the old management team, but now signed directly to the German branch of Polydor, he had high hopes that at least some of BJH's success, to which he had made a significant contribution, would rub off on him. For his band he drafted in two musicians whom he had met whilst working on Rohl's Mandalaband project - Steve Broomhead on guitar and drummer Kim Turner. Those expecting a keyboard opus would have been surprised by the album, *Mæstoso*, which, whilst retaining enough of Woolly's trademark sounds from his compositions for BJH, also explored some different directions. "Sail Away", encapsulating Woolly's views on the split, begins with a very BJH-like multi-tracked lead guitar, but "Quiet Islands" includes an uncharacteristic "reggae clamour", intended, said Woolly, "to imply a polluting force drowning out the real with the ersatz." Next up, the two songs which had made the cut for Barclay James Harvest were pressed into service on the solo album: the gently pastoral "A Prospect Of Whitby" was inspired by a winter break on the north coast with Jill, and features Steve Broomhead's "thousand mandolins", whilst "Lives On The Line" is a frenetic guitar-led piece of chaos in 6/8 time. The first side closes with "Patriots", in which Woolly does Elgar. We're back to frenzy on Side 2 with "Gates Of Heaven (14/18)", a song about the futility of the first World War, then it's the brooding, bluesy rock of "American Excess", surely one of the best songs to be rejected for Barclay James Harvest! An extended version of "Mæstoso - A Hymn In The Roof Of The World" is the album's Magnum Opus: Woolly said of the song, originally recorded by BJH for *Everyone Is Everybody Else*

137

BJH's guest musicians: Kevin McAlea (left) and Colin Browne

but dropped from the running order before release, "In incubation for eleven years and changing a little in every year. The original concept of the pointlessness of national endeavour and the ultimate triumph of humanity now sounds naïve and idealistic - but it fits the music!". The track would have been the album closer, but the limitations of vinyl LPs meant that the huge dynamic range of the track would cause distortion at the end of an LP side, where the stylus moves in a tight circle. Instead, the delicately understated "Waveform" brings up the rear, getting rather overlooked after the pure bombast of the title track.

Unfortunately, it quickly became apparent that the album was not going to get the hearing it deserved. Polydor's priorities, like all big companies, were determined purely by profits, and BJH were now big money-spinners. Perhaps they thought that promoting an ex-member's efforts would muddy the waters for the band, or maybe they just couldn't be bothered, but the effort expended was minimal. A promised single of "Gates Of Heaven" was never released, advertising was discreet to the point of invisibility, and *Mæstoso* sold a disappointing 12,000 copies in all.

Back in the heady world of Barclay James Harvest, one of the band's only regrets about the German leg of the tour was that the promoters had been unable to find a suitable venue available at the right time in Berlin, a city for which the band felt a special affinity. Help was sought from the Berlin Senate's Cultural Committee, which as luck would have it, was looking to organise some major summer events, and so contracts were signed for Barclay James Harvest

to perform a free concert on 30th August, 1980. The venue selected by the
Senate was to be the very steps of the Reichstag, the famous old parliament
building, just yards from the Berlin Wall which had divided the city ever since
the beginning of the cold war, so the music would be heard by many East
Germans living on the other side of the wall. The concert cost £160,000 to
stage, of which the band contributed £50,000 themselves, with much of the the
rest coming from the Axel Springer publishing group (Germany's equivalent of
Rupert Murdoch's News International), the Berlin Senate, MAMA Concerts
(the band's German concert promoter) and Handle Artists. Keith MacMillan's
"Keef & Co." video company was hired to film the show, with Mobile One in
charge of the sound recording, as Handle were planning a film and live album
of the concert. David Walker's plan was that these would repay his and the
band's investment, as he had been shrewd enough to negotiate recording, film
and television rights before the show took place, believing that it could prove to
be a big event.

Just how big the concert in Berlin turned out to be surpassed all
expectations; the official police figure for the attendance was 175,000, and
unofficial estimates have put the actual numbers at anything up to 250,000
people. The band was reaching the peak of its popularity in Germany, and this
was THE gig to be seen at. Behind the scenes, not all was calm; John was
extremely nervous about performing to so many people, asking official

photographer Hannes Schmid at one point in the afternoon not to tell him how many people had already gathered in the *Platz der Republik*, the grassy area in front of the imposing parliament building. In a later interview, Les was asked for his tips for anybody playing a concert at the same venue, and replied: "Whatever you do, don't go looking at the audience in the afternoon; that's what we made the mistake of doing. It was great, but very frightening when you see that amount of people - people just go on for ever and ever and ever. It's a great feeling, it really is. We didn't expect that many people to be quite honest."

John's state of mind was not helped by an accident whereby his main guitar for the show was knocked over, and several of the frets were knocked into the wood of the neck, rendering it almost impossible to tune. John later admitted that at one point he was in such a state that he convinced himself that the concert was a political hot potato and imagined that someone might try to assassinate him on stage. That his mind was definitely elsewhere was amply illustrated by a story that he told against himself in a later fan club interview. Simon Renshaw, the band's outspoken stage manager, saw John walking up the gangway to the stage for the soundcheck, and, in an attempt to clear away onlookers, yelled out, "Everyone off the stage, the band are coming." John obediently turned round and started to walk away, only to be pulled up by Simon's exasperated shout: "Not you, you c***, you're in the f***ing band!".

Stage fright and damaged guitars notwithstanding, the show must go on, and after Ideal, Ginger and Busby Berkeley had warmed up the audience in the hot afternoon sun (local band Wednesday, who were scheduled to appear, pulled out because they weren't given enough time to set up), John, Les and Mel, together with guest musicians Kevin McAlea and Colin Browne, hit the stage at nine-fifteen. The German compère led the huge audience in a countdown from ten to one, powerful white lights illuminated the audience and the band was off into "Love On The Line". Any signs of nervousness quickly disappeared in the adrenaline rush of the occasion, and the band included as many favourites old and new as they could in a much extended set. Two brand new, as yet unrecorded songs were also premièred at the concert, something which BJH had not attempted since 1970. There couldn't have been much more contrast between the songs: the first was John's "In Memory Of The Martyrs", a haunting, slow-building tribute to the men and women who had lost their lives attempting to get over the infamous Wall and flee to the West. No sooner had this ended than the band launched into Les's "Life Is For Living", a summery pop song affirming the joys of life. Both songs were rapturously received. It was over two and a quarter hours before BJH finally left the stage, and even then the announcer had to explain that the band was totally exhausted before the crowds began to disperse. Brief excerpts from the gig were broadcast live on German radio news bulletins, followed by an airing of over half of the show a few days later on Berlin station RIAS, in spite of the technical problems which plagued the recording. In many ways the concert in Berlin marked the apex of Barclay James Harvest's career, and would be a hard act to follow.

8

Diamond Love

The Berlin concert was followed up within a fortnight by the recording of a new single on September 12th. Originally this was planned to be a double A-side of the two new songs featured in Berlin, but at the last minute it was decided not to use "In Memory Of The Martyrs", possibly because it was too long, but to go for the outright commercialism of "Life Is For Living". The replacement B-side in the UK was actually a demo of John's, with his rather out of character vocals backed by a bassline reminiscent of Fats Domino's "Blueberry Hill" piano riff, hence John's title, "Shades Of B Hill". "Life Is For Living", with its catchy tune and

clap-along chorus, was a huge hit, entering the German chart (with "Sperratus" as the B-side) at the end of December with sales of almost 100,000, and going on to reach number 3 in Germany and number 1 in Switzerland. Even in the UK, where the band was, by now, deeply unfashionable, the single received some airplay, and made the Top 75. Not everyone was happy with the success, though, as the band's older fans, especially in Britain, were appalled at what they saw as the abandonment of BJH's progressive and intellectual roots for out and out pop music, and John, too, felt that they had, perhaps, strayed too far from the kind of music on which their reputation was based.

The plus side of the group's more commercial appeal was the obvious one - for the first time in their career, the band members actually began to see some monetary reward for their labours. All three of them bought new houses at the end of 1980 in Saddleworth, one of the more desirable areas of the north-west. Les and Mel settled in Diggle, Les on a farm with room for his and Christine's beloved horses, and Mel and Janet (with the biggest property of the three!) in a house built in 1750 and originally a workhouse for the poor before being converted into a hotel and then into a private residence. John and Olwen weren't far away, either, settling into a farm in nearby Denshaw.

In November the band went into Marcus Music Studios to record their next studio album. If the progression from *XII* to *Eyes Of The Universe* had been relatively seamless, then *Turn Of The Tide* marked a number of major changes for the band. It was the first album to be recorded without any initial input from Woolly (although his presence lingered on in at least one song - "Death Of A

City" had first been performed, albeit in a quite different form, back in 1967). The album was also the band's first digital recording, and their first for many years not to be recorded at Strawberry. One link remained with the studio, however, as Martin Lawrence, who had worked with BJH on *XII* and *Eyes Of The Universe*, was again co-opted as engineer and co-producer, assisted by Liz Biddiscombe. Kevin McAlea and Colin Browne also provided continuity, having played with John, Les and Mel on the 1980 tour and at the Berlin concert.

Whilst recording was in progress, the band's managers were active behind the scenes. At the beginning of 1981, Handle Artists issued a press release stating that

"David Walker and Lindsay Brown ... recently secured the release of Barclay James Harvest from the Polydor label in North America and one of their priorities will be to negotiate a new Record Contract for the band in America and Canada."

Cracking the lucrative American market would have set the band up for life, but several chances had already been missed. "Securing the release" of your band from a major label record deal, even one which had not returned much in the way of dividends thus far, could be seen as something of a gamble, particularly since an alternative had not yet been negotiated. Of course, it's possible that the Polydor deal had already expired, and management was simply putting a brave face on it. Unfortunately, the new record contract didn't materialise, and *Eyes Of The Universe* would be the last new BJH album ever to be issued in North America; from now on they would be completely dependent on the European market to make their living.

Ironically, now that BJH were without a full-time keyboard player, *Turn Of The Tide*, released in May 1981, became their most keyboard-orientated album to date, and the move away from the progressive anthems of the seventies was further accentuated by the clean, almost clinical digital recording. The tempo for the most part is rather plodding, as exemplified by the opening song , "Waiting On The Borderline", with its repetitive synth bass and unchanging beat. Matters improve somewhat with John's "How Do You Feel Now?", a heartfelt, piano-led ballad written in celebration of the birth of his daughter Esther, although John never felt that his performance did the song justice. Les's hypnotic bass introduces "Back To The Wall", which supplies the album's title:

He's been waiting on the other side
He's been waiting for the turn of the tide

"Highway For Fools" is a John Lees rocker, attacking the iniquities of the music business and its emphasis on the pursuit of money over artistic integrity. Les's "Echoes And Shadows" is a thoroughbred ballad from the same stable as

"Play To The World". "Death Of A City", reconstructed by John from the song which the band had demoed in the sixties, injects some pace into the album; the slower choruses are lifted directly from the original, but John re-wrote all the verses and added the driving guitar riff. Several of John's songs from this period share a similar apocalyptic theme of destruction, and it's no accident that one of the new lines refers to "after the day". "I'm Like A Train" includes some lyrical fragments suggested by Mel when Les was short on inspiration, but the end result still feels like filler. Mel gave an interesting insight into his contributions to songs in one interview:

"In the past I've helped with Les and his lyrics. When it comes to the time

for the next album, I usually have just a few pages of ideas, words that are thrown together, and he picks up on that."

"Doctor, Doctor" is not one of John's strongest songs either, in spite of some rather fine "plucked" bass sounds. The song extols the virtues of love as "a natural panacea", but also offers an insight into the depressive phase that John was going through and his withdrawal from prescription anti-depressants. The album finishes

Instrumental excerpts from "Death Of A City" were used in the cult BBC comedy series Not The Nine O'Clock News, providing backing music to visual sketches such as Rowan Atkinson walking into a lamppost ...

with the pair of songs which had been premièred at the Berlin concert - the hit single, "Life Is For Living", now with extra overdubs to give it a fuller sound, and the wistful "In Memory Of The Martyrs", a fine lament which nevertheless seems to be crying out for a better arrangement. Philip John Ireland, to whom the song is dedicated, was John's cousin, who was tragically killed in a road accident in Germany. John saw a parallel between his death and those of the young people killed in trying to make their escape from East to West Berlin.

The album's art direction was by Alwyn Clayden, but the photography and design which illustrated the title so aptly were by Bob Carlos Clarke, then a relative unknown, but now one of the world's foremost portrait and fashion

photographers. The front and reverse of the single sleeve are mirror images, both literally and metaphorically, showing a parched cityscape shimmering in a heat haze on the front, and the same landscape reversed on the back, now flooded and with heavy storm clouds above. Memorable imagery, plus the obligatory butterfly, resulting in one of the band's most attractive sleeves.

In retrospect, "Highway For Fools" can be seen as the first hint that John was beginning to become disillusioned: in an interview with Ray Coleman for *Now!* magazine, given in November 1980, whilst recording of the album was in progress, John said:

"We're not on the road for a lot of fun, but to get on with our job of making music. Success on a gigantic level like lots of the top bands have breeds discontent. We're still hungry enough to keep going. There's that and the fact that, being from the north, there's always this needle between each of the three of us that keeps us on our toes. If we lose the ability to laugh at one another, then the band will definitely split."

There were several occasions in the 1980s when John seriously considered his position within the band, and the immediate post-Woolly period seems to have been one such occasion for soul-searching.

Overall, *Turn Of The Tide* was a slightly disappointing effort, suffering from early eighties synthesiser overload and some unimaginative arrangements. The clean digital sound and leisurely tempo make it rather anodyne, and recent opinion polls show that the album is not generally regarded as one of the band's finest moments, particularly amongst older fans in the UK.

Nevertheless, riding the crest of the wave created by the band's growing popularity and the success of "Life Is For Living", the album attracted enough advance orders in Germany to qualify for a gold disc before it was even released, and entered the Swiss chart at No.1. In the UK it reached a more modest position of 71, but this was, at least, an improvement on its predecessor. EMI chose this moment to issue the third of their *Best Of* compilations of BJH's early work, but, considering that they had only four original albums from which to select material, three volumes of the "best of" seemed to be stretching the description somewhat. In fact, of course, the LP was more of a "Rest Of", collecting up most of the songs not included in the first two volumes.

The European tour promoting *Turn Of The Tide* took in ten UK shows, then continued through Norway, The Netherlands, Belgium, Luxembourg, France, Italy and Switzerland, but not, on this occasion, Germany, for which they had other plans. The trek got off to an inauspicious start when after only seven dates, as the band was alighting from the coach for the sound check at Bristol's Colston Hall on 21st May, Mel was knocked down by a stolen car which was

Right: Presentation of German gold discs for Live Tapes and Turn Of The Tide on the island of Sylt, 24th April, 1981

trying to outrun the pursuing police. Fortunately, he suffered only cuts and bruises, but that night's show and the ones in Southampton and Leicester had to be cancelled. Mel was able to continue the tour from Oslo onwards, with the three gigs being rescheduled at the end of the tour at the beginning of July.

The live set drew fairly heavily on *Turn Of The Tide* - with no less than seven songs from that album and five from its predecessor, this was definitely not a band resting on its laurels. There was still room for some of the old classics, and "Hymn" was firmly established as the finale, but by now all of the Harvest-era material had disappeared from the repertoire, even "Mockingbird". The reviewers praised the shows for their professionalism, musical quality and light shows, but criticised them for a lack of warmth and communication with the audience. Barclay James Harvest had always been a quiet and relatively static band on stage, preferring the music to do the talking, but with the defection of Woolly they also lost their main raconteur and master of the bizarre introduction, and it was this aspect which was noticeably absent at the live shows. *Record Mirror*'s review seemed a trifle harsh, though, with Robin Smith claiming that he had "seen more life in a stuffed gibbon"!

On stage at the Hammersmith Odeon, May 1981 - "who are you calling a stuffed gibbon?!"

In October 1981 German magazine *Pop Rocky* sent editor Elias Fröhlich and photographer Hannes Schmid over to England to do a series of "at home" features with the band. Unusually for BJH, possibly because Fröhlich was a personal friend of John's (or perhaps because the magazines were not available in England!) readers were allowed a glimpse of the band members' homes and lifestyle. Les was photographed cooking,, and with his favourite horse and his cat. Mel was seen with his Land Rover and Renault 5 (!) and with his wife, Janet and their dog, Holly. He was quoted as saying that he was working on his own compositions ("but I don't think they are good enough for Barclay James Harvest"!). Mel went on to say that he had recently bought a drum computer, and that he was giving his ideas to John to work on, as he had more contact with John than with Les - this was how the B-side track "Blow Me Down" later came about. John was pictured with his Porsche, but said that he was about to sell it because it attracted too much attention! He showed the journalists his small home recording studio and his collection of everything to do with BJH, which filled up several drawers.

Although Germany had been omitted from the 1981 tour schedule, BJH were not about to abandon their most important market. Plans to release a live album of the Berlin Reichstag concert were dealt a blow by the poor quality of much of the recording, due in part to the problems with John's guitar, but mainly down to some bad hum which rendered large portions of the tape unusable. Reluctant to give up on a permanent record of such an important event in the band's career (not to mention the substantial amount of money invested in the original concert), the record company, management and band decided to use as much as they could of the raw live tapes and to re-record the remainder in the Strawberry North studio to make up a single LP. This was achieved during the second half of 1981, which accounts for the long gap between the concert and the appearance of the album. At the same time, a documentary film of the concert was being prepared for cinema release across Europe.

The first results of their endeavours appeared in December 1981 with a German-only live single of "Child Of The Universe", backed, appropriately enough, by "Back To The Wall". The single made it into the German Top 30, but was really just a taster for the main event: in January 1982 Polystar, the TV-advertising arm of Polydor GmbH, released a limited edition 11-track album, *Berlin - A Concert For The People*, featuring two songs, "Love On The Line" and "Rock 'N' Roll Lady", which would not be on the standard LP once the limited version sold out. "Limited" is a relative term in this context, as 250,000 copies of the Polystar version were pressed - coincidentally, the number of sales required for the award of a gold disc in Germany! A combination of this marketing ploy, the intense interest and publicity which the original concert had generated, and the fact that the "live" album was, in effect, a "Greatest Hits" package, sent *Berlin* crashing straight into the German album chart at No.1, achieving the coveted gold disc status on the day of release.

A mammoth tour of Germany (plus a couple of Austrian and Danish dates) was organised to coincide with the launch of the live album. On February 24th, 1982, the day after the opening night, the band attended the première of the *Berlin* film. This took place at the Berlin Film Festival, and the film received a standing ovation from the assembled German media! At a Deutsche Grammophon reception on the same day, the band were presented with their gold discs for *Berlin*, platinum awards for half a million sales of *Eyes Of The Universe* and triple gold disc sets for three quarters of a million copies of *Gone To Earth*. As a gesture of thanks, the band also handed over a cheque for a further ten thousand German Marks to the Berlin Senate's programme to sponsor young bands and artists.

The German outing was a huge success, with extra concerts being added in arena-size halls as the tour progressed, so that by the end of April, the band had played over forty concerts to a total audience of more than four hundred

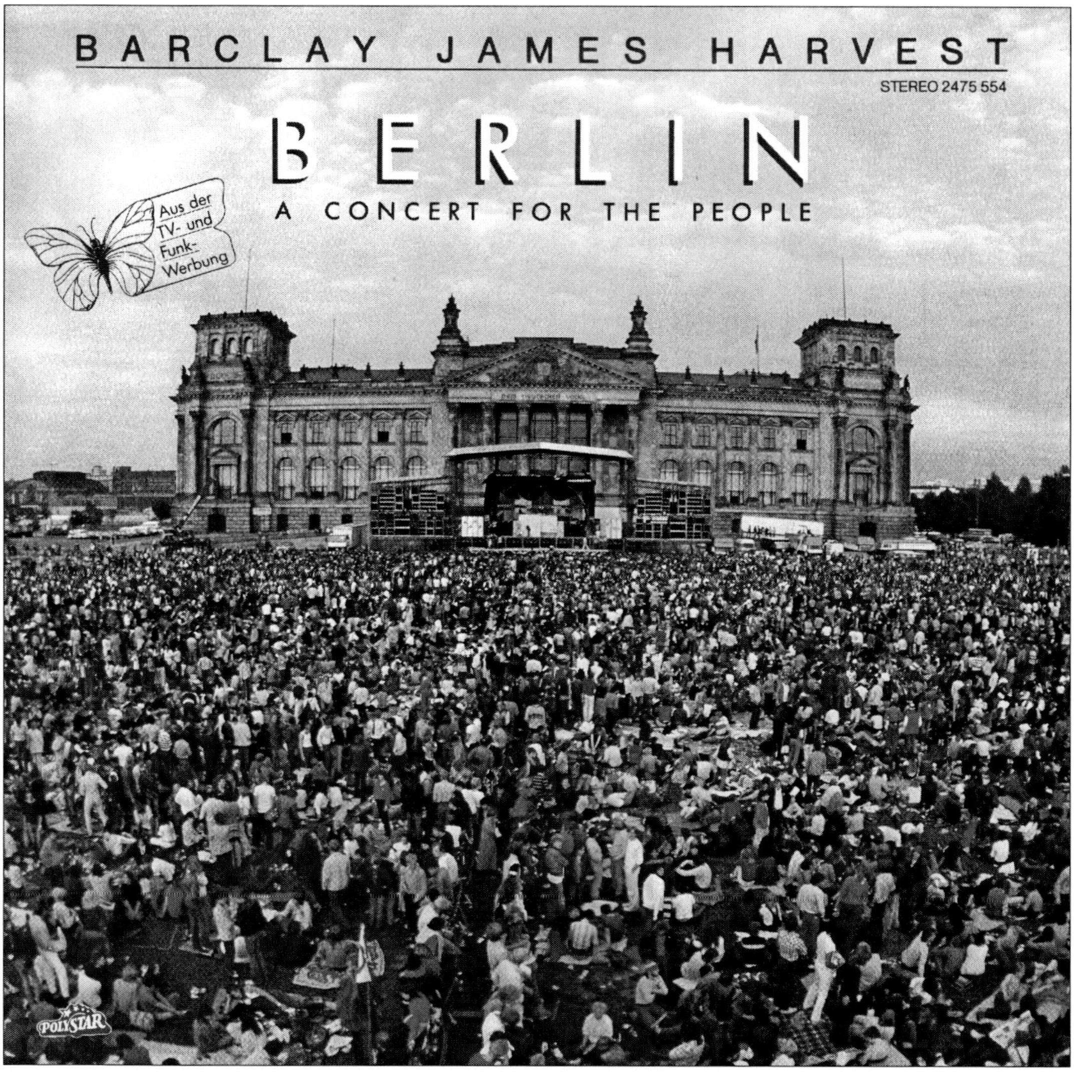
BARCLAY JAMES HARVEST
STEREO 2475 554
BERLIN
A CONCERT FOR THE PEOPLE
Aus der TV- und Funk-Werbung
POLYSTAR

Above: the German Polystar 11-track edition of the Berlin LP

Below: Les, Mel and John at the awards ceremony in Berlin

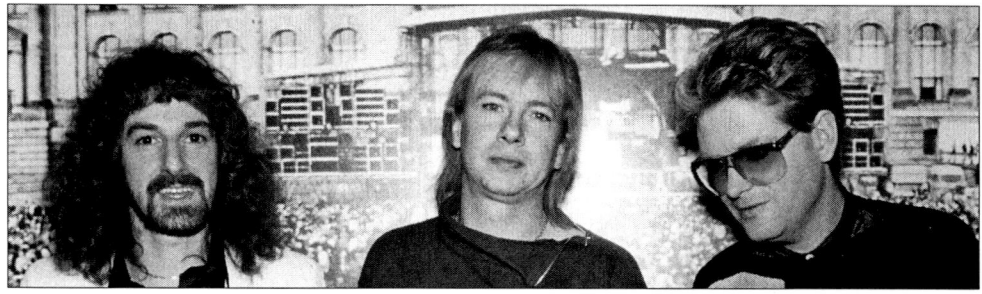

thousand fans. The band were stunned by the enthusiasm of the crowds, and John got so carried away with his call and response during "Hymn" that he lost his voice after the first gig! He even managed to speak to the crowd in German with the aid of a cassette provided by his sister Edna, who had married a German and settled with her family near Düsseldorf, where she taught art and English. By the beginning of April, the schedule was beginning to take its toll on the band's health; after the first of four shows at Munich's Olympiahalle, Les collapsed backstage before the final encore, and was rushed to hospital, where a kidney infection was diagnosed. In true "show must go on" tradition, Mel, John, Colin and Kevin finished the show with "Hymn". Fortunately, after medical treatment Les was fit enough to continue with the tour. The promoters, MAMA Concerts, were so delighted with the record-breaking ticket sales that they presented the band with gold tickets and a large cake!

Above: Mel, David Walker, John and Deutsche Grammophon's Rudolf Gaßner receive gold plaques for Berlin.
    Right, above - gold ticket awards for the German tour
    Right, below - Marek Lieberberg (MAMA Concerts), John, Lindsay Brown, Les, Mel and Marcel Avram (the other half of MAMA)

Fans in Britain had to wait until July for the *Berlin* album, when the nine-track version of the LP was finally released, in order to coincide with cinema and BBC television screenings of the film of the concert. Curiously, for the UK release the title was subtly altered to *A Concert For The People - Berlin*. Perhaps the record company felt that the original version was a touch too Germanic for British tastes! In any case, boosted by a BBC TV broadcast of the concert, the album became BJH's highest chart entry in Britain, entering the album chart at number 15. Some reviewers commented on the studio overdubs on a supposedly "live" album, and dedicated fans spent hours studying the differences between the original radio broadcast and the LP, but notwithstanding the origins of the album, it was a huge success by anybody's standards.

Left: ah, that 80s New Romantic image! (publicity shot for the UK release of the Berlin album)

Immediately after the German tour, the band members took a break, Les in Munich and Mel and John in Portugal. John was with Olwen and Esther in the Algarve, near Almancil, and they liked it so much that they stayed for about three months! All too soon, though, it was time to start recording the next album. The venue was to be Frankfurt's Far Studios, which belonged to Frank Farian, best known for writing, singing and producing many of Boney M's greatest hits. For the duration of the recording Handle Artists arranged rented apartments for the band members in Germany, partly to keep accommodation costs down, and partly to reduce their tax liabilities in the UK. John stayed in Frankfurt, whilst Les and Mel were in the same apartment block in Bad Homburg, a short distance away. Almost immediately the recording ran into technical difficulties with the new digital equipment, which was unfamiliar even to the studio staff, and many takes were lost due to effects being incorrect or a failure to record anything at all. The sessions had to be abandoned, incomplete, in September, as the second half of their European tour was about to get underway in France, Switzerland and the Benelux countries. Once more box office records tumbled, and BJH's rising popularity in France was underlined by several of their albums going gold in the same year.

The huge costs and logistical organisation required for a major tour are demonstrated by the supporting cast for BJH's 1982 jaunt: 35 roadies (including 11 sound and 7 light roadies), 3 road managers, 4 T-shirt sellers, 2 cooks and 1 cleaner, plus 40 local security people per show; 4 trucks plus 4 coaches with 12 beds each, 10 different keyboards, 17 guitars, 350 spotlights and a 72-channel mixing desk! Little wonder that Mel told one interviewer that the tour would actually cost the band money ...

Whilst Barclay James Harvest were appearing at vast arenas around Europe, Woolly was also performing live. Together with Steve Broomhead, Kim Turner and bassist Terry Grady, now billed as a band under the name Woolly Wolstenholme's Mæstoso, they played around twenty dates as support act to Judie Tzuke. The contrast was marked - Mæstoso played like a new band, which, in effect, they were, with energy and enthusiasm, if not always with the same degree of perfectionism as the Barclays' cooler, more detached presentation. Woolly's banter enlivened the set, drawn partly from the *Mæstoso* album, but also featuring songs from both ends of his stint with BJH ("The Iron Maiden" and "In Search Of England"), plus a number of powerful new songs such as "Too Much, Too Loud, Too Late", "Has To Be A Reason" and the epic "Deceivers All", a thinly-disguised diatribe aimed at the record company. The tour may not have sold many albums, but they certainly enjoyed themselves doing it!

The UK dates were followed by a tour in Germany and Austria early in 1982, as Mæstoso performed as special guests to Saga. Whilst the shows were quite successful, they proved to be not nearly as much fun as the trek with Judie Tzuke, but the real hammer blow was still to fall. The band had already begun recorded their next album, *Black Box*, which was to be issued under the Mæstoso band name; the artwork was ready and it promised to be a very strong release. Polydor, however, took another look at the sales figures for the first album and decided otherwise. At about the same time, guitarist Steve Broomhead left the band, and the Mæstoso project was effectively dead in the

On stage with Mæstoso at the Amsterdam Paradiso, February 20th, 1982 [photo: Marco de Niet]

water. Woolly headed home to consider his future, and decided that his musical career was at an end - as he put it in a later interview, "I felt like I'd had rock and roll beaten out of me". He continued to work in the studio with David Rohl on the odd soundtrack for children's TV series such as *Cockleshell Bay*, *S.W.A.L.K.* and *The Squad*, plus Cosgrove Hall's animated films *The Pied Piper* and *The Wind In The Willows* (although the music for the latter was not adopted), but he and Jill were becoming increasingly involved in non-musical activities. From a vegetable plot in the garden of their home in Greenfield, Saddleworth, they graduated to a farm in the Colne area of Lancashire and thence to serious organic farming on a hundred acres in Llandeilo, Dyfed. Most of the profits from the BJH days were invested in the business, and it would be many years before fans would have the opportunity to appreciate Woolly's musical talents once again.

9

Renew Our Faith

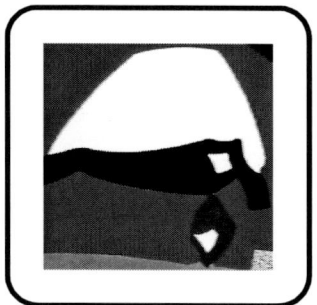

No sooner was the French tour over in early December, 1982, than the band returned to Far Studios to continue work on the new album. The producer selected for the new album was Pip Williams, one time member of Eurovision hopefuls Bardot, but best known for his production work, and now managed by David Walker. Williams, a trained guitarist, arranger and producer, had known David since the early seventies, and was exactly the kind of strong character that Walker considered necessary to keep a tight rein on the band members' diverging opinions as to the appropriate musical direction to pursue. It also helped that the band had known him as a friend for a few years before working with him. His credits included The Moody Blues' *Long Distance Voyager* and Status Quo's *Whatever You Want* and *Rocking All Over The World*, plus Mud and Kiki Dee - through the latter project, he had worked with Bias Boshell, who now joined the sessions as the main keyboard player, although Kevin McAlea still filled that seat for "Midnight Drug". The engineer was Gregg Jackman, former Chief Engineer at RAK Studios where he had met Pip Williams. Jackman also engineered for The Moody Blues as well as BJH. Pip Williams imposed his will on the proceedings and had firm ideas about the way the album should sound, something which John later acknowledged was a necessary evil, even though he wasn't entirely happy at the time:-

"I didn't have a good time - I don't think anybody did, really - and at the end of the day it showed. The producer probably kept us all together, we've got to thank him for that, but I think to do that he had to give such a strong influence that the Barclays really got smothered a bit."

Producer Pip Williams (above) and engineer Gregg Jackman (right)

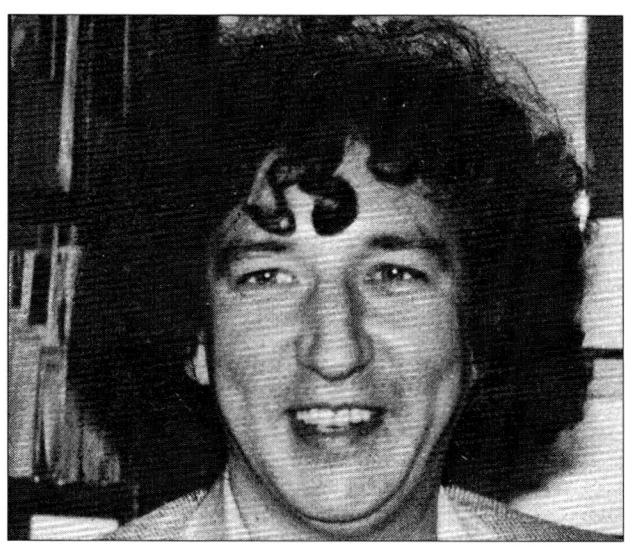

Guest keyboardist
Bias Boshell

Bias Boshell, known to his parents as Tobias, was a founder member of cult favourites Trees at the end of the sixties. His "The Garden Of Jane Delawney", a Trees album title track, was later covered by All About Eve, and he also wrote the hit single "I've Got The Music In Me" for Kiki Dee. His densely-layered keyboards set the tone for the new BJH album, and Pip Williams brought his distinctive pop style to the recording. Whilst Pip's strong influence homogenised the mix, it also made for a rather anonymous sound - nonetheless, he got the job done.

The album was trailed by a single of "Just A Day Away", released on April 5th in Germany and 9th May in the UK. From the outset, it was apparent that Polydor were prepared to throw their weight behind the band - the single was boosted by the release of a rather lurid, red and blue disc cut in the form of a butterfly, with "Looking From The Outside" from the same album billed as the B-side, which helped the single to reach number 68 in the UK chart. Unfortunately there was a breakdown in communication between the record company and the pressing plant, which resulted in the initial batch of picture disc singles being pressed with the wrong B-side (one of the extra tracks on the limited edition German LP of the Berlin concert, "Rock 'N' Roll Lady"). The error was corrected for later pressings, but such a large batch had already been manufactured that the "correct" version is now sought after by collectors. In Germany, even without the aid of gimmicks, the single eventually reached #40, even though it was by no means the strongest track on the album. It's a pleasant enough love song, but the arrangement does it few favours, with a rather unconvincing synthesised "Tijuana brass"-style trumpet solo towards the end, and a syrupy string arrangement. One sign of the times for BJH was that whilst Radio 1 showed no interest in the single, the "housewives' favourite" station, Radio 2, gave it a fair amount of airplay! The single was supported by a video featuring the band dressed as convicts on the chain gang, wielding pick-axes under the watchful eye of a mysterious oriental female guard and a black obelisk straight out of *2001 - A Space Odyssey*.

A week after the release of the single in Britain, the *Ring Of Changes* album was launched in a fanfare of publicity. It so happened that the new format for audio recordings, Compact Disc, was about to be launched onto the market, and Philips, the inventors, also owned the PolyGram group of companies, who were thus expected to back the format. Barclay James Harvest's polished style was thought likely to appeal to exactly those people who would be sufficiently interested in high fidelity (and sufficiently affluent!) to be targeted for CD, and so Polydor not only included *Gone To Earth, Turn Of The Tide* and *Berlin* in the first hundred or so titles to be released on silver disc, but promoted *Ring Of Changes* as the world's first digitally recorded album to receive a simultaneous release on CD, LP and chrome cassette. Veteran DJ and long-time BJH fan Alan Freeman was on hand to do his bit as the album was presented to the press at an expensive launch party on a boat on the River Thames in London, whilst similar events were held at a castle in Hamburg and half way up the Eiffel tower in Paris - *Ring Of Changes* had arrived!

The first thing the listener hears is real strings, arranged by Pip, and performed by the New World Philharmonic Orchestra conducted by David Katz. The neo-classical "overture" introduces the "Ring Of Changes" theme before the band plunge into "Fifties Child", a John Lees number lamenting the lost idealism of those who grew up in the sixties and seventies, and espousing the now passé ideals of peace and love. The keyboard-dominated "Looking From The Outside" sees Les continuing where "Waiting On The Borderline" had left off, and in "Teenage Heart" John revisits his youth and recalls the agonies of young love. The band come closest to rocking out on "High Wire", painting a picture of a relationship where the protagonist is badly-treated, and predicts that his lover will come to a bad end, but can't resist coming back for more. In "Midnight Drug" John returns to the theme of contrasting the natural highs of love and the artificiality of chemically-induced pleasure (*cf.* "Hymn"), but this song is more personal, being written about a friend whose lifestyle was giving John cause for concern. The song is also notable for the shared vocals, with Les taking lead on the middle eight before John picks up the tale again. A hypnotic bass-line and multi-tracked backing vocals *à la* "Giving It Up" introduce "Waiting For The Right Time", a bittersweet romance. The single,

"Just A Day Away (Forever Tomorrow)", is followed by "Paraiso Dos Cavalos" (Portuguese for "Horses' Paradise"), which was inspired by John and his family's stay in the Algarve, and the title of which is taken from the name of a riding school in Quinta do Lago. John described how it came about in a 1989 fan club interview:-

"When I was in Portugal I learnt to ride. My wife is really into horse-riding, as is Les's Christine; the two of them sort of grew up together and were always interested in horses. My wife had a bad fall - the horse bolted and ran away, she went under the horse and got kicked badly, and it put her off. When we went to

165

Portugal, she got confidence enough to start riding again, so I decided to learn and it was then that I got the idea for "Paraiso Dos Cavalos". Olwen's now very involved in horses again, and goes out with Christine."

It's a lovely song which effortlessly evokes long days of "summer sunshine and cool green wine", even if John somewhat ominously goes on to say, "if I had known then we'd be there still". The string arrangement works better here, and a harp is also used to good effect. Fan club members voted this their favourite song from the album shortly after its release, and it has stood the test of time well. Another song written at the same time was the beautiful "Star Bright", but this one would not appear on record for over fifteen years. Finally, Morse code spells out "ring of changes" to introduce Les's title track, reflecting John's love of amateur radio, a hobby he shared with his father. The album's theme of cyclical change is continued in the lyrics and in the reprise of the orchestral motif at the end, bringing us neatly back to where we came in.

A lot of thought had clearly gone into the concept and packaging of the album, with its expensive gatefold sleeve featuring a cut-out front and the circular theme which permeates the songs and the design. Still, *Ring Of Changes* marked another step away from the old style and closer to mainstream rock/pop. *Ring Of Changes* peaked at a slightly disappointing 33 in the UK album chart, but fared much better in Germany, where it earned the band another gold disc, and in France.

With rather less fanfare, this period also saw the release of the band's first commercial video, a straight transfer of the earlier TV broadcast featuring highlights of the 1980 Berlin concert. The tracklisting is identical to the album, missing an opportunity to include extra footage from the concert, but the mix is different, as the television soundtrack doesn't have all the overdubs of the LP. Complementing the standard VHS and Betamax video cassettes was a new format, a curious hybrid of existing video, LP and CD technology called

Laservision which had been launched the previous year. These 12" discs came in LP-sized sleeves, but were silver in colour and read by laser like the new Compact Discs, even though the encoding was analogue rather than digital. The format was not a commercial success, and this was the only BJH release on Laservision.

The UK "Waiting For The Right Time" single and "Ring Of Changes" German issue in the rare withdrawn sleeve

A second single was planned to extend the shelf life of the *Ring Of Changes* album, and the song chosen was Les's title track. Since the original version clocked in at well over seven minutes, it was edited down to four and a half minutes and remixed for radio, with a release date of July 15th scheduled in most European territories. At that point, though, it seems that there was a last minute change of heart, and it was decided instead that Polydor UK, France and Spain would issue "Waiting For The Right Time" instead, also edited and remixed, in 7" and 12" formats. The band wasn't involved in the hasty editing of the song, which wasn't so much mastered as master butchered. In Germany the record company stuck with the original plan to issue the title track, but even there the traditional efficiency was lacking and confusion reigned - the "Ring Of Changes" single came out with a picture sleeve featuring a particularly unflattering picture of the band. Less than two weeks later it was withdrawn and replaced with a new sleeve using the same colour picture as used on the UK "Waiting For The Right Time", with only the title bar altered. Both singles featured the same flip side, John's previously unreleased "Blow Me Down", based on a collaboration with Mel and including a nod to its inspiration, Free's "Heartbreaker", in the middle eight. Obsessives may like to note that the German and Spanish singles included a count-in at the beginning of the B-side, which was absent from the UK cut - a collectors' item in the making!

Miming to "Ring Of Changes" on German TV channel ZDF's Thommy's Pop Show Extra, December 1983, with Bias Boshell and Pip Williams on keyboards

Plans for tours in the U.S.A., Australia and Japan never came to fruition, and instead of embarking on the customary European tour to promote the album, the band broke with tradition by going back into the studio in September 1983 to make another album. This time the venue was Wisseloord Studios at Hilversum in Holland (apparently because it was cheaper than recording in the UK), with Pip Williams again in the driving seat, assisted by Gregg Jackman as engineer. Female backing vocalists Vicki Brown (wife of Joe and mother of Sam), Stevie Lange and Joy Yates were brought in to perform on one song, but ended up singing on much of the album. John explained why:

"When you've got that many albums in the marketplace, you need to be looking for something different all the time, and it was felt that the girl singers would complement some of the things we were doing. When we actually brought them in it was great and so we're even gonna take it a stage further now."

Les, John and Mel pictured in Amsterdam between recording sessions

Les too, was keen on innovation:

"We're trying to bring new people into the band and new ideas, and that's why the albums are selling so well. The band has maybe sixty to seventy per cent say in everything that goes on - songwriting we obviously have total control over, recording we have maybe ninety per cent control and business-wise about sixty per cent control. Everything that is done for Barclay James Harvest, we have to see it first, to make sure that it is in keeping with the band and is not something just to make money."

Also featured on the album are string arrangements written by Pip Williams and performed by The David Katz Strings, plus Bias Boshell on keyboards. Tarred with Pip's pop sensibilities, the whole enterprise sails dangerously close at times to pure schmaltz, but *Victims Of Circumstance* is probably also their most commercial work in terms of instant accessibility.

Recording was completed in January 1984, and the album was trailed by a single of the title track. Issued in 7", 12" and clown-shaped picture disc formats on March 16th, the single was backed by an instrumental version, plus "Love On The Line" from the limited Berlin album on the 12". A promotional video for the single was directed by Keith MacMillan, depicting a nightmare society (shot in Fulham!) of zombies blindly following their leaders - hope is not lost, though, as at the end of the video a child stops the doomsday clock at one minute to midnight.

The very striking album sleeve was chosen before recording started and is closely based on a poster for a Berlin cabaret club and *bierkeller* called *Senta Söneland*, painted by the famous illustrator Jo Steiner in 1912. Lindsay and David commissioned an artist to design some album covers, and he came back with the design and the title *Victim Of Circumstance*. David Walker suggested to John and Les that they should try to write a song with that title, and, as John

told the *Friends Of Barclay James Harvest* newsletter in March 1985, "Strangely enough I had written a song *["Rebel Woman"]* when the Korean 'plane was shot down by the Russians and the chorus was 'Victims Of Circumstance'. It was funny because I hadn't mentioned this and then this guy came up with it. Then Les wrote a song around the title."

The album itself appeared on April 6th. "Sideshow" gets things off to a start which is very similar to *Ring Of Changes* - sonically and musically, these albums are very much a pair. A string-backed guitar introduction heralds a song about media intrusion and their relentless focus on the negative aspects of human existence, but also inspired by the positive example of the Band Aid project. It's a strong composition, but slightly formulaic, and the arrangement is too close to that of "Fifties Child", although this one is notable for the fact that John and Les share the lead vocals. The tempo increases with "Hold On", one of Les's rockier songs which became a live staple, and the momentum is maintained with "Rebel Woman", John's driving protest song about repression

in the Soviet Union (not, as some listeners thought, in Thatcher's Britain!). The poppy "Say You'll Stay" provides a contrast with the closing number on the first side, the piano-led ballad, "For Your Love", written about the fans who waved lighters and sparklers at the end of live shows. Side two begins with Les's title song, with an anti-war lyric which sits rather uneasily with a lightweight arrangement, highlighting the female backing vocals and Pip Williams's Spanish guitar fills. John was moved by the report in a local newspaper of a car crash to pen "Inside My Nightmare", in which he puts himself in the shoes of someone whose girlfriend is killed by his own dangerous driving. The song rocks out in suitably manic fashion, but the message is undermined by the banshee wailing of the chorus and ultimately fails to convince. "Watching You" describes a crumbling relationship with pop sounds and ersatz reggae rhythms, and the album closes with Les's, "I've Got A Feeling", a wistful ballad with strong melodies but somewhat formulaic lyrics.

Overall, *Victims* is a frustrating album, with some strong songs struggling under the weight of stifling pop and AOR arrangements, and rather too much filler in between. For both *Ring Of Changes* and *Victims Of Circumstance* Polydor spent lavishly on album launches and special edition boxed sets for the media, including glossy biographies, enamel badges and posters. Now they went to the extreme of producing an "Interview Album", consisting of the band's recorded answers to set questions which were included on a cue sheet. The idea was for radio DJs to read out the questions, then play the appropriate answers as though it were a live interview! Stunts like this were not popular with the media, who completely ignored the interview albums (which soon fell into the hands of eager fans and collectors).

Fans' polls consistently rate *Victims* as one of the band's weakest efforts, although at the time of its release in April 1984 it was very successful, particularly in attracting younger fans. France went overboard for it, sending both the album and the title track single to Number 1. Germany also made it another gold record, and even in the UK it reached a respectable #33. However, the band's older followers were generally not impressed, Les and Mel had misgivings, and John later said (of both *Victims Of Circumstance* and its predecessor) that they should have wiped the tapes.

Around this time, John bought the old Friarmere Vicarage in Delph and converted part of the building into a twenty-four track recording studio. It was intended primarily for his own writing and rehearsal work, but was also used to record demos for promising young acts John discovered, or who had been sent up to him by the record company. John told Berlin radio station RIAS that in his spare time:-

"I go round looking at bands, trying to find people, acts, other musicians, who haven't had the kind of exposure or opportunities I have, trying to give them some kind of facility to record."

Steel, from Birmingham, who later toured as support to Magnum, were one such band who got an early break recording at Friarmere. Another protégé of John's was a young bassist and singer by the name of Craig Fletcher. John gave Craig's band, Off The Rails, the use of his studios and acted in a semi-managerial role for them. Unfortunately, Off The Rails' chances of fame and fortune were dealt a severe blow after three showcase gigs for record companies; first the drummer fell off his stool during the third gig after over-indulging in the hotel with the A&R men the night before. The band asked if there was a drummer in the house and a stranger got up and played kit for the rest of the gig. The final nail in the coffin, though, was when the lead singer asked David Walker if he was Jewish because he had a big nose. Bye bye huge record deal ...

One of the benefits of BJH's higher profile was that companies involved in making music gear were now keen to associate themselves with the group's success. By 1984 BJH had endorsement deals for Pearl drums, Paiste cymbals, Washburn guitars and effects, Yamaha keyboards and AKG Acoustics microphones. Washburn even developed a guitar especially for the band, named the "Harvest", and asked them to try out four handmade copies before the company put the instrument into mass production. John approved of it so much that he bought one of them and wrote many of the songs from this period on it. One of the others was bought by Sam Brown, soon to become a solo performer in her own right, best known for her hit single and album, "Stop".

Publicity shot for Washburn, with Les's yellow bass and three "Harvest" acoustics

Backing vocalists on the first part of the 1984 tour, Sam Brown (left) and Jan Ince

Not having toured *Ring Of Changes*, it was now time for BJH to go back to Shepperton to rehearse for a record-breaking trip around Europe, playing over fifty shows in seven countries to a total audience of over three hundred thousand, including their first British concerts for three years. The choice of songs to play was a difficult one - with two new albums to promote, none of which had been heard live, should they concentrate on them or stick with the tried and tested "oldies"? Bravely, they chose the former, playing thirteen songs in all from *Ring Of Changes* and *Victims Of Circumstance* at the expense of crowd-pleasers like "Mockingbird", "Child Of The Universe" and "Loving Is Easy", although they still found room for "Poor Man's Moody Blues", "Berlin", "Life Is For Living" and, of course, "Hymn".

The shows were a huge success commercially and, to a lesser extent, artistically. Some songs which had foundered under the weight of unsympathetic arrangements in the studio suddenly came to life in the live arena. "For Your Love", in particular, was a revelation, transformed from a slightly lacklustre effort into a powerful ballad with some beautiful piano work from Kevin McAlea. However, the presence of Sam Brown (taking over her mother's album role for the live concerts) and Texas girl Jan Ince, best known for her work with Kit Hain, on backing vocals, whilst indubitably adding to some songs, seemed to be surplus to requirements on others. The girls wore white dresses on stage, and their non-stop dancing, which might well have suited a less cerebral band, merely constituted an annoying distraction from BJH's music. The spectacular light show and video screens also took attention away from the band, but in the cavernous venues which were now the norm for BJH, were probably essential to keep the interest of the large part of the audience which could barely see the stage in the distance.

*On stage in 1984
[photos: Frank Rybinski
and Kevin Goodman]*

This was, perhaps, the most successful period in Barclay James Harvest's entire career, but musically it seemed to many fans, especially those who had grown up with the band's earlier work, that they had lost their way. John felt much the same thing, and his unhappiness with the last two studio albums extended to the tour. Word spread amongst the band's followers that this was to be the last ever BJH tour, to the point where the *Friends Of Barclay James Harvest* fan club newsletter was later forced to print a denial, asking plaintively, "Where do these rumours start?". Embarrassingly (and probably unbeknown to the club), the answer was, apparently, from within the band itself! Les was quoted in the German press before the tour even began as saying that the three members of the band had decided that this would be their last tour, at least for some time, adding that this was not just a cynical ploy to sell tickets. The article did, however, add that BJH would definitely carry on making albums, and that they might change their minds about playing live in a few years' time. On tour Les rebutted the story, and by the following March John was telling the fan club that they would definitely not stop touring, and that the whole thing was "a foul rumour started by the press". It seemed that the alleged quotes from the band in Germany had lost something in translation ...

John's mood was probably not improved by the fact that he was in pain from a broken rib, incurred in an accident on the German leg of the tour. The final straw, though, was when, one day after "Victims Of Circumstance" reached the number one spot on the French singles chart, John broke his finger coming off stage after a concert in Lille on June 2nd. Accounts vary as to whether John tripped over some wiring or just missed his step, but according to eyewitnesses, one moment he was chatting to the road crew, the next he simply

disappeared. With a broken rib it had been possible to play on, but it was out of the question to play guitar with a broken finger. Sixteen concerts were cancelled and two hundred thousand tickets, worth over a million Pounds, had to be refunded. The band's families were flying out to join them on tour at the time, but, as Olwen Lees later recalled, she ended up instead spending a few days in the south of France, quaffing champagne, before returning home with John to England. The cancellations were not quite the disaster that they might have been, though, as the tour, like virtually any others on that kind of scale, was fully insured. The lucky brokers were music specialists Robertson Taylor, who handed over a cheque for a grand total of £227,755.40p, which covered paying off the 37-strong road crew, cancellation expenses and all the other costs incurred by the band. For the disappointed fans, too, all was not lost, as John's finger healed quite quickly, and by September 5th the band was in Geneva to resume the tour, with most of the original dates rescheduled, and even a couple of extra ones added for good measure. The news of the insurance payout was broken to Olwen the day after John set off again, and she told the local paper that John, Les and Mel were probably unaware that the claim had been settled. She went on to observe wryly:- "The ironic thing is that John played and sang with a broken rib for four weeks before he broke his finger. We're just waiting to see what he breaks next!".

Fortunately the remaining concerts passed without further mishap, still featuring Bias Boshell, Kevin McAlea and Sam Brown, although Jan Ince had prior commitments and was replaced on backing vocals by Helen Chapelle. A special extra show was added at the very end - a starring appearance at

London's Wembley Arena. Originally planned for September, but put back to October 13th to fit in the rescheduled dates elsewhere in Europe, this was to be the band's biggest ever headlining show in their home country. Although they had begun the 1984 tour with six shows in the UK, the (relatively) small venues prevented them from deploying the full light show, and demand for tickets had proved higher than expected. In the event, around 8,000 fans attended the show, a fine performance which was also filmed for TV and video release. John betrayed his nerves by forgetting the words to "Fifties Child" at the beginning of the show, but after a slightly shaky start the band excelled themselves, and the British press reviews were uncharacteristically positive.

At the end of September another single was released: "I've Got A Feeling" was a new version with added saxophone, and came in edited 7" and extended 12" versions. Curiously, the 12" version never reached the shops in the UK, although white label DJ copies were sent out. Germany, too, had only the 7", with the 12" apparently only available to the public in France.

In November the band visited Germany again to record a TV special for Thomas Gottschalk's *Tommy's Pop Show*, where they mimed to "Rebel Woman" and "Victims Of Circumstance". Around the same time they were approached by Frank Farian, with whom they had become friendly while recording *Ring Of Changes*, to help out with a Live Aid-style benefit single for Ethiopia. The record, a cover version of Paul Simon's "Mother And Child Reunion" was released as the Frank Farian Corporation. The recording actually started life as an unreleased track from the 1983 sessions for a Boney M album, *Ten Thousand Light Years*, with a lead vocal by Reggie Tsiboe. The track was resurrected and remixed with additional vocals by Liz Mitchell, Amy and Elaine Goff, the School Rebels and Raff, plus John and Les, although you'd be hard pushed to hear their contributions. They are visible on the promotional video, though, even with John doing his best to look inconspicuous at the back! The single was initially released only in Germany (where it reached no.24 in the singles chart), Switzerland (no.28) and Spain, although it later appeared in the UK under Reggie Tsiboe's own name. Farian himself had an interesting career both under his own name and as the mastermind behind protégés like Boney M and the notorious Milli Vanilli, and scored a worldwide hit with his Far Corporation cover of "Stairway To Heaven".

10

Back To The Wall

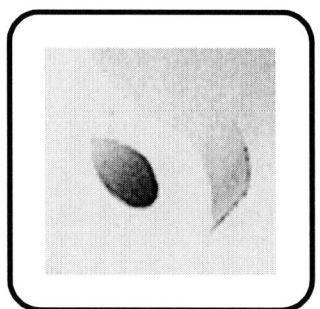

BJH spent some time at the end of 1984 mixing the Wembley video soundtrack. TV producer Mike Mansfield (of *Supersonic* fame) was drafted in to produce additional footage for the *Mirror Image* series on Channel 4. Filmed on Lindisfarne Island off the Northumbrian coast in the absence of the band or any creative input on their side, the result was, frankly, risible. The "conceptual" parts of the film bear a marked resemblance to an advertisement for Turkish Delight, scenes of the band actually playing are all too rarely seen, and all in all it's best heard but not seen! The programme was shown by Channel 4 on May 16th, and the broadcast version included interviews with Les, Mel and John which were not on the video version released shortly afterwards.

Apart from the video, the only "new" release from BJH in 1985 was their first

ever CD compilation, *The Compact Story Of Barclay James Harvest*, put together by their management and record company. The CD contains a number of Polydor-era classics plus alternative versions of familiar songs, notably the

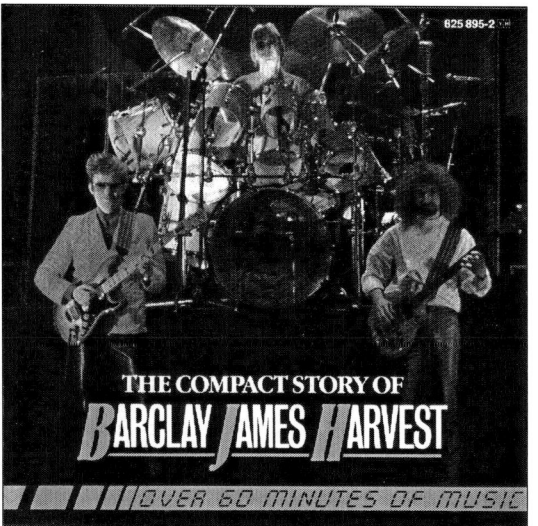

single version of "Ring Of Changes", the rare extended remake of "I've Got A Feeling" and an otherwise unavailable take of "Poor Man's Moody Blues" recorded live at the Wembley show.

An ominous note was sounded on March 26th, 1985 when writs were served on John, Les, Mel and Woolly, plus EMI Records, Polydor, RAK Publishing and EMI Music Publishing, on behalf of Robert Godfrey, claiming joint authorship of ten early compositions, five from *Barclay James Harvest* and five from *Once Again*. The writs further claimed that there had been an unwritten agreement that he would be treated as the fifth member of the band and that he would share equally in any "fortunes which might thereafter accrue". Through their management, BJH announced that they would fight the case, but it was a Damocletian sword which would hang over all of the band's activities for at least another decade.

Plans had been made for a possible American tour in April/May 1985, but once again nothing came of it. Instead the band took some time off for what they aptly described as "a well-earned rest". Mel spent some time in Munich, where he became friends with fellow drummer Nigel Glockler of heavy metal stalwarts Saxon. The Sugar Shack was musicians' favoured club in Munich at the time, and Mel and Nigel either met down the Shack every night, went to dinner, or both, ending up with their reserved stools at the bar!

Asked why there had been a long break between albums and tours, Les told Berlin radio station SFB:

"Up to then, we made almost one album every year. It got to a situation where as soon as we'd finished the album we were out on the road and then after the tour maybe a couple of weeks off and back into writing again. We figured we needed a little bit of time off and to spend a little bit more time in the studio experimenting, rather than having to rush the album together."

John actually spent some of this time considering his future in the band, not for the first or the last time. Eventually he decided to continue with BJH, using it as "a vehicle" to get his songs heard. In fact, this is an image that John has frequently used to describe the individual members' relationship with the band as a whole. It's a common problem with any group which stays together for any length of time - a number of young people come together with dreams of fame and fortune, bound by a common love of particular kinds of music and a sense of being united against the establishment world. As the years go by, aspirations and tastes change, and idealism gets lost along the way. A cursory look at any of the Barclays' contemporaries - Pink Floyd, Led Zeppelin, Yes, Deep Purple, Genesis, Supertramp and many others spring to mind - shows that the one common factor which keeps bands together is that the name becomes a kind of trade mark without which, except in very rare cases, the individual performers struggle to make their mark. John recognised this, and realised that he still had a lot to offer within the confines of the band.

John also managed to retain his sense of humour: interviewed by Timmy Mallett for the new Sky Channel, he was asked how the band was going to celebrate its twenty-first anniversary:

John: "Splitting up!"

On the band's long-winded name:

"It just meant that when people went into record stores they'd say, 'Can I have that record by, er, Barc.., er - give us The Stones', so we're responsible for other peoples' success!"

Saddleworth Moor, October 1986

Another, happier cause of the delay in the appearance of new material was the birth of John and Olwen's second child, John Joseph, on 13th January 1986, on John's thirty-ninth birthday. It had been a difficult time for the family, but after the event John was able to express his feelings in the way he does best, by returning to penning songs for Barclay James Harvest.

Fortunately, the band members were in agreement about their next move - no more female backing singers, dodgy haircuts or poppy productions, but a back to the roots album drawing on the traditional BJH strengths of great songwriting and melodies.

John's Friarmere set-up had been intended primarily for use as a rehearsal studio, but Pip Williams, first choice as producer for the new album, was busy working on the Moody Blues' *The Other Side Of Life*, so BJH decided to use the new studio to begin work on their album. Gregg Jackman, who had previously undertaken engineering work for the band, was drafted in to help, and ended up co-producing the album. Asked whether the expense of the previous digital recordings had influenced the decision to go back to analogue, John replied:

"No, cost wasn't a factor in that, it was the fact that we didn't really think that it made any difference. OK, if you mix analogue as well, then obviously the quality isn't there, but if you record analogue and mix digitally, I really do defy people to tell the difference. Some things don't record that nicely on digital, because there's a kind of natural compression with analogue when you're overloading drums and things like that - you don't get anything like that with digital."

New material was demoed as early as September 1985, with a planned release date for a new album with the working title *Elements* in the spring of 1986, but recording seemed to go on forever. Unused to the luxury of unlimited studio time, the band took their time over getting exactly what they wanted, and when Les felt that a few tracks still didn't sound quite right, some extra work was done with Pip Williams at Chipping Norton Studios.

Les had other things on his mind, too, as in November 1986 he and Christine became the proud parents of a baby boy, Christopher. Away from the glare of the media spotlight when the band was on tour or had a new record to promote, the individual members guarded their privacy jealously, and this time no announcements were made to fans or the press. When later questioned about this in an interview for the *Mittelbayerische Zeitung*, Les explained:

"I didn't think it was relevant. One of the reasons was that the band were still quite big in Germany and in Switzerland and a certain Swiss magazine wanted to do a article on us. This particular magazine is like newspapers in England like *The People* and the *News Of The World*, and they wanted to make more out of it. Why should I talk about my personal background? I'm a musician, I'm an entertainer; my life is private and I like to keep it private".

It was more than a year before the first fruits of the recording work emerged in the shape of a new single, released in November 1986. "He Said Love" was BJH's most overtly Christian song to date, something about which Les, in particular, was apparently not best pleased. He told SFB radio:

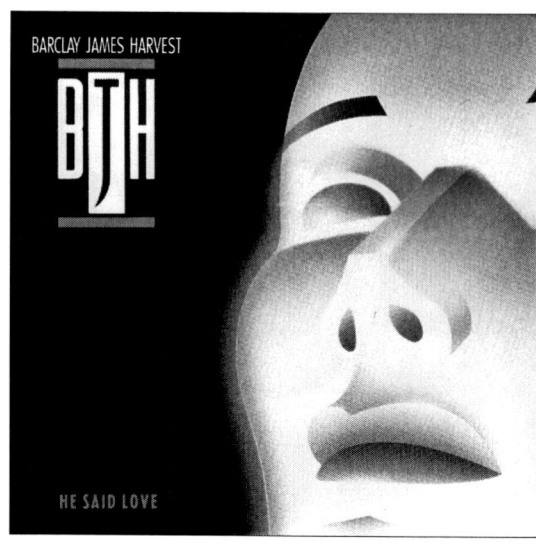

"John writes all of those, he wrote 'Hymn' and he wrote 'He Said Love'. It's NOT necessarily the way that the rest of the band feel. It's not something that I would like to get into."

John concurred, telling Timmy Mallett:

"We all work independently within Barclay James Harvest, the framework, and our inspirations come from different places. There are two writers in the band, and we don't actually participate in each others' material."

He told *Pop Rocky* magazine the full story behind the sentiments of the song:

"My wife Olwen was pregnant again after three miscarriages. We then went to a specialist, who thought that she might have cancer and would have to have an operation. At that time I just prayed like mad, and indeed my prayers were heard and everything went well. My wife didn't need the operation and had a healthy boy, so I wrote 'He Said Love' as a thank you."

Musically, it owes a lot to "Hymn", and that probably explains why it was chosen as the single from the album. As part of the promotion for it, the band travelled to Germany in November to appear on *Peter's Pop Show Extra*, where they and Kevin McAlea mimed to "He Said Love" and "Prisoner Of Your Love", which seems to have been tentatively planned for release as the second single from the album. Being released close to Christmas, "He Said Love" picked up some seasonal airplay, but didn't make the charts. Some felt that the B-side, Les's classic ballad, "On The Wings Of Love", would actually have made the better choice of single. Inexplicably, the latter song wasn't even included on the vinyl LP or cassette which followed in February 1987, now entitled *Face To Face*, although it does appear on the CD format and, ironically, went on to become a firm live favourite.

Face To Face did, indeed, mark a return to a more traditional BJH style. The cover features a modernistic, androgynous face with the trademark butterfly discretely tucked away in the eye, but on the back, to the relief of older fans, the band appear without make-up, dressed in jeans and casual jackets in the reassuringly familiar surroundings of Saddleworth Moor. The contents of the sleeve continued the theme: the opening "Prisoner Of Your Love", begins with synths and breathy backing vocals which could have fitted seamlessly onto *Victims Of Circumstance*, but it develops in more muscular vein. The religious celebration of "He Said Love" gives way to the excellent "Alone In The Night", the atmospheric, almost ethereal opening contrasting nicely with the powerful guitar riffs which herald the chorus. "Turn The Key" is unashamedly poppy, whilst "You Need Love" (omitted from the vinyl LP format) is a bittersweet piece about about the difficulties of sustaining a long-term relationship after the first flush of excitement.

The band seemed to have rediscovered their political consciousness, too - Les's "Kiev" is a ballad in the "Whiter Shade Of Pale" mould, drawing attention to the plight of the people affected by the Chernobyl disaster, whilst "African" is a savage indictment of racism and exploitation, particularly by the Apartheid regime then in power in South Africa. John described its genesis:

" 'African' was written off the back of that mining disaster where all those people were killed; it had to be literal, it had to be brutal."

There were some worrying signs, though, as the gulf between Les and John's vision of Barclay James Harvest seemed to be widening.The pure pop of "Following Me" sits rather uneasily after the outraged vehemence of "African", whilst the hypnotically dreamy "All My Life" is rudely followed by the tongue-in-cheek rocker "Panic". Overall, though, the album plays to the classic BJH strengths of melody, harmony and superb musicianship, nowhere better than in the closing "Guitar Blues". It wasn't even a new song, as John told the fan club:

" 'Guitar Blues', interesting song, that. It goes back a long way, it was written for *Ring Of Changes*. There were a couple that didn't get on that album and that was one of them, so it went on the *Face To Face* album."

In fact there had been some debate about the advisability of doing a song with a Moody Blues-ish title on an album produced by Pip Williams, and the song was shelved. The lyric is ambiguous - it can be read as a lament for a lost lover, but it also makes sense as a tribute to the man who was closest to John in the original Barclay James Harvest, i.e. Woolly. Whatever the subject matter, the soaring string arrangement and inspired guitar solo ensured its popularity, and it is widely regarded as the high spot of the album.

The consensus was that *Face To Face* was, at least in parts, a return to form which boded well for the future. After a three year delay since the last studio album it was not altogether surprising that the sales struggled to match those of its predecessors. The young French fans who had sent *Victims Of Circumstance* to Number 1 proved to be a fickle audience, and the album just crept into the British chart without the benefit of much in the way of publicity, although Germany again sent the album into the Top 10 and to gold record status. In retrospect *Face To Face* is generally regarded as something of a mixed bag.

John admitted to the band's fan club magazine in April 1989 that he had been surprised by this:

"We were terribly disappointed about the reaction to *Face To Face*; we'd made a conscious effort to go back and look at the catalogue that we'd produced over the years, to try and take something from that, and we didn't really get the kind of reaction we thought we would. I thought that *Face To Face* was a great album, I thought it really worked; the songs of mine in particular I was very pleased with."

Polydor Germany issued a second single for that market only, a radically remixed version of John's "Panic". There's no record as to who was

responsible for this mix, although it seems likely that Gregg Jackman was involved. In any case, there is general agreement that the new interpretation is a great improvement on the rather lacklustre original; clever use of loops to extend the song and a much harder edge lend themselves well to the jokey subject matter, wherein John advises the listener not to panic when the music comes to an end, but exhorts them simply to put the record on again! Les explained why they band had moved away from their usual sound:

"We've always done up-tempo rock numbers in the past, but this time in the studio we had a little bit more time to experiment with sounds and voices and things, and we just tried on that particular number to see how far away we could get from the normal Barclay James Harvest sound into something that was a little more commercial. It was just an experiment, but it seems to have worked quite well."

In addition to the standard 7" and 12", "Panic" was the band's first CD single release - clearly Polydor weren't yet familiar with this new-fangled format, as the cover proclaims "45 rpm"!

The spring tour which followed confirmed the impression of a return to form, with less emphasis on the pyrotechnics and more on the music. Les told German radio audiences who would be guesting on the tour:

"There are two guys from the last tour, Kevin McAlea and Bias Boshell on keyboards, and we're also using Colin Browne. He did the Berlin concert with us, and he'll be doing some guitar work and backing vocals, but we're not using

the girl singers this time, a lot of people will be pleased to hear, myself included! Last time round we had a step forward, we thought, with two girl singers! That was an experiment - you have to try these things to see if they work. It was OK, it was an experience, but I for one didn't think it worked properly - I think it detracted from what the band was about."

Les also revealed plans for a second big Berlin concert:

"The possibility is that we are going to do a festival in East Berlin this summer. We have been approached by East Berlin people to do the gig and we really, really want to do it if we can feasibly fit it in. It would be great."

Mel, speaking on SWF3 radio, explained how they chose the songs for the live set and how to deal with stage fright:

"I usually find a lot of Scotch helps! It usually goes after the third number ... Set-lists are the worst decision you've got to make. People want us to do the new songs, but we've got such a huge back catalogue that the choice is very difficult. Also, each of us has got his personal favourites. So, next week we will be putting together a list of songs that will be about three to four hours long. Then we will start the rehearsals, then we'll take this concept to London and argue for another four days with the management who disagree with us totally! Then we go back to rehearsals."

The new songs sounded more powerful in live performance, and, mindful of the risks of alienating audiences by concentrating too heavily on new material, the band found room in the set for some of the classics which hadn't been given an airing for five years or more, including the opener, "Nova Lepidoptera", "Mocking Bird", "Child Of The Universe" and "Medicine Man". John told German journalist Kathrin Brunner-Schwer:

"I like to put a very wide spectrum of my music in, although I have been criticised for that. If people want to hear titles like 'Mocking Bird' or 'Medicine Man', then why not? I'm not ashamed of those, I'm more ashamed of what we did on *Ring Of Changes* and *Victims Of Circumstance*. I didn't think it was very good at all from my point of view."

On expectations that the band should change their musical style, John disagreed:

"I certainly listen to a lot of modern music and I'm influenced by a lot of modern stars, but the basic morality of the material that I'm writing is the same, and to expect me to change I think is a little bit much, really. As long as people want to see me for what I am and what I'm doing, then that's fine. You have to take us as we are."

By now, the whole operation involved sophisticated technology which ensured smooth running of the hugely complex shows, with the drawback that the band's ability to improvise musically was strictly limited. Mel explained:

"Once the tour starts, and we've worked out the lights, then it's all set, and we have to keep it as it is. There are sampling machines, the lights, and everything is controlled by a computer. If we had to change something half way through the tour, then we could put two new songs in, but we'd need a day off for that. Certain things like the keyboard solo, we could extend that by eight bars, but actually re-approaching songs, certainly from the lighting and the keyboard department, can be a bit traumatic sometimes."

The indoor shows were followed by several open airs in Germany in June and July and, as the band had hoped, culminated in a second historic Berlin concert after BJH became the first western rock band to be invited to perform an open air concert in communist East Germany. The authorities were preparing to celebrate the 750th anniversary of the founding of the settlement which became Berlin, and BJH, with their known empathy with Germany in general and Berlin in particular, were an obvious choice. The gig was originally scheduled to take place on the Island Of Youth in the middle of the River Spree. Within two weeks of tickets going on sale, though, at the princely price of 4,05 East German Marks (then equivalent to about 20 pence on the black market), applications soared past 50,000, and the venue was relocated to the nearby Treptower Park, close to the Berlin Wall. In the event, so many fans turned up on the day that the ticketing arrangements were abandoned altogether and they were allowed in free. The official figure for the attendance was 130,000 to 170,000, but the actual number was in all probability rather higher.

Treptow soundcheck, above, and East German press agency shot, right

191

The 1987 tour: pictures from Birmingham, Babenhausen, Frauenfeld and Zürich (left, John with Olwen and John junior) taken by Kev Goodman, Janet Richardson and Micki and Siggi Scherrer

On stage in Paderborn [photo: Janet Richardson]

Much to the band's relief, the technical problems which had bedevilled the West Berlin concert seven years earlier were not in evidence in the east - a triumph for socialism (and for the band's own planning, which included flying in their own stage)! The set was an extended version of the one from the earlier tour, and the event was recorded for posterity by East German television and radio. Unsurprisingly, perhaps, the authorities didn't risk broadcasting the concert live, but chose to air it as a TV and radio simulcast two weeks later, with two songs excised from the set, either because the concert was too long,

Backstage in Frauenfeld [photo: Janet Richardson]

or because of official nervousness about controversial political content. Given that the missing songs were "Kiev", Les's ballad expressing solidarity with the victims of the Chernobyl disaster, and "Berlin", a lament for the divided city, the latter explanation seems more likely. A week or so later West German TV broadcast the same truncated version, but when East German radio repeated the concert a couple of years later, both of the missing songs were restored - a hint of a softening attitude towards censorship, perhaps, or just a clerical error?

During the band's trip behind the Iron Curtain, they were escorted at all times by an official, but still managed to see something of East Berlin. John summed up the band's attitude when he said, "The wall is terribly depressing. I wish that more bands would play over there, because the more people go over there, the greater the chance that the damn wall will be torn down one day."

October 1987 saw the first release of the band's Harvest-era material on Compact Disc, in the form of a "Best Of" collection entitled *Another Arable Parable*. Compiler Paul Cox told new fanzine *Nova Lepidoptera* how it came about:

"Once it became apparent that CD was here to stay, I wanted to get involved in the medium as soon as possible. I've done enough compilations and reissues now - I just present them with the package, really. My initial intention was to replace the three 'Best Of' volumes with one definitive set. The powers that be at EMI approved the project immediately, although they proclaimed a vinyl edition unnecessary. I think the set flows nicely. It was nice to have it included in the launch of EMI's mid-price range - it was originally scheduled for August release at full price."

Completed by sleeve notes from long-time fan Ryszard Szafranski, *Another Arable Parable* proved a popular introduction to the group's early material, and in Germany EMI later relented and issued a vinyl version, too. With renewed interest in the band and their back catalogue, it seemed that they were back on the right track again.

11

A New Tomorrow

As night follows day, showcase concerts are followed by live albums, and the East Berlin spectacle was no exception. Plans to call the album and video *Back To The Wall* were, unfortunately, altered in favour of the Russian political catchphrase of the day, *Glasnost* ("openness"), as popularised in the media. It could have been worse - it could have been called *Perestroika* … Although the video stands as a worthy record of the event, unadulterated by dodgy concept footage, the packaging and presentation of the album left a lot to be desired; the running order seemed wilfully perverse, and whilst this may be excusable on vinyl LP and cassette formats where two sides need to be balanced, there is no excuse on CD,

especially when the bonus tracks, "Turn The Key" and "He Said Love", were placed after the actual closer, "Hymn", creating an unfortunate sense of anti-climax. The sleeve design, too, was uninspired, giving rise to the comment that it was actually an accurate reflection of the contents - a snapshot of the concert sliced into ribbons and put back together badly! However, the actual recordings were fine, showing the band on good form, especially on the *Face To Face* material, where "African" and "On The Wings Of Love" come across as the definitive versions.

The album was released in April 1988 to coincide with an Easter Saturday BBC1 TV broadcast of highlights from the concert, and the video followed in May. However, only the most loyal fans were eager to invest in a fourth BJH live album, and sales were disappointing - even in the band's German stronghold, *Glasnost* barely scraped into the Top 50.

The release of the *Glasnost* album coincided with the launch of a new official fan club for the band. *Friends Of Barclay James Harvest*, which had been started back in 1977 by Woolly's wife, and continued for nine years after Woolly's departure by Chrissie McCall, had run into difficulties. The relative inactivity of the band in the late eighties made it difficult to attract new members, and without much news to report, the frequency of newsletters tailed off, so that existing members had little incentive to renew. However, just around the time that the future of the club was looking uncertain, a BJH fanzine called *Nova Lepidoptera* appeared, produced by Keith Domone, co-author of this book and a member of FOBJH since its inception. Copies of the fanzine were sent to the club and to the band's management; following a request for proposals for the club from Lindsay Brown and a meeting with Lindsay and Mel, a new official fan club was set up with the blessing of band and management. The unimaginatively named *International Barclay James Harvest Fan Club* was

Les relaxes at home, July 1988

initially run by Keith and Madge Domone with the help of fellow fan and fanzine subscriber, Kev Goodman. The new club name was purely down to the fact that nobody had a better suggestion on which everyone could agree, and it was adjudged better to make a fresh start rather than keep the old FOBJH name.

One of the first things in which the new club became involved was tracking down Woolly Wolstenholme for his first in-depth interview since he had left Barclay James Harvest some nine years earlier. The request for his address must have sent a few tremors through the management camp and the band, as nobody really knew what his attitude towards his erstwhile friends and colleagues would be, and the club's printing of the interview was made conditional on it being vetted by the management first. Fortunately Woolly, whilst disillusioned with the music business, still bore no animosity towards any of the band members. The meeting with Woolly and Jill at their farm in Colne, Lancashire, shortly before they moved to Llandeilo in South Wales, led to a number of unexpected bonuses. The first of these was the release of a limited edition cassette tape of five unreleased songs from Woolly and Mæstoso. Comprising "All Get Burned", the "lost" B-side of the unreleased "Gates Of Heaven" single from *Mæstoso*, plus four songs which had been written and recorded for the *Black Box* album, the cassette was released on the fan club's own Swallowtail label in December 1989. Frankly, the sound reproduction was poor and the artwork was amateurish, but it offered a taster of what might have been, and with only two hundred and fifty copies made, it couldn't fail to become collectable!

After *Glasnost*, the feeling within Barclay James Harvest was that they had reached something of a crossroads in their career, and that they needed a very special album to re-establish themselves. By March 1989 work had already begun on their next studio album. In pursuit of a more contemporary sound, a new producer was sought, and eventually found in the shape of Jon Astley. Jon comes from a musical family - sister Virginia Astley was already a well-established solo artist, Jon himself had released two excellent solo albums, *Everybody Loves The Pilot (Except The Crew)* and *The Compleat Angler*, and his brother-in-law is one Pete Townshend, who also dabbles a bit in music, apparently. More recently, Astley has become better known for his remastering work on the back catalogues of Abba and The Who, but at the time his pedigree was predominantly in production, working with artists such as Eric Clapton, Sad Café and Corey Hart.

Astley worked with Andy MacPherson as a production team at Andy's own Revolution Studios in Cheadle Hulme, near Stockport, and the pair quickly established a rapport with the band. Andy Mac enthused about the band's music, with which he had previously been unacquainted, whilst John paid Jon Astley the ultimate compliment:

"For once we are enjoying doing it, we're having a good time. The producer, Jon Astley, is working very well to get us working as a unit again. The guy to me is very like Woolly in temperament and attitude, and it really is having a good effect."

Les, too, was happy with the new team, although he felt that Andy MacPherson deserved more credit:

"Jon did pre-production more than anything and he had a lot of ideas, but when it comes to the actual production of the album I think it should have been credited the other way round: Andy MacPherson and Jon Astley. It's completely in the dark at the moment as to what we're going to do for the next album - the only definite, or rather 99.9% definite, is that we will be recording at Revo, and we will be using Andy Mac."

Revolution's Fairlight sampler enabled the band to get the precise sounds that they wanted, although the downside was that much of the recording was not "live" in the traditional sense - Mel's drums, for instance, were simply sampled into the Fairlight and "played" via the keyboard. The results were certainly convincing, with many fans later commenting on the excellent drumming on songs such as "African Nights", but Mel was honest enough to admit in an interview for the fan club magazine that he hadn't actually played the part in question:

"That was Steve Pigott - he had this idea of doing something with the end, so we sat down and worked this thing out."

Mel also added a self-deprecating aside:

"It'll be interesting if we do it on stage to find out if I can do it!"

and gave an interesting insight into the working dynamics between producers and band:

"Jon Astley was there on the pre-production and actually putting the songs into shape, and that gave me more time to work on ideas to do with drums and everything. Once they were in a kind of rough outline shape with no vocals on or any of the top colours, then it would be taken upstairs, because we were working downstairs with the programming, and then we'd all get involved with it. Jon Astley set songs in directions that possibly they wouldn't have gone without him but that's always the case with producers. With Pip Williams there were some songs that went in ways that never in our wildest would have gone that way, but the record company got Jon Astley and ourselves together, and we decided we wanted the classic Barclay James Harvest brought up to date, and I think it's worked."

A number of musician friends of the production team were drafted in to produce particular sounds on the album, including some familiar names on the Manchester scene - old friend Ritchie Close contributed additional keyboards, Sad Café's Ian Wilson and Mike Hehir provided backing vocals and some guitar sounds, Steve Butler also sang backing vocals and Steve Pigott of Living In A Box produced the dramatic keyboard effects in "Lady Macbeth". Veteran saxophonist Andy Hamilton also made a guest appearance, on Les's Chicago-style big ballad, "Where Do We Go".

Polydor executives were impressed with the first results of the recording sessions, and there was a real feeling around the band that this could, indeed, represent a renaissance for Barclay James Harvest in the 1990s. The record company began to invest more effort in promotion, producing a four-track CD sampler with a colour inlay, "teaser" postcards which were sent out to fans, and items such as "bullet" keyrings and pens to push an album-trailer single. "Cheap The Bullet" hit the shops in February 1990 and didn't disappoint, with its relentless driving rock beat married to some typical John Lees anti-violence sentiments. The B-side, too, Les's "Shadows On The Sky", was an impressive advertisement for the album, featuring some thought-provoking lyrics and an unusual "backwards" guitar solo. The single version of "Shadows On The Sky" is quite different from the one which eventually appeared on the album, as Les explained:

"That was an edited version. It was all right, but it wasn't musically correct; there was half a chorus missing on the second chorus where it went into the middle eight, there were odd vocals missing. I think on the original mix we put

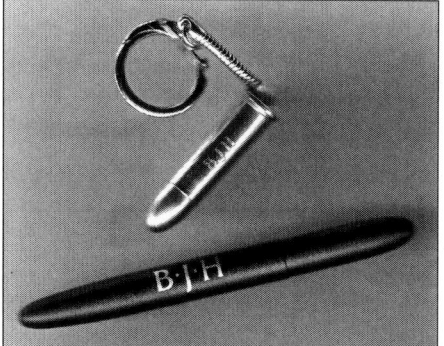

"Cheap The Bullet" CD single with promotional bullet keyring and pen

the oral exciter on it and tended to overdo it a little bit. We were pretty close to distortion on a couple of tracks on the original mix; that's certainly what happened to 'Cheap The Bullet'. We had to be very, very careful bringing that up for a single, because it was very close to distortion, so you have to compensate, you roll off a little bit of bass to push the vocal out."

The single was issued in 7", 12" and, for the first time in the UK, CD formats, and was also notable for the fact that nowhere on it did the name "Barclay James Harvest" appear, being replaced by the "BJH" acronym. Apparently the record company thinking was that the band's existing fans were already very familiar with the short form, but that the unconverted and the media might be more sympathetic to an "unknown" band than to a dinosaur rock act of the seventies! The "BJH" lettering of the new logo was designed by Les, whilst the stylised butterfly was based on a map of airline routes!

For the first time ever, there was enough belief in the record for a proper video to be shot. Costing £30,000 to produce, the video was produced by Tony van den Ende and complemented the song perfectly with images of news, violence and bullets cut into footage of the band looking suitably mean and moody. The reaction in the UK was quite encouraging, with the BBC's local London radio station, GLR, giving it some heavy rotation, and "Cheap The Bullet" sold well enough to be placed at Number 11 in the official "Hot Metal" sales chart! Unfortunately, national radio chose not to playlist the record, and the video was barely aired at all, preventing any further chart action.

Worse still, there were mutterings at Polydor Germany, in stark contrast to the enthusiasm shown by the UK branch, about the song being "too heavy" for the German market, and at the eleventh hour, after copies of the single had already been pressed, the Germans decided to go with a different single, throwing marketing plans into confusion. Polydor GmbH have a history of selecting album title tracks as singles, almost regardless of musical merit, presumably on the basis that it is then easier to market one "title" instead of two. Had the band decided to call the album *Cheap The Bullet*, things might have turned out differently, but they went instead for *Welcome To The Show*, the title of Les's song about the superficiality of the music business! It's debatable whether this was a good move, given that the title could easily be assumed to refer to a live album, but the German record company, with a stereotypical lack of irony, seized on it and released their own single of the title song.

Record company politics aside, *Welcome To The Show* was a triumph. Regarded by many as their best work of the post-Wolstenholme era, the album has a diversity about it which invites comparisons with earlier classics, whilst Jon Astley's and Andy MacPherson's input gives it a real band feeling.

The opening "The Life You Lead" chugs along in an up-beat, Bee Gees kind of way, with lyrics about the choices we make in life - indeed, the original

working title of the song was "Choices". In stark contrast, the brooding "Lady Macbeth" is a direct descendant of "Medicine Man", as John returns to the Shakespearean theme of "Something Wicked This Way Comes". John described in an interview for the fan club magazine how he was stung by criticism of another song into writing this one:

"I've just been pulled up for being too blatant in the lyrics! The song in question is really literal, it's a story about something that happened on one of the first albums we ever recorded. The song was written in about two or three hours, and it was one of these that just flowed out; because of its literal use of names and things like that, I actually had to change the lyric, because people thought it sounded amateurish! I started thinking maybe I should write a devious one now, so I went out and wrote a very devious one, and that's one of the ones that we've recorded now."

Fans' speculation as to the subject of "Lady Macbeth" favoured Maggie Thatcher, but John's deviousness had extended to a little gender-bending, whilst leaving enough clues for the really determined. The pounding single, "Cheap The Bullet", precedes the more reflective title track, wherein Les gently mocks some of the absurdities of the music business where "the blind lead the blind". Les also played the Dire Straits-ish guitar at the end of the song. "John Lennon's Guitar" is, of course, the "literal" one for which John had been criticised. It recalled the incident in 1970 when the band were recording the *Once Again* album, and Norman Smith was regaling them with tales of his work with The Beatles. Delving in a studio cupboard, he produced the blond Gibson Epiphone Casino which John Lennon had played on many Beatles sessions, including their last ever live performance, on the roof of the Apple building in London's Savile Row in January 1969. John Lees was thrilled by the chance to play one of his hero's guitars, and did so for the original recording of "Galadriel" - some of the magic must have rubbed off, as he produced a BJH classic in the process.

The landscape photos used in the booklet for Welcome To The Show were taken on Saddleworth Moor, not far from the band's homes. The one on the cover of the CD sampler (left) shows the hill known locally as Pots And Pans, with the war memorial built in 1923 to honour those killed in the Great War

Mel gives an interview at one of his favourite pubs, The Commercial in Uppermill, April 1990 [photo: Kev Goodman]

"Halfway To Freedom", Les's anthem to the people of the former Soviet Union and Eastern Bloc, proved prophetic - between the song being written and the album being released, events had overtaken everyone and the Berlin Wall had finally come down. In the album's sleeve notes, "Halfway To Freedom" is dedicated to the people of Germany. Les described his motives for writing the song:

"After doing the East Berlin concert I was convinced that the Wall was definitely going to be down before Christmas. It wasn't specifically about Germany, I must confess that. I think what sparked it off was Romania, because I'd been following that for quite some time. I just couldn't believe what was happening out there."

"Halfway To Freedom", alongside "Cheap The Bullet", "Lady Macbeth" and "The Life You Lead", was also included on the promo-only sampler CD, but an early mix of "Halfway" was used, with some minor differences from the finished track.

"African Nights" and "Psychedelic Child" take a nostalgic look back to the band's early experiences. The former sees Les reminiscing about touring South Africa in September and October 1972, supported by Gary Farr, a singer-songwriter who released a number of solo albums between 1969 and 1984. The latter harks back to the hippy era of the late sixties. The lyric is a "stream of consciousness"-style listing of contemporary references. Most are fairly obvious, but a few which may be unfamiliar to younger readers include: "My Little Red Book", the first single by American band Love in 1966, The UFO Club, a well-known psychedelic venue in London and "Ballad Of A Thin

Man", a track from Bob Dylan's 1965 LP *Highway 61 Revisited*. Blow Up, credited as the inspiration for the song, were a local band, friends of John's who recorded at his studio, and Josh was their manager. "Where Do We Go" is a big ballad drawing heavily on the style of one of Les's favourite writers, Chicago's Peter Cetera, and "If Love Is King" is another John Lees lyrical enigma and features a hypnotic hookline, making it another standout track.

The growing importance of the Compact Disc format was reflected in the inclusion of two extra songs on the CD (and cassette), the single B-side, "Shadows On The Sky", and "Origin Earth". Both were included in the album at the last minute, as Mel revealed:

"Les had got another song, but he didn't want to use that – he wanted to use 'Shadows'. Jon Astley was back down at his place in Twickenham, because he was working on his solo album, so Les, myself and this other guy went in and put the basis of 'Shadows' down. It was based on a Zulu chant. The song that was going to be on was virtually finished and that was just put on one side for this new thing at the last minute. It didn't have a name, it was just a rhythm track with very moody chords. It had got a melody which he'd hummed to me and Jon Astley had programmed it to the format Les wanted, but he came up with 'Shadows', then within the last three weeks John arrived with 'Origin Earth'. It's an ongoing thing - a lot of the time someone just gets a better idea."

The subject of "Shadows On The Sky" was big game being hunted to extinction, as Les elaborated:

"It's actually about the elephants and rhinos; it's hard to explain if people haven't been to Africa, but you can actually see for miles and miles, and if you see any animal it looks like a shadow on the horizon."

The inspiration for "Origin Earth" was the book *Eon* by Greg Bear, a copy of which was given to John by sci-fi buff Kev Goodman during an interview in April 1989. The tale concerns a mysterious structure which appears in orbit around the Earth, and turns out to be not from some alien civilization, but from the future of Earth itself.

The album artwork was designed for Nexus by Storm Thorgerson, best known for his work with Hipgnosis for Pink Floyd and others, and the photographs of the band were taken by Peter Chatterton at the University of London Observatory near Hatfield.

The German record company's single choice of "Welcome To The Show", whilst it wasn't a hit, garnered significant airplay and, coupled with a number of television appearances, helped to propel the parent album into the Top 10 in Germany and Switzerland. The album went on to sell over 250,000 copies in Germany, qualifying it for a gold disc, and it also performed very well in less obvious territories such as Norway. Another single was plucked from the album - Les's anthemic "Halfway To Freedom" was the perfect choice to be performed at a big live television gala to celebrate the fall of the Berlin Wall.

The show, *Guten Abend, Deutschland*, was the first ever joint presentation by East and West German television channels, and featured six of the best-known German TV presenters, three from each side of the old divide. BJH were there, too, at the Friedrichstadtpalast in the heart of East Berlin on 6th May, 1990, "performing" to an estimated audience of twenty-five million, with the single released to coincide with the TV show.

Autograph signing session at World Of Music, Berlin Steglitz, 5th May, 1990 [photos: Gregor Lellek, Birgit and Micki Scherrer]

The final German single release from the *Welcome To The Show* album was "John Lennon's Guitar", which was issued in September 1990 in 7", 12" and CD single formats. The band, plus Kevin McAlea and Colin Browne, travelled to Germany to promote the single with an appearance where they mimed to the song in front of a large backdrop of John Lennon on the *Gottschalk* TV show.

Emboldened by the small success of Woolly's *Too Late* cassette, the fan club began to get involved in a number of reissue projects. An advertisement in *Record Collector* magazine by a German record company looking for seventies rock music to release on CD prompted a discussion with Woolly with a view to offering them his *Mæstoso* album. They jumped at the idea, and, after several false starts, the disc finally appeared on S.P.M./World Wide Records in association with Swallowtail in June 1990. The mastering of the disc left a little to be desired, with drop-outs audible in the epic title track, and the booklet was a disaster - all the lyrics were omitted in favour of an advertisement for the record company, whilst the sleeve notes were heavily edited and mangled into something which bore little resemblance to English. The front cover was also marred by poor reproduction and the addition of a red blob advertising the fact that Woolly was an "ex-member of Barclay James Harvest". Still, at least *Mæstoso* was now available on CD at last, and drop-outs notwithstanding, sounded pretty damn good!

For live concerts, fans had to wait until the autumn, and British audiences were disappointed that there were only two concerts in England, effectively warm-ups for the German tour. The opening night, on home territory at the Manchester Apollo, was the band's first live performance for more than three years, but for the most part there was no sign of rustiness after the long lay-off. After the excellent Manchester-based trio To Hell With Burgundy had got things underway with their melodic, folk-tinged songs, BJH were ready to tread the boards once again. Surprisingly, they opened with "Mocking Bird", breaking with the conventional wisdom that the best-known songs are saved for the end. It soon became apparent that the band had taken fan club members' requests on board, and neglected "oldies" such as "For No One", "Crazy City", "Jonathan" and "Play To The World" made welcome returns to the live set. The choice of songs from *Welcome To The Show*, though, raised some eyebrows, with only four new songs in the set, and no place for favourites like "Lady Macbeth", "If Love Is King" and "Where Do We Go". Revelation of the night, though, had to be the live rendition of "John Lennon's Guitar": beginning with

John at the microphone, empty-handed and looking oddly naked without a guitar, whilst an old Gibson stood in the spotlight next to him. Perversely, the studio recording of the song contained no lead guitar, and it seemed that the live performance would follow suit. However, after the verses and a keyboard middle eight drawing on fragments of Beatles' melodies, John picked up the guitar and proceeded to play a blistering solo, with the band swinging into action behind him in what can only be described as a Barclay James Harvest boogie - not a word that one would normally associate with this particular band!

As ever at the beginning of a tour, the UK dates suffered from one or two technical problems, but one of these at Manchester lifted the lid on a BJH trade secret, when several members of the audience commented that the performance of "Hymn" had been surprisingly weak. Unlike most bands, the Barclays have generally eschewed the use of backing tapes in live shows, deservedly enjoying a reputation as a fine live act. However, there have been a couple of exceptions down the years - the stage introduction, where an atmospheric recording leads into the first live number, and "Hymn". Although the original recording sounds deceptively simple, BJH-loving guitarists have found it extremely difficult to recapture that sound, since on *Gone To Earth* it was achieved by multi-tracking

numerous twelve-string guitar recordings. As far back as the 1977 tour, the band decided to bolster the live sound with a backing tape of the twelve-strings, plus the horn parts towards the climax of the song. A question was even raised once in the original *Friends Of Barclay James Harvest* newsletter about why Mel wore headphones for "Hymn" - the real answer, of course, was that he needed to hear the click track from the tape at the mixing desk so that he could tap the drumsticks together as a cue for the rest of the band. In Manchester in 1990 the tape failed to roll, and the band were left with no choice but to play the song without it - odd how until then nobody ever noticed that the live performances of the song were always very similar, and exactly

the same length! It's also amusing to realise that, in a very real sense, Woolly was a presence on stage at all the live shows after he left the band …

The tour ran to thirty-three shows, the vast majority in Germany with a sprinkling in France, Switzerland, The Netherlands and Luxembourg, with the size of the venues and attendances ranging widely, from the relatively small Zenith club in Paris to the massive Hallenstadion in Zürich, almost full with about 10,000 fans. One concert which was advertised in the UK press but never took place was one of a series of gigs by various bands in association with Central TV. The shows would be broadcast in the *Stage 1* series on TV before being released on video, and a BJH concert was set up for Nottingham on November 4th at the end of the tour. In the end, though, it proved impossible to agree terms in time, and the plan was temporarily shelved.

Back in the summer of 1989, BJH's management had been approached by reissue specialists The Connoisseur Collection about a possible BJH compilation of Polydor-era material. It transpired that Mark Stratford at Connoisseur was a bit of a BJH buff, and hit on the idea after reading an article about the band in *Record Collector* magazine which mentioned a number of rare or hard to find recordings. Provisionally titled *For Every One*, and scheduled for May 1990, the compilation was shelved for a while due to record company nervousness about a possible impact on sales of *Welcome To The Show*. Fortunately, once the new album had been released and had proved highly successful, Polydor relented and gave the go-ahead. Retitled *Alone We Fly* (from the climax of "Hymn"), and with a revised tracklisting based on fan club input, the double LP and single CD and cassette included many recordings which had never appeared on album. *Alone We Fly* was released on 22nd October, and the timing couldn't have been better - the band were still on tour in Germany and audiences were leafleted with a flyer advertising the compilation and the fan club. The lack of any Polydor-era "Best Of" compilations other than the full-price, CD-only *Compact Story* left *Alone We Fly* without any competition in the market, and over the full five-year term of the license from Polydor sold an amazing seventy-seven thousand copies.

Not to be outdone in the reissue stakes, EMI began to look again at the band's back catalogue; in Germany *Once Again, Mocking Bird - The Early Years* and *The Best Of Barclay James Harvest, Volume 3* appeared on CD in June 1990. The intention was for a second batch of CDs, comprising *Barclay James Harvest, Barclay James Harvest and other short stories, Baby James Harvest* and a double *Best Of* CD to appear a few months later, but they were never pressed, leaving the first three on the shelves as an apparently random selection and leading disconsolate collectors on a wild goose chase as they unsuccessfully tried to track down the missing *Best Of, Volumes 1 and 2*...

EMI UK took the altogether more sensible step of putting together a definitive triple LP/double CD and cassette of the band's early years, compiled by the fan club, with access to the band's Abbey Road recording log sheets in search of any unreleased gems lurking in the vaults. As it turned out, there were one or two interesting items, including a hitherto unknown "live in the studio" recording of a rocky number from 1970 called "Too Much On Your Plate", plus an incomplete version of Woolly's "White Sails" from the same era, both of which had been considered for inclusion on *Once Again* but eventually rejected. The band (including Woolly) was consulted, but felt that neither recording was suitable for the EMI compilation. In the case of "White Sails", the piece existed only as the individual tracks, marked up for editing, and the Abbey Road engineers used vintage equipment to recreate the whole piece from the individual tapes. There were no vocals, and the recording consisted mainly of Robert Godfrey playing what sounded like a classical piano concerto - *Variations On A Theme By Woolly Wolstenholme*? With the benefit of hindsight it was just as well that it was left in the vaults, as it would undoubtedly have featured in the 1995 court case between Robert and the band with him (quite rightly in this particular case) claiming to have written most of it. All was not lost, though, as the band and EMI gave the fan club permission to release "Too Much On Your Plate" as a free flexidisc, which duly turned up in the December 1991 issue of *Nova Lepidoptera*.

Fortunately, the Abbey Road archives were not the only source of unreleased material. Long-time fan Steve Hibbard had managed to acquire three acetates of unreleased recordings from the Harvest label's original manager, Malcolm Jones. Recorded in 1968 at Advision Studios in London's Bond Street at around the same time as "Early Morning", the acetates were in reasonable condition and contained three lost gems - "Pools Of Blue", a John Lees song written from the point of view of a blind girl, "Eden Unobtainable", a fine Les Holroyd composition which the band had once recorded in session for John Peel, but had never released, and "I Can't Go On Without You", a wistful Tim Hardin-style

piece from Woolly. The band agreed to the inclusion of these songs on the Harvest collection, and the ever-obliging engineers at Abbey Road put them through their new Sonic Solutions "No Noise" system to remove hiss, clicks and pops, with excellent results. *The Harvest Years* was released in May 1991, and, in addition to the three previously unreleased songs, included all of the band's EMI-era material which had not been available on CD up to that point. At about the same time The Connoisseur Collection, encouraged by the success of *Alone We Fly*, licensed a reissue of *Barclay James Harvest Live*, the 1974 set which by now was the only Polydor release not available in CD format. That hit the shops in July in double LP and single CD and cassette form, bringing one step closer the goal of making Barclay James Harvest's entire catalogue available again!

12

A Difference Of Opinion

Whilst the Connoisseur and EMI compilations unearthed previously unheard material which was fascinating for fans and collectors, of much more interest to the band was another compilation album which was being planned at the beginning of 1991 - the difference was that this one would be put together by their own record label and backed with the might of TV advertising in Germany. John and Les were already writing and demoing new material for the follow up to *Welcome To The Show*, but even that took second place to the preparations for the "Best Of" album and associated tour, which would mark the 25th anniversary of the formation of Barclay James Harvest. *Best Of Barclay James Harvest* was released on the Polystar label in Germany and on Polydor in France on October 1st, 1991, and was launched with a TV campaign which parodied a well-known German advertisement for *After Eight* mints - the original slogan of "the fine English way" became "the fine English way of making rock music"! It was a good career move, as the album went Top 10 in Germany, qualifying for gold within three months and went on to sell over four hundred thousand copies across Europe. Die-hard fans were less impressed, grumbling with some justification about the inclusion of one previously unavailable recording (the Treptower Park live take of "Mockingbird") as a marketing technique to persuade those who already owned all the other albums

to buy this one as well. The cover design of an "old-timer" vintage car with the number plate BJH 91 also caused some comments along the lines of "we know that the band are old-timers - why rub it in?"! The fact remains, though, that the band's enhanced profile and income from that one compilation kept them going for most of the nineties. Plans to issue a version of the album in the UK in February 1992 were put on hold when a brand new song was recorded. "Stand Up" was penned by Dutch brothers Rob and Ferdi Bolland for a concept album in a form reminiscent of the Alan Parsons Project, entitled *Darwin - The Evolution*. The album, issued under the name The Bolland Project, featured guest appearances from a host of well-known musicians, including Ian Gillan, Suzi Quatro and Falco. The songwriters had previously written Status Quo's smash hit "In The Army Now", and manager David Walker, who was responsible for Quo and BJH, undoubtedly hoped that the same trick would work for the Barclays. John and Les were invited to The Netherlands in January to sing lead vocals on "Stand Up", a latter day environmental protest song, and the results were good enough for it to be released as a single in Germany under the Bolland Project banner.

The Dutch and German CD single of "Stand Up", with Les and John featured on the artwork

A special arrangement was made between their Dino label and Polydor, allowing the single to be released under the Barclay James Harvest name in the UK, and Polydor UK therefore decided to delay the release of the *Best Of*. Unfortunately, not only had advertising already been placed, but copies of the CD and cassette had already been manufactured with the original tracklisting (featuring "Kiev" in place of "Stand Up"), giving rise to another instant collectors' item when a few copies "escaped".

With the success of the *Best Of* under their belts, it was time to celebrate their silver jubilee year in time honoured BJH style - with another tour. The release of a "greatest hits" compilation can often mark the end of an era for an artist, if indeed it doesn't effectively draw a line under their entire career. BJH's 25th Anniversary Tour reinforced that impression, being a determinedly back to the roots affair. For the first time since the mid-seventies, the band played more concerts in England and Wales than in Germany. Sadly, Scotland missed out because two scheduled concerts at Aberdeen and Glasgow had to be cancelled because of circumstances outside the band's control - rumour had it that the Glasgow one was pulled due to a clash of dates with a more bankable act, The Chippendales! The list of venues, too, read like one of their standard seventies schedules, seeing them revisiting old haunts like the Wolverhampton Civic Hall, Croydon Fairfield Halls, Cambridge Corn Exchange and even the odd college gig.

When the band finally hit the boards at the Liverpool Royal Court Theatre, it seemed that they had truly come full circle. As the band surveyed the few hundred fans who barely half filled the scruffy venue, they must have had doubts about the wisdom of the tour. The show threatened to turn into farce when, half way through the opening number, "Mockingbird", a wash of keyboards crashed in, not just at the wrong moment but in a completely different key! The bemused performers looked accusingly at each other, with guest keyboardist Kevin McAlea pantomiming "not me!". The sound man quickly realised what had happened - as usual, the stage show had begun with a taped introduction, but the DAT tape also contained the old version from the 1990 tour, and it was this which had made an unexpected entry when the tape wasn't faded down at the appropriate moment. When they made it through to the end of the song, John observed wryly: "twenty-five years, and we still can't get it right!" and coined a catchphrase for the rest of the tour.

*Les celebrates his
birthday in Bremen*

After that shaky start, things could only get better, and BJH quickly settled into their more usual professional routine, with some fine performances and many of the shows full to bursting point. The set leant heavily on the band's history, and the light show, too, looked back, with slides of their album sleeves projected on the screen above the stage at John's suggestion. The idea might have been even more effective if the appropriate sleeves had been used for the

*Kevin McAlea
and Colin
Browne on tour
in 1992*

221

songs performed, but then again the band have frequently had difficulties in remembering which song came from which record! Some imaginative laser effects helped to make for a memorable light show, although some of this was lost when the decision was made to shorten the rather long set by dropping "Alone In The Night" and "On The Wings Of Love". The February 16th concert at London's Town and Country Club was filmed by Central TV for the second series of *Stage 1*, and broadcast on March 16th at the peak viewing time of four-thirty in the morning! A number of live recordings from the same show were also released on the four different single formats of "Stand Up" in May, including, to the fans' delight, "Play To The World" and the excellent live arrangement of "John Lennon's Guitar". With these bonus tracks and the added attraction of a lavishly presented limited edition CD in a butterfly-shaped package, the single came close to cracking the UK charts, but eventually stalled at number 82 when the shops ran out of stock, as not enough had been pressed!

In many ways the best of the UK shows was the last one, a charity concert in aid of the local hospital's scanner appeal on BJH's home territory at the Oldham Queen Elizabeth Hall. In fine form by now, and playing to an audience which included many friends and relatives, the band were visibly relaxed, and John, in particular, was more forthcoming in his introductions and between song patter than anyone had seen him for years. The whole show had an emotional feeling about it, with the thought never very far away that this could be Barclay James Harvest's valediction, and indeed the concert would prove to be the last one that the three-man BJH line-up ever played in the UK.

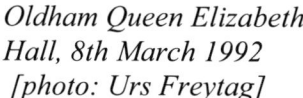

Oldham Queen Elizabeth Hall, 8th March 1992 [photo: Urs Freytag]

The UK *Best Of Barclay James Harvest* finally made it to the shops at the end of June. The old-timer design was dropped in favour of a mauve version of the BJH logo and butterfly from *Welcome To The Show*, but by the time *The Best Of* eventually hit the racks, the momentum was largely lost, and the compilation failed to emulate the success of its German counterpart. The UK version was the first front line release from Barclay James Harvest not to be released on vinyl (the German Polystar LP being the last BJH album ever to appear in that much-loved guise), although curiously, Polydor UK did issue it in three different formats - CD, cassette and a brand new format in the technically advanced but ill-fated Digital Compact Cassette. Also in the shops that June was a video, an extended version of the *Stage 1* TV broadcast of the Town And Country Club show, *The Best Of Barclay James Harvest Live*, released by Virgin Video under a complicated arrangement between the band's management, Central TV and Polydor. Another welcome development was the reissue of the band's entire Polydor back catalogue on CD, as many of them had been deleted in the UK for a number of years. Never slow to cash in, EMI Germany got in on the act with a double CD compilation, *Twice As Much*, covering much the same ground as the earlier *Harvest Years* set, whilst the 1978 concept album *The Eye Of Wendor: Prophecies* by Mandalaband, with instrumental contributions from BJH, made its debut on CD courtesy of Mark Stratford's new RPM label. The digitisation of BJH's original studio albums was finally completed in November when reissue specialists Beat Goes On licensed the Harvest-era albums from EMI and released them as a pair of two-on-one CDs.

After the nostalgia of the 25th Anniversary Tour, it was time for BJH to get back to the business of producing a new album. Given the success of the *Best Of*, it was important to get new material on the market quickly, to remind their public that the band was still in business and to capitalise on their higher profile. Recording began at Friarmere in December 1992 with Martin Lawrence making a welcome return as co-producer, Kevin McAlea on keyboards and Darren Tidsey assisting with programming.

Shortly before recording began, John completely rebuilt and re-equipped Friarmere, moving the studio into the basement and converting the rest of the building into flats. The new studio set up was digital, based around three Alesis ADATs and an Akai hard disc recorder, which allowed the band members to record instrumental parts individually and to synchronise them with a computerised time track. In practice the members of the band were rarely in the studio at the same time, as they worked in isolation on their own songs, and there was practically no live playing on the recording.

Caught In The Light does contain some strong songs, including Les's opener, "Who Do We Think We Are?", about mankind's mistreatment of the Earth. Before the release of the album there was some debate about its length, and a number of cuts were made to reduce the running time to an eventual 70 minutes. When work on the album began, Les came up with an extra verse for the song, incorporating the album title, but it was never recorded, although it still appears in the lyric insert:

> All around we're caught in the light of a thousand suns
> Riding the wind of eternal years
> Watching the Earth die before our eyes
> Hearing the world crying in our ears

The vocal effects on the chorus were achieved with vocoders, the devices popularised by Peter Frampton. "Knoydart" is inspired by one of John's favourite places on the west coast of the Scottish highlands, and most of the lyrical references are to places on that peninsula. The first line of the lyrics should read "heading for Mallaig", the town from which the ferry crosses the Sound Of Sleat (the correct spelling) to Knoydart. Spanish John, Ladhar Bheinn, Kinloch Hourn and Inverie are all places on the peninsula. The "ugly bastards", to whom the song is dedicated, are a group of John's friends with whom he visited Knoydart. The lyrics conjure up the wild and beautiful landscape, but the arrangement, with chiefly computerised instrumentation, spoils the effect.

Les's favourite of his own songs from *Caught In The Light* is "Copii Romania", written about the turmoil in Romania following the collapse of the Communist regime. The English subtitle is "Children Of Romania", and all proceeds from the song were donated to the fund for the orphan children of Romania. It's a slow ballad with the lyrics incorporating some local colour in the form of the *lautari* (gypsy violinists), and "the mighty *Karpatii*", the Carpathian mountains. "Back To Earth" is John's very personal tribute to his father, written following the death of his father in 1992. The lyrics are very moving, but again the lack of a band performance shows with some unsympathetic synthesised bass and MIDI drum sounds. John dedicated the song not only to the loving memory of his father but also to all those who mourn the loss of someone they love. "Cold War" is dedicated to Les's cousin Marguerette, living in the former Yugoslavia at a time when the Balkans were racked by civil war. The classical guitar at the end was also played by Les - in fact, it was his first instrument, before he took up piano and later bass.

In "Forever Yesterday" John charts the shameful history of the Highland clearances. In the 19th century the Scottish highlanders were mostly tenant farmers, using the traditional runrig system, whereby each farmer had several non-contiguous strips of land. Their English absentee landlords were content as long as the land was unsuitable for more profitable use. However, new breeds of sheep such as the black-faced Lintons and Great Cheviots were capable of surviving on the bleak highland hillsides, and the landowners saw the chance of huge profits. The farmers were unceremoniously evicted, often by force, and a large number went to the New World. John Morrison (Murdo) and Neil Morrison, who are credited with the inspiration for the song, used to live on Knoydart, and it was whilst John Lees was there on holiday that the history of the clearances first came to his attention. "Forever Yesterday" was another victim of the misguided attempt to shorten the album, when the coda, featuring a particularly fine guitar solo, was excised from the CD, although, unaccountably, left on the cassette issue. Questioned as to the reasons for this in a 1993 interview, John's state of mind at the time is evident:

"I never understood that, really. By that stage I'd just had enough anyway. I was very unhappy about the whole situation and wasn't prepared to argue about it".

Even in its butchered form, it's an affecting piece, and in full it's magnificent. A churchy-sounding keyboard sets the scene for "The Great Unknown", a reflective song about love and growing older, before the guitar and drums burst in for the second half. Some beautiful vocal variations and more vocoders complete the effect. "Spud-U-Like" is subtitled "David's Rock Song", as David Walker was particularly keen on its inclusion on the album. The song was some years old, but Martin Lawrence persuaded John to finish it and record it for this album. As well as being the name of a chain of fast-food restaurants,

Top: the original artwork for the cover of Caught In The Light, rejected by the band.

Below: first sketches for the eventual sleeve by Rodney Matthews, reproduced with permission from Rodney's book, **Countdown To Millennium**

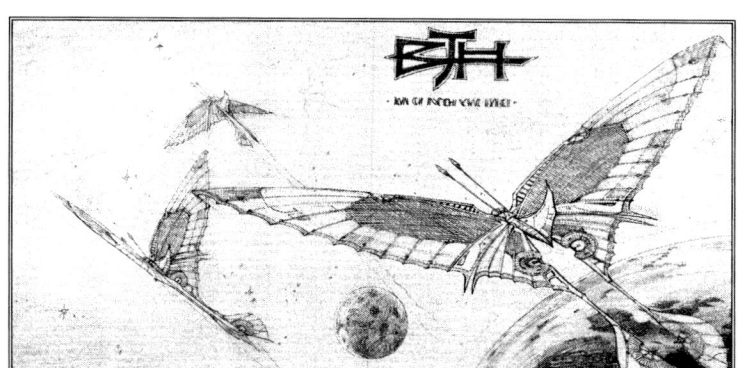

specialising in jacket potatoes, "Spud-U-Like" was also a video game, hence the rather unusual title for a song which unfavourably compares the superficiality of video games with the more lasting pleasures of rock and roll. The song divided listeners into those who enjoyed its undemanding, tongue-in-cheek rock and those who found it superficial and the sound effects merely annoying. Les described *Caught In The Light* as "a very personal album", and "Silver Wings" certainly falls into that category, all too successfully capturing the anguish caused by the end of a relationship in a beautiful but bittersweet song. With the benefit of hindsight, it could also be read as a commentary on the difficult patch which the band themselves were going through at the time, although that may be to read more into it than the composer intended.

In "Once More", aside from the obvious rewriting of "Mocking Bird", John also quotes musically from "Galadriel" and mentions "Pools Of Blue", which was written at the same time. Recorded at a time when doubt had been cast on the authorship of "Mocking Bird", this was John's way of proving its pedigree. Les returns to the subject of a relationship where all is not well in "A Matter Of Time" before the album closer, "Ballad Of Denshaw Mill", based on an old Saddleworth legend which has its basis in fact. Denshaw Mill was a woollen mill which operated until the late 1880s, and was already derelict by the time of the first war, when the events described in the song took place. The line "a hole as rotten as ever fouled the green earth" is from a verse by local poet Ammon Wrigley, and the area is part of the Friarmere division of Saddleworth, known locally as the Darkside. Harold McKlintock, to whose memory the song is dedicated, was an old friend and neighbour, and a source of inspiration to John when he wrote the song, which was first presented for inclusion on *Ring Of Changes* - and rejected.

Even the album artwork proved controversial, with John's original concept (a painting combining the best elements of Monet's water lilies and The Beatles *Revolver* cover) hijacked by Polydor, resulting in a hideous design which was immediately rejected by the band. Les is a fan of the work of Rodney Matthews, and had a calendar featuring his paintings. Les commissioned Matthews, who had designed many album covers in the past, including Asia's *Aqua,* to paint a replacement based on Les's concept of butterfly-shaped spaceships, and this was what finally appeared on the finished album. In his book *Countdown To Millennium,* Matthews explains how it came about:

"I was pleased to be invited to participate in the cover design for this album because I can remember my band Squidd supporting Barclay James Harvest at a Bath University gig in the early 1970s. The design concept of this image belongs to Les Holroyd who explained how all their album covers have a butterfly included somewhere.

As I was producing the first two rough sketches, my wife Karin who also trained as an illustrator, happened to be in my studio and remarked that she considered a lighter, rounder butterfly would be more appropriate for this style of music. Karin did a sketch to illustrate her meaning and, with a few amendments, it was chosen by the band.

It was my intention that the planet should appear above to create a feeling of vertigo. Unfortunately everyone's expectations are not always the same and the design has been printed upside down on two occasions! Several titles were proposed for this album, including *Silver Wings* and *Feel The Silence*."

In retrospect, by most people's standards *Caught In The Light* is a very good album; the problem was that by BJH's standards it was below par. Even in its truncated form it clocks in at seventy minutes, with few up-tempo songs - it's interesting to speculate how what is effectively a double album by seventies standards would compare if edited down to the regulation vinyl running time of forty minutes or so. The overall mood is of sadness and regret, understandable given the circumstances of the band and its members at the time. Predictably, on its release in June 1993, the album was panned by the critics and, with the record company unimpressed and giving it the minimum of backing, sales were dismal - something of the order of forty thousand, compared with over two hundred and fifty thousand for *Welcome To The Show* a mere three years earlier. Polydor's main contribution to advertising the album came in the form of a promo-only CD single featuring an edited version of "Who Do We Think We Are", the album version of "Cold War" and, for reasons best known to themselves, the full-length "Forever Yesterday", complete with the guitar solo which had been chopped off the CD album!

The record company also produced some large butterfly mobiles for shops in Germany, and they advertised CD, LP and cassette versions of the album, although in fact no LPs were pressed, making *Caught In The Light* the first BJH studio album not to appear on vinyl. This may have been indicative of the decline of vinyl, or perhaps a sign of Polydor's decreasing interest in Barclay James Harvest. The band's own commitment was also called into question by their curious decision to perform only two songs from the album ("Back To Earth" and "A Matter Of Time") at eight concerts in Germany which were ostensibly intended to promote *Caught In The Light*.

John was very disappointed by what he saw as a progressive decrease in the collaboration between band members and creative input on each others' songs. In an interview with the fan club magazine he described his feelings about the album thus:

"I have to admit to disappointment. When we started recording, I'd visions of us getting back to the old days when we worked together as a group on arrangements and put our own style and instrumentation on each others' songs and, most important to my mind, the rich vocal harmonies which were such a

On stage at Fulda, June 1993 [photo: Thomas Vollmer]

Martin Lawrence (left), acting as sound engineer on the 1993 open-airs, and tour manager Roy Lemon, a.k.a. 'The Balding Brummie'!

distinctive feature of our early records. The reintroduction of Martin as co-producer was an attempt to try and reverse the situation. Unfortunately it was not to be, and the amount of creative input on each others' songs continues to decline on each new album."

Since he was speaking with the benefit of hindsight, his views may well have been coloured somewhat by the album's poor sales performance, but there's no denying that it sounds like two solo albums welded together and released under the Barclay James Harvest name. It's also true to say that his songs suffered most from the recording regime, with "Knoydart" and "Back To Earth" particularly affected. Further friction was caused by the truncation of some songs and the issues over the album artwork.

Les suffered a double personal blow in June, when both his mother, Mary, and his sister, Carol, died within days of each other.

To cap a particularly bad year for the band, a follow-up tour which was

planned to take in shows in Germany, Switzerland, Austria, The Netherlands and France was cancelled. The official reason given was that an economic downturn in Germany had affected ticket sales for all artists, and whilst there was some truth in this, the bottom line was that the band could no longer rely on its hitherto solid support in Germany, its core market. John's opinion as to the reasons for the postponement were unequivocal:

"My personal theory goes back to the loss of creative input by everyone on all the songs - 'The BJH Sound'. Over the years it's resulted in an ever-widening difference in mine and Les's style of music. Add to this the TV shows we've done that were just not the kind of show that this band should have been doing. At this particular moment in time I can't see the point in going on, because I don't want to see the band devalued any more than it is at present. We should just take time out from the whole thing, and if in two or three years' time things improve, the credibility of the band and its music is once again in demand, then everybody could get back together and discuss the possibilities." The future looked grim, and John expressed the view that the band should take a sabbatical in the hope that the situation would improve and enable them to

John at home, considering the future of Barclay James Harvest

pick up where they had left off. When asked whether there was likely to be a rescheduled tour, he dismissed it thus:

"I don't think there will be, or an album - not with my involvement."

Manager David Walker expressed his frustration with the situation in the band:

"My attitude is this: 'Fine, if you don't want to listen to what I've got to say, then I won't say anything.', and Barclay James Harvest and I did get to that point. They stopped listening to each other, so there was no chance of them listening to people like me and Lindsay. The record company are the first ones to say, 'We don't want any more of these so-called Barclay James Harvest recordings', and the fans said the same. I'd love to see them get back together with Woolly, to be honest."

The hiatus continued through 1994, although in June the "lost" material from Woolly's abandoned *Black Box* album was made available at long last. Independent reissue specialist Voiceprint, in association with Swallowtail, released a CD comprising the entire *Mæstoso* album plus more than half an hour of rare recordings from 1982, under the title *Songs From The Black Box*. All five songs from the original Swallowtail *Too Late* cassette now appeared on the CD, with two (Has To Be A Reason" and "Too Much, Too Loud, Too Late") in different mixes, whilst "Even The Night", "The Will To Fly", "Sunday Bells" and "Open" had never been released in any form before.

Polydor's waning interest was reflected in their decision to put plans for a *Best Of Barclay James Harvest, Volume 2* on ice, although there was still interest from the German branch of the company, and it came as no great surprise to anyone when Polydor UK declined to take up an option on a further two studio albums, putting an end to BJH's twenty-year relationship with the label.

13

It's Over, My Friend

The only ray of hope for the future of Barclay James Harvest at the end of 1994 was a projected "unplugged"-style acoustic concert or series of concerts in Britain, with John reported as being particularly keen. In the event, even the unplugged project fell by the wayside, overshadowed by the culmination of the Robert Godfrey affair. Writs had been served on the band and their record and publishing companies back in 1985, claiming joint authorship by Godfrey of ten early BJH compositions, five from *Barclay James Harvest* and five from *Once Again*, and breach of contract over an alleged agreement that he would be treated as a fifth member of the band and receive a commensurate share of their earnings.

The case finally reached the High Court in The Strand on February 6th, 1995, after a series of legal wrangles, with BJH's solicitors trying to prevent the case reaching the court by challenging the validity of Godfrey as Plaintiff receiving Legal Aid for a writ which they asserted would not cover the cost to the taxpayer even if he were to win. In response, his legal representatives successfully appealed four times, presenting new submissions and altering the claims. Before the case was heard, Godfrey dropped his claim to co-authorship of one song, and during the proceedings abandoned his claims to three more ("Taking Some Time On", "The Iron Maiden" and "Ball And Chain"), leaving a core of six songs in dispute. It took two weeks for all the evidence to be heard, and a further month before the Hon. Mr. Justice Blackburne handed down his judgement on 21st March, 1995.

The judgement itself was a legal landmark, whilst at the same time allowing both sides to claim victory! In the first action Godfrey claimed that he had been given to understand by John Crowther that he would receive his fair share of royalties "in due course". He further claimed there was a verbal agreement that he would be treated as a fifth member of the band and would therefore be entitled to a fifth share of any earnings which might accrue as a result of their joint efforts. The judgement on this action came down squarely on the side of the defendants: "The plaintiff does not persuade me that on the balance of probabilities there was any common understanding such as he now asserts, much less that there was any enforceable agreement."

If the band's team was feeling smug at this stage, reading the next part of the judgement would have wiped the smiles from their faces. On the claim of joint authorship of six songs, the somewhat surprising finding was that a contribution to a recording does not have to be part of the original song (i.e. it could be an arrangement), nor does it have to be equal in terms of quantity, quality or originality to the work of the other collaborators, in order to qualify as significant and therefore entitle the writer to joint authorship. In the Godfrey vs. Lees and others case, these guidelines led the judge to find that Godfrey had made a substantial contribution to "Dark Now My Sky", "When The World Was Woken", "Mocking Bird", "Galadriel", "Song For Dying" and "The Sun

Will Never Shine". In the case of the latter two songs, the judge described the joint authorship claim as "very borderline", but nevertheless decided that Godfrey "establishes, albeit to varying degrees, that he was a joint author of all six musical works".

There was a sting in the tail for Godfrey: the judgement applied only to the arrangements of the original recordings of the work. If there was any money to be had, the only one of the songs in question which had made any significant contribution to the band's earnings was "Mocking Bird", but the judgement meant that later live versions, for instance, without the orchestral arrangement, would not be covered. Given that only income from the six years prior to the writ being issued (i.e. from June 1988 to June 1994) was at issue, the amount involved would be negligible. No *Berlin* or Polydor *Best Of* sales would count, only the sales of compilations which included the original EMI recordings, such as *Another Arable Parable* and *The Harvest Years*.

Godfrey was to be denied even that victory, though. The judge decided that, because of the extraordinary length of time which had passed before the claims were legally made, Godfrey would not win any royalties or other rights over the works in question. The crucial part of the judgement reads as follows:-

"It would be against all conscience if, in these circumstances, the plaintiff should be permitted to step in and reap for himself a share of the band's hard earned success. In my judgement the plaintiff is estopped from claiming any relief to which he might otherwise have been entitled.

Conclusion.

I dismiss the two actions."

With that, the case was over. Fascinating to music business legal specialists, no doubt, and a warning to anyone intending to collaborate with other writers or arrangers to ensure that matters of authorship are clearly laid down in their contracts, but from the point of view of both Robert Godfrey and Barclay James Harvest, the only winners were the legal profession. John, Les, Mel and Woolly had to pay a great deal of the costs of mounting their defence (in the order of £150,000) which could not be reclaimed since Godfrey's case was funded by Legal Aid. In fact the band's costs would have been far higher if Les, Mel and Woolly hadn't themselves been granted Legal Aid towards the end of the case. John didn't qualify, but he was helped out by manager David Walker acting as his "McKenzie friend", the term for a kind of legally unqualified "prisoner's friend". Godfrey gained nothing, at least financially, and the taxpayer had to foot the bill for his costs, a total of £400,000. Godfrey later stated that he had not expected to win, and issued the writs purely to prove his point. The Enid web site quotes Robert as saying,

"I would of *(sic)* settled for a declaration of my authorship, an apology and £2,000. It all concluded (as I expected that it might) with a hollow moral victory for me."

For those who were not personally involved in the court case, it was not without its lighter moments. The judge showed impeccable musical taste when referring to both "Mocking Bird" and "Galadriel" as "most attractive work", and belied the stereotype of judges as old duffers in his dry summation of the evidence from each side:

"I had the impression that the plaintiff, who gave his evidence fluently and fairly, was, if anything, a little too forthcoming in his recollection of the details of these distant events to render his account wholly reliable. In contrast, the evidence of the first, second and third defendants *[John, Les and Mel]* exhibited an undue reluctance to remember anything about the plaintiff ..."

John's wife, Olwen, took the stand to describe how she had first heard "Mocking Bird" in 1968:-

"I remember John playing 'Mocking Bird' to me for the first time, just on the guitar on a sunny day outdoors."

When it was suggested to her that this rendition probably didn't include the orchestral arrangement, she replied:-

"I probably heard the orchestra in my head"!

Les would have been pleased to hear the judge, trying to relate the faces in front of him to the pictures on the debut album sleeve from twenty-five years earlier, say:-

"Mr Holroyd doesn't seem to have changed at all, but you'll have to help me with the others".

He would have been a lot less amused at the evidence of the band's first roadie, Jim Tetlow, who apparently got the job because, firstly, he lived just down the road, and, secondly, because he owned a van! When questioned about Robert's assertion that the band must have been expecting him to arrive in Diggle, as Les had met him at the railway station, Jim replied to the effect that Les wouldn't walk down the road to go the pub, let alone trudge two miles across the moors to the railway station! Wisely, Les didn't dispute this flagrant piece of character assassination ...

After all the dust of the court case had settled, the band had to put the case behind them and make some difficult decisions. All of the band members were demoralised and disillusioned, and for John, at least, it was by no means certain that the band should carry on. However, when the band and management met up in July, he was persuaded that keeping the band going would not only prove that it had not been destroyed by Godfrey's actions, but would also be financially advantageous, given the plans for a second Polydor *Best Of* album. The idea was for the band to record at least a couple of brand new songs at Friarmere, which would then be included on the compilation as an incentive for die-hard fans who already owned all the earlier releases.

When the proposed release date for the Polystar/Polydor set was put back, BJH had more time to work on new material, and decided to carry on composing new material with a view to recording an entire album. In September, the band met again and two songs were chosen to be recorded for Polydor. Les's "Yesterday's Heroes" was his strongest song for many years, a moody, powerful piece which contrasted with John's "River Of Dreams", on the face of it a commercial up-tempo number with a singalong chorus. What the songs had in common, though, was their genesis in the traumatic events surrounding the court case. The lyrics of "Yesterday's Heroes" are aimed squarely at those who consider the band to be a spent force, with particular reference to "those who try to keep the flame from burning". Similarly, the jauntiness of "River Of Dreams" masked a bleak theme of dreams unfulfilled. Encouragingly, the adversities which they had had to face collectively seemed to have brought the band closer together and an atmosphere of real co-operation and shared aims prevailed once more.

The new songs were premiered at four live concerts in October 1995. The opportunity to appear at a prestigious Pop and Rock Festival in the Swiss Alps at Visp gave them the perfect platform to prove that BJH were back in business, and three low-key German dates acted as rehearsals for the larger event. Sharing the bill with BJH in Switzerland on the Friday were May Day, Katrina And The Waves and Alan Parsons and his band - the latter was an inspired choice, as not only do the two bands attract similar audiences, but Parsons, of

239

course, knew BJH from his work on *Once Again*. After his own excellent live set, he stayed behind to watch BJH wow the crowd of 5,000, then joined them in the dressing room afterwards for a chat. BJH seemed rejuvenated in many ways. The new songs were very well received, and the live set also found room for songs which hadn't been aired for a long time, such as "Nova Lepidoptera", "Loving Is Easy" and, the biggest surprise of all, "The Song (They Love To Sing)", making its first live appearance since 1981! The general feeling was that the band was back on peak form.

Late 1995 witnessed the arrival of an important new way for the band to reach their fans when the official Barclay James Harvest web site was launched. At that stage few people had heard of the World Wide Web, which would soon become a global phenomenon, and Barclay James Harvest were amongst the very first bands to have their own site. Set up by the fan club with the blessing of the band's management, the site quickly became a vital way of communicating news of new releases and live dates to fans who were otherwise starved of any information about the group in the mainstream media.

Above: Les in St. Wendel, October 1995

Right: Mel surrounded by his kit in St. Wendel

[photos: Rolf Tombült]

John on stage in Neu-Ulm, 4th October, 1995

February 1996 marked the release of EMI's *Four Barclay James Harvest Originals*, a small but perfectly formed box set of the group's first four albums on separate CDs, each contained in a miniature facsimile of the original LP sleeve. More importantly, the same month saw John, Les and Mel back in the studio recording the new album. Then in May came the news for which the band's

241

followers had been waiting - a new deal had been signed, this time with Polydor GmbH, the German arm of Polydor. Although it may seem irrelevant as to whether their contract was with the UK or German branch of the company, there were some significant differences: Polydor GmbH had often been frustrated that BJH were signed to Polydor UK, as this meant that the UK called the shots as to release timings, cover artwork etc., despite the fact that the vast bulk of sales were in Germany. In recent years the UK had shown little interest in promoting the band, especially for 1993's *Caught In The Light*, but still insisted on keeping control. The band's managers felt that signing direct to the German end would give them the best of both worlds - a record company which understood the band's music and was prepared to push it, whilst at the same time having access to over twenty years' worth of catalogue which could be exploited on the back of the new material. The deal was for two albums, and gave Polydor GmbH exclusive rights for the world excluding North America.

In June the fan club did an on the spot report at Friarmere for the club magazine, and found the band in good humour, with Les enthusing about his new Rickenbacker guitar, and John even describing how he and Les had ended up playing acoustic guitars together on one session, something which hadn't happened for many years.

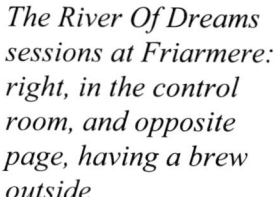

The River Of Dreams sessions at Friarmere: right, in the control room, and opposite page, having a brew outside

In July the band took a break for family holidays, and there was another hiatus when co-producer Martin Lawrence was absent because of a prior engagement touring with Joe Longthorne. Whether the delays affected morale within the band, or whether the initial enthusiasm simply wore off, it's hard to say, but the reports coming out of the studio became less enthusiastic, with John being particularly unhappy with the state of affairs. He felt that the spirit of co-operation which had marked the recording of "River Of Dreams" and "Yesterday's Heroes" had evaporated, with Les and himself working separately on their own songs - the very thing which had upset him so much about *Caught In The Light* and which he had been promised would not happen this time. John expressed his frustration in a 1998 interview:

"Two songs were recorded like we're recording now *(for Nexus)*, 'River Of Dreams' and 'Yesterday's Heroes', and they've definitely got a different feel from all the other tracks. As soon as we got the deal with Polydor and we came into the studio it went right back to square one, people working on their own. All those songs were wasted, because they never turned out like they were supposed to turn out."

Les had a somewhat different view of what went wrong:

"I still think it sounds quite fresh compared with the last few albums, but I think we could have taken it a stage further, and personally I think we should have done it in a different studio. I think we should have got away from the area and totally isolated ourselves from all the normal domestic things that go on around you. It's like being on tour - you're either on tour or you're not. At the end of the day you don't go home and start mowing the lawn! It tends to drag on, because people go oh, you know, 'I'll just take the afternoon off because I've got to do this with the kids'."

Mel, on the other hand, was happy with the results:

"I think it's as good as anything we've done, in fact in some ways I think it's a lot better than some of the things we've done in the past. I've got to say that it took a little bit longer than was expected, but it was just one of those things. John had booked his holiday and stuff like that. In terms of the overall sounds and the songs, yeah, I was happy. Whether the songs turned out as expected when they were written, I couldn't tell you, but they all sound good to me. It's a nice Barclay James Harvest album - it covers all bases from rock 'n' roll to melancholy and anywhere in between."

Recording dragged on into 1997, and by the time that the album was finally completed, a year had elapsed since they first began work at Friarmere.

Whilst waiting for the new studio album, a number of reissues provided some consolation for impatient fans: Connoisseur followed up the stunning success of *Alone We Fly* with another fan club-compiled set of rarities and obscurities. *Endless Dream* covered various single mixes and B-sides, plus two never before released takes - the 1974 Barclay James Harvest recording of Woolly's "Maestoso", originally planned for release on the *Everyone Is Everybody Else* album, plus a different version of "Child Of The Universe" from the 1975 sessions for an American single, but this version wasn't used (despite being superior to the cut which was selected!) and had been gathering dust in the Polydor vaults for more than twenty years. Also of interest to collectors were a September 1986 German EMI CD called *Premium Gold Collection* (later repackaged for the UK as *The Best Of Barclay James Harvest - Centenary Collection*), which was notable for including John's solo version of "Child Of The Universe" without his permission! A Dutch company called Disky also got in on the act in June 1997 with yet another selection of early material, called *Mocking Bird*.

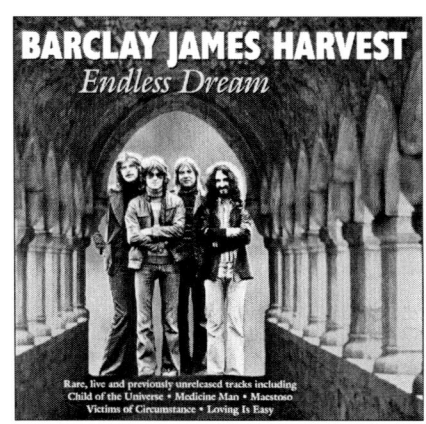

In spite of the difficulties, the new album, *River Of Dreams*, was really rather good. Released on May 26th in Germany and Switzerland, there was enough of the band spirit about the recordings to convince most fans that it was a genuine BJH album and a significant improvement on *Caught In The Light*. The opening "Back In The Game" was a determined statement of intent from Les: Jeff Leach's string overture leads us into the acoustic guitar intro before John steps in with some fine lead guitar reminiscent of the band's mid-seventies sound, and the song also features the trademark harmony vocals from Les and John which had been so sorely missed in recent years. "River Of Dreams" (incidentally the first time that John was given the title track of a BJH album) begins with a country-ish introduction before developing into a catchy sing-along, in stark contrast to the undoubtedly autobiographical lyrics, which deal with looking back on life in disillusionment. "Yesterday's Heroes" continues the retrospective theme, the hypnotic Pink Floydian opening leading into powerful guitar riffs which soon made the song a live favourite and potential BJH classic. John's next song, "Children Of The Disappeared", is a brilliant evocation of the climate of fear which affects the parents of young children in these less innocent times, with the title also making reference to the political activists who vanished in South American dictatorships. Musically, the sparse, piano led beginning and end and the beautiful string accompaniment recall the melodies of Love's *Forever Changes*, whilst the middle section which leads into a classic Lees guitar solo takes BJH into previously unexplored areas - still innovative after all these years! A magnificent, emotionally affecting song. In contrast, "Pool Of Tears" shows John's lighter side with a song about lost love. There is a touch of "Origin Earth" about the melody, but with an unusual feel, probably due to the input of "Jazzy" Jeff Leach. Early pressings of the CD misspelt the title as "Pools Of Tears", but later printings have it correctly in the singular.

"High, low, here we go!", sings Les on "Do You Believe In Dreams (Same Chance For Everyone)" - not, perhaps regrettably, a football anthem, but a song with a romantic flavour and harmonies which recall earlier classics like "Jonathan". "(Took Me) So Long" is a classy ballad showcasing some more of Les's classical guitar expertise as well as some moody lead playing from John, and was one with which Les was particularly pleased:

"My personal favourite was 'So Long'. I wanted to spend more time on that - I would have liked to have taken it further. It went down very quickly and it would have been rather nice to experiment a bit longer, on all of the tracks really, to have spent more time on it, particularly on the vocals - I wasn't really too happy with the vocals at the time, I had a cold and one thing and another, but there comes a time when you've got to go for it and get it out of the way."

The wilfully obscure lyrics of the enigmatic "Mr. E", with its musical nods to The Beatles, led to a great deal of debate amongst fans, but it seems likely

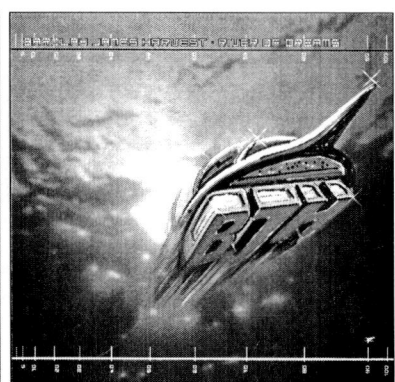

A selection of artwork presented to the band for possible use on River Of Dreams: the "water drop" design was selected, but changed from purple and yellow to shades of blue, with different lettering, for the final version (right)

that both "Mr. E" and Les's "Do You Believe In Dreams (Same Chance For Everyone)" were written, at least in part, about the situation in and around the band over the previous few years. The nearest John ever came to lifting the veil from "Mr. E" was when he introduced it on stage by saying, "E is for emulation, envy, ecstasy. I know what *I* mean - you find your own meanings!". He told fans that the song has many meanings, and anyone who found them all would be doing very well! Ultimately, the subject, as John intended, is a mystery ...

No doubts in "Three Weeks To Despair", as John tackles the subject of homelessness. Inspired by two articles in *The Sunday Times* written by Margarette Driscoll, the song has a dreamy melody, almost like a lullaby, but the chilling quotes from a homeless man whom John and Martin interviewed in Stockport are enough to touch the most cynical heart. Whilst the pair were working in the studio, just listening to an early mix of the piece with the homeless guy's voice-over, they were so affected that they didn't realise for some minutes that the song had actually ended. Mel rated it as the best song on the album:

"I like 'Three Weeks To Despair'. I know it's not a very 'up' subject, but it was the way it was done - the rhythm track was done pretty quickly, so there wasn't a lot of birth pain with it - it just seemed to be a magical thing. We all seemed to be touched by the muse at the same time, and it went down a treat. The song, as well, especially in this part of the world where we live, you can see things like that happen. You see it every day, and your heart does go out to them."

Finally, Les's reflective, acoustic-led, "The Time Of Our Lives" builds up to an anthemic close and ensures that the album ends on an upbeat note.

For many of the band's loyal following, *River Of Dreams* was a welcome return to form, but ultimately the dissent within the band itself, coupled with indifference from the record company and the press, probably meant that it was doomed from the outset. The initial launch looked quite promising, with a one-track promotional CD single of the title track garnering a reasonable amount of

A Barclay James Harvest cake (?!) was produced to promote River Of Dreams. Puzzlingly, the butterfly design used was taken from the XII album, complete with Woolly's face etched in finest marzipan ...

airplay, and the album charting at respectable, if unspectacular, positions of #71 in Germany and #33 in Switzerland. Les, Mel, John and Martin Lawrence travelled out to Germany at the end of May to do radio and cable TV interviews. Initially they had planned to take acoustic guitars and perform "unplugged" spots live on radio, but in the end they simply recorded two songs at Friarmere and took the tape with them. John's "River Of Dreams" was an obvious choice to promote the album, but the second song was a surprise selection - "Life Is For Living", performed solo by Les in a completely new arrangement for acoustic guitar. These recordings gained some useful exposure with four broadcasts on German radio in conjunction with live band interviews.

Back home, though, it was a different story: UK fans, already disappointed that BJH had not played any live concerts in their own country since 1992, were devastated to discover that Polydor UK had not bothered to release *River Of Dreams* at all. The band's managers, including Lindsay Brown who was actually working for Polydor UK as International Director, were unable to get any kind of response out of the company before the deadline for licensing expired, and were then incensed to discover that they couldn't even offer the album to another company without paying a hefty licensing fee override to Polydor GmbH or renegotiating the original contract. To the band's faithful at home, it appeared that BJH had finally turned their back on Britain for good.

Sales of the album proved to be disappointing, restricted as they were to only two countries. A second promo-only CD single, of "Back In The Game", was ignored by radio programmers, and plans for a re-recorded, edited version of "Yesterday's Heroes" to be released to radio were abandoned - much to Les's annoyance, since he had already done all the work on it and sent the tape to Germany. He, like many fans, felt that "Yesterday's Heroes" had real potential for getting airplay and bringing the album to the attention of a wider audience, but it wasn't to be. The relationship between the band and their new record company was already deteriorating rapidly.

The band appeared at two big open air festivals in Germany at the beginning of July, co-headlining with Art Garfunkel over Emerson, Lake and Palmer. In Halle Art Garfunkel went on last, whilst the next night in Dortmund BJH took the headlining spot. The attendance was a respectable five thousand and the set, including "River Of Dreams", "Yesterday's Heroes" and "Back In The Game" from the new album , was well received, but there was little sign of record company or media interest.

The release of *River Of Dreams* was quickly followed by another back catalogue reissue, this time in the form of the 1972 compilation *Early Morning Onwards* making its debut on CD, This one, on a new label called Brimstone, was more significant, though, as the label was not only the International BJH Fan Club's first venture into running a "proper" record label, but, more significantly, marked Woolly Wolstenholme's first tentative steps back into the music business as co-owner of the label.

A BJH tour was set up for September in an attempt to boost *River Of Dreams'* flagging sales. The lack of availability of the album anywhere other than Germany and Switzerland precluded live concerts in any other countries, confirming the worst suspicions of fans elsewhere. By this time John was thoroughly disillusioned with the whole business, but was persuaded to go on tour anyway:

"It didn't feel right. There was constant competition within the band, and eventually it tears itself apart. I'm as guilty as anybody else, but if you're trying to promote something and you don't believe in it, then you won't give it 100%."

Unsurprisingly, Les saw it differently when asked if he had enjoyed the tour:

"*I* did, yeah. I'm writing good songs, I'm doing them well, I'm performing well, and I personally thought I was performing very well, better than I'd done for a long time. It's just annoying when at the end of the day, people don't think it's happening. I would work live, it doesn't matter if it's five people or 5000 or 50,000, but we're not given the opportunity, more than anything from the record company we were with. I don't think Polydor in Germany are interested. I could be wrong, but there's no use in pushing it. The reaction from the media was quite good, but when we actually got out there there was an incredible

absence of the record company from every event we played. These were big gigs, headlining over Art Garfunkel and people like that. There was a complete lack of interest, and I was extremely annoyed. I know that John was disappointed when we went on the road that there weren't that many people around, but there weren't that many people around for anybody unless you happened to be Bryan Adams! But, if you want to be Bryan Adams, or even Chris de Burgh, you've got to go out and work. You can't go on the road after a two or three year absence and expect it all to be laid there on a carpet for you. This is not 15 or 20 years ago, this is 1998 when the market is completely flooded with all types of music, and we're in a totally different generation to what's happening now. No-one owes us anything, that is the bottom line. The promoters don't owe us anything, the record companies don't owe us anything and the fans don't owe us anything."

Mel, too, was happy to be on the road:

"It was great! I always enjoy touring. The only thing I will say about it is that I would have liked to have done more gigs, because once you've gone through the rehearsals and you've got a few under your belt then you're in the mode, and rather than being four or five weeks it could have been eight, nine, ten weeks. Firstly you could play to more people, obviously you're getting tighter as well and it just becomes more enjoyable. Once I'm in tour mode I could just go and go and go. Having said that, you've got to remember that I haven't got a family. For me, when I'm on tour I'm an eighteen year old again. My mind is eighteen, but whether my body would wear it I don't know!"

Les at Hamburg Docks, 11th September 1997

Asked afterwards about the feeling within the band on that tour, Mel was still upbeat:

"It's always good. Obviously we've known each other for a long time, we know each other's foibles, so we give each other enough space, we know when people need time alone. Gone very much are the days when you all go out for a meal every night and you all hang around together. Of course, if there was a night off we all went out and had a chinwag and talked about what was going on. I've never had any problem with morals - er, morale! Being on the road with x amount of people, there's always going to be somebody who's not in the same mood as you at any one time, but you need each other."

Professional to the end, the band turned in some good performances, playing five songs from the new album - the title track and "Yesterday's Heroes", of course, plus "Back In The Game", "(Took Me) So Long" and "Mr. E". Audiences were surprised that both "Mr. E" and "Life Is For Living" were not performed as a band - "Mr. E" featured John on acoustic with the only backing being Colin Browne's harmonica, whilst "Life Is For Living" was performed completely solo by Les, accompanied by his own acoustic guitar. During these solo spots, the rest of the band left the stage, reminiscent of the days when Woolly and the orchestra were left to it for "Moonwater".

Unfortunately, the solo spots were an all too accurate reflection of what was happening behind the scenes. John made no secret of the fact that he didn't want to be there, and by the end of the tour he and Les were barely speaking to each other. On at least one occasion it seemed that they wouldn't get through the whole tour, but as ever they felt that they couldn't let their audiences down. In the end the band somehow made it through to the Bern Theater im National on 27th September 1997, with those who came to see them blissfully unaware that Bern was the last gig that this line-up of Barclay James Harvest would ever play.

John, Les and Mel make their last appearance on stage together in Bern, backed by Colin Browne and Jeff Leach   [photo: Olivier Gille]

14

Some Things Change

By the end of the *River Of Dreams* tour, relations between the band members had reached crisis point. John was convinced that they should return to the way things were done in the early days, working together as a band on each other's songs and going back to the style which had first brought them success. Les believed that this would be a retrograde step and could see no reason to change anything, and Mel was just happy to be working. The management were concerned by the dwindling audiences and lack of record company interest. Something had to give, so a series of meetings was convened to determine the future of Barclay James Harvest, if any. John left David Walker in no doubt as to his view that the band was not working and that they should rest it for a while. He was not prepared to do any more concerts or recording with BJH for the time being, and if that meant Les and Mel working without him, then they would have to come to some arrangement.

There was a further complication to the equation: Woolly was back on the scene. It was a critical point in Woolly's life. The court case brought by Robert Godfrey had hit him particularly badly, contributing to a nervous breakdown in 1995, and whilst he made slow progress in recovering from that, he was left with a feeling of dissatisfaction with what he felt was the pointlessness of his life. His marriage had broken up and he had left the farm in Wales to live with his parents in Chadderton again in 1996. He became more involved in the arts, a side of his personality which had had little outlet during the years on the farm, writing poetry and one or two new songs, with a tentative view to recording a new solo album at some point. In June 1996 he had met up with John again, when they spent an evening in *The Bull's Head* pub in Delph reminiscing about the old days. The pair had also been in occasional contact through 1997, rubbing shoulders at John's fiftieth birthday party and at a reunion of their Art School year. It wasn't until early 1998, though, when John finally decided that he wanted a break from BJH, that he hit on the idea of persuading Woolly to join him in a solo project.

David Walker now had a problem - solo projects were all very well, but would they be marketable? The brand name of Barclay James Harvest still meant something, but who owned it? Legally, it was actually a limited company with Les and John as directors and with equal numbers of shares owned by John, Les and Mel. That meant that unless Les or John agreed to give up their right to the name - unlikely - or bought out the other one, then they had an equal claim on it. David made discreet enquiries as to the viability of a band without John or without Les. The consensus in their main markets, especially Germany, was that a group including John would be more favourably received, but that neither would be great money-spinners. David still believed that the three-piece band could be resurrected when the market improved, and Polydor Germany still had an option on a second album to follow *River Of Dreams*.

Walker therefore devised the plan of announcing that the band would take a sabbatical whilst the members worked on solo projects.

David now came up with the idea of calling the solo albums *Barclay James Harvest Through The Eyes Of John Lees* and *Barclay James Harvest Through The Eyes Of Les Holroyd* respectively. The use of the BJH name would give extra credibility to the solo projects, whilst still leaving the door open for them to work together again in the future. There was a difference in opinion as to these names, though: Les believed that the names were just a suggestion for one-off album titles and not meant to be taken literally, whilst John understood that these were the agreed names for the solo projects. A number of meetings between David Walker and the band members followed, and Les and Mel reluctantly agreed to the idea of the sabbatical. So it was that in March 1998 David Walker announced through the fan club magazine that the band would be taking a sabbatical for a couple of years, using the time to undertake solo projects.

Now free to work on his own music, John wasted no time in inviting Woolly to take part. Woolly was still involved with Brimstone Records, which followed its debut release, *Early Morning Onwards*, with a first appearance on CD for the rare quadraphonic version of *Once Again*. Ultimately, though, these minor undertakings provided more by way of distraction than real purpose in his life, so John's invitation came at just the right moment for Woolly, and he agreed to the proposal. This strengthened John's resolve not to compromise concerning the existing band, and when asked about the possibility of a Barclay James Harvest reunion, he was quite open:

"There is a way, as a four-piece, but not in any other form as far as I'm concerned. I can't see it, unless somebody comes along with a couple of million quid! I just think that it's come to the end of the road, it doesn't function as a unit. I wouldn't close the door on it - if something came in I'd consider it, but we should really pull away from it for a while."

Les, interviewed in July 1998, was less enthusiastic about the sabbatical:

"It was decided that for whatever reason, it wasn't happening, so it was time to take a break. The only thing I can say is it was a majority decision, but it wasn't mine. At this point in time, although there is a break, we are actually talking about various future projects. I personally think we should go out on the road - the band as it is now. I don't envisage any major changes in the band. John obviously is off doing his own thing at the moment, but I've no doubt at all in my mind that if someone came up with an offer for Barclay James Harvest to do something, I've no doubt at all that we'd get together."

Les was unequivocal in rejecting any thought of a reunion with Woolly:

"No. That's gone, that's past. As far as I'm concerned Barclay James Harvest is the band that exists now. The band that existed for the majority of the time was from 1978 onwards. That's 20 years, and you can't just say, 'Well it's not working, therefore we'll get the four together.' You can't recreate something for the sake of the few people that want it. I can't see any benefits to the four members getting back together again."

From Mel's perspective, the sabbatical wasn't really his issue:

"It was more about John and Les, I think. For me, I think it's a time to reassess what direction we're going to go into, rather than just keep going through the process of another album and a tour. It was getting a little bit flat. The court case took a lot out of us - looking back now, I don't think we realised how much it did take out of us. It's only when you get working again that you realise how much it's drained you. I certainly think that from John and Les's point of view that it's more of a reassessment. It's being adult about it - there's no great arguments, it was just, 'is this really what we want to be doing or should we take time away from each other and see what happens?'"

Events moved swiftly: by now BJH's co-manager Lindsay Brown had left Polydor, having been head hunted by Terry Shand, former owner of Castle Communications, for his new label, Eagle Records. Lindsay was in place as International Director, and Eagle, specialising in artists who made their name in the seventies, was the obvious place to go with John's project. As an untried "new" act, John and Woolly in effect had to audition for a contract. Working at Friarmere studios, the duo quickly established that the old rapport was still there, and Woolly set about learning the new studio technology which had evolved during his long absence from the scene. They quickly completed a demo of a song which had been around since 1968, when the original quartet had included it in a session at Intercity Sound, but which had never been properly recorded by the band. "Sitting Upon A Shelf" is a melodic, very sixties sounding song, with echoes of Traffic, Donovan and (whisper it!) The Moody Blues. The people at Eagle liked what they heard, and John was offered a deal for an album, although there were strings attached. The new label was keen to acquire an interest in some Barclay James Harvest classics, so made the deal conditional on the album including some re-recordings of old BJH songs alongside the new material. The deal also included an arrangement whereby John's original solo album, *A Major Fancy*, would finally get a CD release, also under the Eagle imprint.

John and Woolly wanted the new album to be a real band effort, rather than a studio creation, and the pair decided to invite Mel to join them on the basis of all credits and monies being split equally, a move which would not only give them a drummer familiar with their way of working, but also give added credibility to the project. Mel was initially keen, but never got as far as arriving at the studio to begin work. He had evidently decided on reflection for reasons of his own not to take part, although he had indicated in an interview a few weeks earlier in the fan club magazine that he was happy to work with both John and Les on their individual projects if they wanted him to:

"If they asked! If they needed a drummer, and they wanted someone of my style and technique, I would love to do it. They know I'm always available. If they're having trouble with drum sounds or they've got a drummer and need someone to explain a few things, then I'm more than willing. We're still good friends! Any or either of them, I'd be more than happy to help."

Possibly Mel consulted others before changing his mind, or perhaps he simply decided that such a move would have made a reunion of the whole band less likely and left Les completely isolated. In a later interview he expressed his regret that he hadn't given it a go, but felt that he had made the right choice in the end:

"I regret not having had a go at it. Listening to it, I'd rather go this way with it rather than the way John and Woolly have gone, and I mean that in the nicest way ... there's no profit in revisiting something that is past, because it's never the same. If it can be recreated, then good on 'em, but to me it was a thing in time. The side of developing and looking at things differently, with this new band, it excites me, that side of it, working with new ideas and new people."

David Walker issued a further statement in July 1998 through the fan club, intended to clarify the position for the band's most loyal followers, and reproduced here in full:

"Having read the interviews in NL, it is easy to detect that John and Les have a serious difference of opinion as to where Barclay James Harvest are at, or indeed which way they should go.

Neither is right or wrong, as they are both very passionate in their views. Having worked with them for many years, it became blatantly obvious to Lindsay and I that a break was essential. It is my wish that by having a break and involving themselves in solo projects, they will either enjoy solo success or come to appreciate again what it was that they gave to each other as opposed to what they didn't.

Each of them has been given the opportunity to record a solo album entitled *Barclay James Harvest Through The Eyes Of John Lees* or *Barclay James Harvest Through The Eyes Of Les Holroyd.*

John has already produced a few tracks which the record company have enthused over, and contracted him to complete an album.

Les has written some material and as soon as he is ready to make a presentation to the record company, I will arrange this.

So far as Mel is concerned, I know that John has invited him to participate, and I'm sure that if the situation arises, Les will have no hesitation in doing the same. Naturally, the final decision rests with Mel.

I'm sure that you will all appreciate that, as well as being their manager, I have been a staunch fan of Barclay James Harvest for many years, and I'm excited about this opportunity afforded to both John and Les. There is no getting away from the fact that both individually and collectively they have contributed their all to Barclay James Harvest, and it will be very interesting to see, given a free hand, in what direction they choose to go.

David Walker"

Back at Friarmere, two local session musicians were recruited to complete the new band, and recording went ahead between April and November 1998. John had known bassist Craig Fletcher for many years, having provided rehearsal facilities at Friarmere and acted as mentor to his band Off The Rails, and Craig introduced John to drummer Kevin Whitehead, with whom he had played in a number of local bands. The two younger musicians quickly settled in and, whilst their styles were certainly different from those of Les and Mel, made a valuable contribution to the "group" feeling of the album, which marked a move away from the sampled, rather sterile sound of recent BJH output to a less technically perfect but more live-sounding, authentic rock feel. The use of a real acoustic drum kit undoubtedly made a large contribution to that sound, and although Woolly wasn't able to procure a Mellotron in time for the recording, he managed to coax enough of his own unique keyboard sounds out of the MIDI-based kit in the studio to make his presence unmistakable.

Whilst the record company had a great interest in the old songs, it was the new ones which the fans were keenest to hear, and here an early decision was made by John and Woolly to credit all of the songs to both writers, in the same way that the early BJH songs credited the entire band. In some cases it was apparent which pen provided the original inspiration (the classical textures and dramatic resonances of "Float", for instance, could hardly have been by anyone other than Woolly), but each writer had a considerable creative input on the other's songs, with one song, "Festival!", being co-written in the studio. John was delighted to get back to this way of working, away from what he saw as the destructive competitiveness of the latter-day Barclay James Harvest:

"I don't know whether people understand how the original Barclay James Harvest worked, but it was a partnership between four people. When Woolly left it became a limited company. When Barclay James Harvest first started off,

Woolly and John with Herr Roth of Saar TV, February 1999 [photo: Stefan Lauer]

it didn't matter who wrote the song, it was split four ways. In the early days it was credited to 'Barclay James Harvest', then it went to credits to whoever had written it, but monetarily it was still split four ways. Somewhere along the way that changed. People weren't satisfied with that, they wanted to get their own royalties and not share them. When we went back to this project, I really felt that if things were shared, it got rid of this element of competition, which is really destructive. When we're writing, it's a meltdown of ideas and it's very difficult to say that one person wrote this. You can tell from the style who's had the most input, but there are things going on that are every bit as important to the finished song as the actual writing of the song itself - you can't see the line! We had a couple of days together to see how things went initially. We weren't any different to when we were at school together or when we were in the early bands. It became obvious that it was something that hadn't changed. I have my way of looking, he has his way of looking, and when the two come together, I think you get a pretty magic sound - other people might not think so! Woolly was the soul of Barclay James Harvest, and when he left the soul went out. Of any of us, he was the one that wasn't doing it for fabulous wealth and riches, he wasn't the one that was looking for the pot of gold and the superstardom, and he was the least competitive of all of us."

Some of the old songs re-recorded at Eagle's behest are entirely predictable for obvious commercial reasons, but John and Woolly also managed to include some lesser known ones in the list, so that "Hymn" and "Mocking Bird" were balanced by "The Iron Maiden", "Titles" and "Loving Is Easy". Woolly later noted that they spent more time on the old songs than on the new ones, striving to give them a new twist without losing the spirit of the originals. To a large extent they were successful, with the new takes on "Mocking Bird", "Titles" and "The Iron Maiden" being particularly popular, sometimes to the extent of outstripping the original. "Mocking Bird" is given a new instrumental introduction, "Hors d'Oeuvre", then the pair alternate lead vocals on the new version of the song itself, which also features a folky double-speed centre section and a cornet solo by Ian Brownbill. "Titles", originally written using Beatles song titles to comment on the falling out of Lennon and McCartney, gains an extra verse:

> Imagine nowhere man
> In my life's where you'd be
> Band on the run can't buy you love and I agree
> It was a long and winding road
> Before I'd see
> The fool upon the hill was really me

Conspiracy theorists were quick to interpret these lines as John's views on Barclay James Harvest, but in fact they were Woolly's words, reflecting on his own years in the wilderness. "The Iron Maiden" has more gravitas than the original, with an extended guitar part and added recorder, plus a musical quote from Pachelbel's *Canon*. "Hymn" provoked more mixed feelings - whilst "Mocking Bird" had been through numerous incarnations over the years, acclimatising fans to change, "Hymn" had retained its original arrangement unchanged over twenty years, even down to the horns and massed twelve-string guitars being played on a backing tape at live shows (a rare use of such an artificial aid for the Barclays). The shock of the new, even though it is not a particularly radical re-work (lead guitar instead of horns, an extra D major chord and some singing by Sarah Pickering), proved too much for some fans. "Loving Is Easy" is probably the least successful of the remakes - intended to be less ponderous and obvious and more laid back, it somehow falls between two stools.

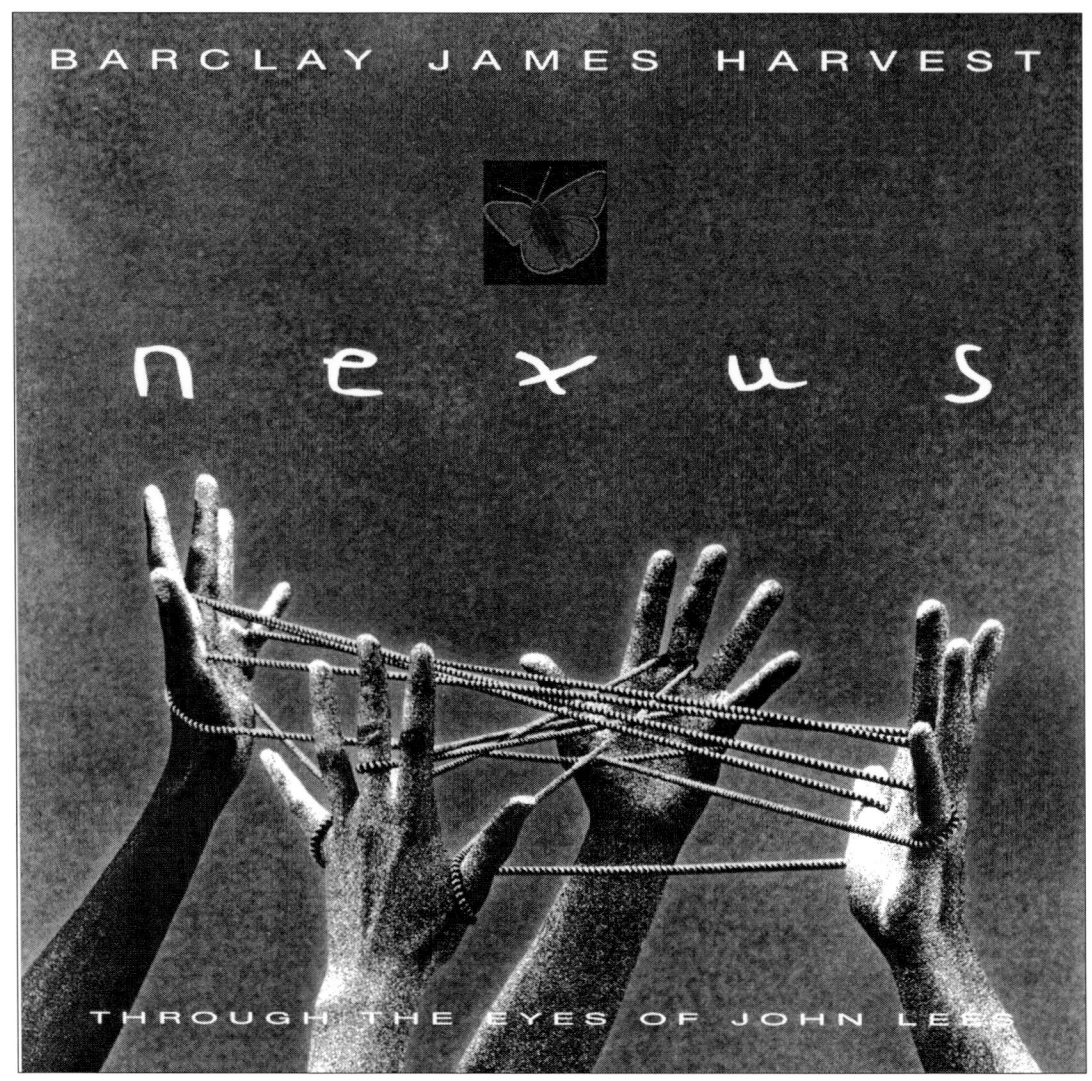

Elsewhere the past provides inspiration: "Festival!", aptly subtitled "(May contain nuts)", is, according to Woolly,

"a song 'assembled' in the studio. One building block is a guitar riff from an unrecorded BJH song called 'Wandering'. Throw in some of the tonality of 'Lives On The Line', a grim waltz and liberal references to hippydom, middle-age, mud and... *voila!* (The crowd is a real, genuine BJH audience!)."

Some fans loved the infectious melody and self-deprecating lyrics, such as "And life has done its trick
Our waists are thick but never mind our hair is thin",

whilst others didn't get it at all - "One of the worst songs ever", opined one, much to Woolly's delight!

"Brave New World" is a re-write of a John Lees song first demoed at Abbey Road on acoustic guitar in 1971. The references to "Galadriel" and "Brother Thrush" give a clue that the re-written parts refer to BJH, and John is clearly philosophical about the recent traumas, singing

"It's everyone's fault and nobody's blame".

As mentioned previously, "Sitting Upon A Shelf" dates back to the very beginnings of the band, whilst "The Devils That I Keep" is Woolly's autobiographical attempt to banish his own personal demon of clinical depression. This and "Float" started life as parts of one song, and they have similar themes, although "Float" is, perhaps, of a more optimistic nature. Musically, it's classic Wolstenholme/Barclay James Harvest, building serenely to a climax with a huge E flat major chord towards the end. Finally, there's "Star Bright", written in Portugal at the same time as "Paraiso Dos Cavalos", and a fine song with a bittersweet lyric and superb guitar solo which ends the album in classic Barclay James Harvest style.

The album artwork and even the title were to prove controversial. Although saddled with the unwieldy *Barclay James Harvest Through The Eyes Of John Lees*, John and Woolly felt that the album should also have a "proper" title. The record company contract was solely with John, and Woolly was happy to take a back seat as he didn't wish to commit himself to a particular record label or management deal at the time. Eagle were keen to play up the Barclay James Harvest connection, so it was decided to bill the band as Barclay James Harvest Through The Eyes Of John Lees, and the album, initially referred to by Woolly's working title of *Codex* (a literary work or a pile of books, which Woolly thought sounded like pills - "take two and go to bed!"), was re-christened *Nexus* (a bond or a linked group, an obvious reference to the re-established bond between John and Woolly and the fact that this line-up was linked to, but not the same as, Barclay James Harvest).

The artwork was designed by Woolly to reflect the "link" theme of the title. Much has been made of the fact that there are four hands in the picture (all left hands!) but in fact the photo itself is a stock library shot and so the viewer shouldn't read too much significance into it. The controversy arose when Eagle sent proofs to Handle in January 1999, where it was spotted that although the front cover had the wording "Through the Eyes Of John Lees" at the bottom, the back and the disc itself referred only to "Barclay James Harvest". David Walker immediately contacted Lindsay Brown at Eagle, insisting that this should be remedied in the next print run, to avoid giving fans the impression that this was a Barclay James Harvest album. He also pointed out that it was only by arrangement with Les and Mel that Eagle were able to use the name Barclay James Harvest for promotion purposes.

The appropriate corrections were duly made, and the "Through The Eyes Of" was also moved up to just below the "Barclay James Harvest" on the front to make the distinction from a BJH album more obvious.

The album was released in February 1999, and the initial signs were very encouraging. In the UK *Classic Rock* magazine included "Sitting Upon A Shelf" on their free cover CD and gave the album a nine-star review out of ten. In Germany there was much interest in the return of Woolly, although a great deal of confusion was caused by inaccurate press reports about the actual line-up of the band, in some cases complete with a picture of John, Les and Mel! The Barclay James Harvest Through The Eyes Of John Lees band travelled to Germany in February to promote the album and to attempt to set the record straight, but wildly inaccurate press reports continued to appear, promising just about every possible permutation of the original four members on stage, and confidently stating such gems as that Woolly had performed at the 1980 Berlin concert and that John had spent the last twenty years rearing sheep! Despite the mayhem, both CD and ticket sales were healthy, and *Nexus* sold 20,000 copies in the first fortnight, soon outselling *River Of Dreams* in Germany. Unlike its predecessor, it actually appeared in UK shops, too, alerting the band's home fans to the fact that the individual members of BJH were still recording.

In the hotel bar in Siegen, following their first concert together for twenty years. [photo: Wiebke Conrad]

Any lingering doubts about the *Nexus* project were swept away on the opening night of the tour in Siegen; the grin plastered across John's face throughout the concert spoke volumes, whilst Woolly, making his first appearance on stage of any kind for seventeen years, and his first with John in almost twenty, betrayed little outward sign of nerves. As he launched into the Mellotron intro for a majestic version of "She Said", it was like he'd never been away. The fans who had been with the band since the early days were ecstatic, and even those of more recent vintage, whilst lamenting the absence of Les and Mel, still generally agreed that the concerts were superb. Some even commented that only now did they

Above and right: Bad Breisig, Tennishalle [photos: Gregor Lellek]

understand what people had meant by saying that "the spirit of BJH was missing" without Woolly.

For the tour, the quartet of John, Woolly, Craig Fletcher and Kevin Whitehead were augmented by master of the keyboards Jeff Leach, who had already worked with BJH on the *River Of Dreams* album and tour, and whose presence would allow Woolly more freedom to play guitar and come to the front. The live set certainly answered criticisms that BJH gigs had become predictable, whilst retaining enough of the traditional crowd pleasers to ensure that nobody went away disappointed - "Mocking Bird", "Poor Man's Moody Blues", "Loving Is Easy" and "Hymn" survived the purge, albeit with subtle

Above: the return of the recorder for "She Said" [photo: Andreas Gab]

Right: Woolly in Berlin

Facing page, top: "It's a plug for the new album"

Below: "So I told John to get us somewhere with a double bed, a bar and a view ..."

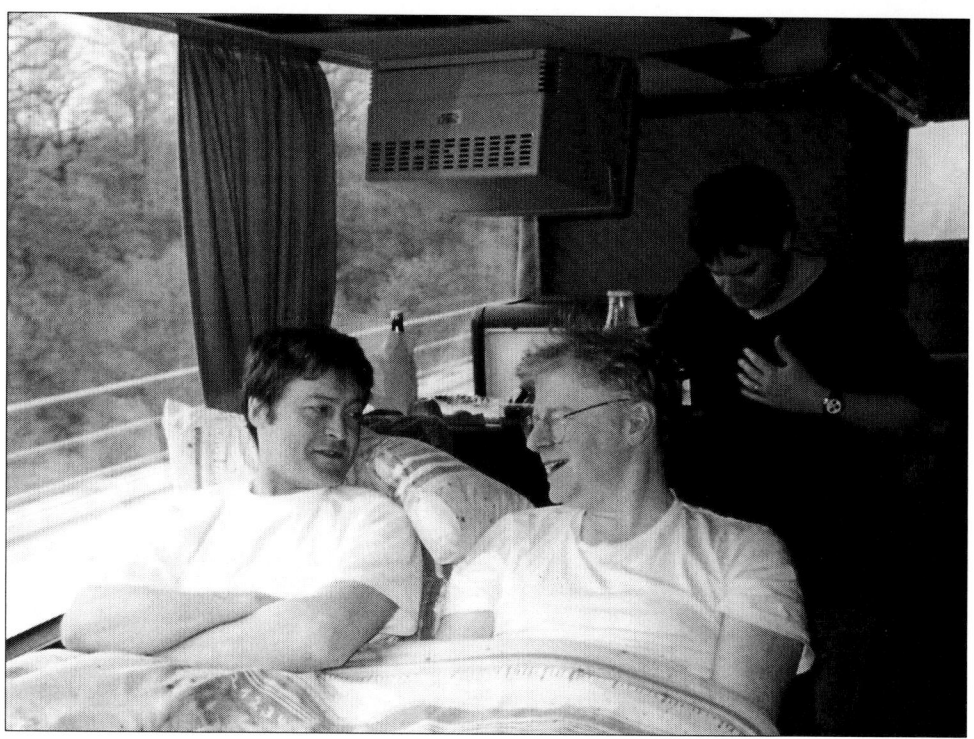

changes, but at the same time there were more than welcome returns for classics such as "She Said" and "Galadriel", neither of which had been performed live for twenty-five years, plus "Brother Thrush" and "Harbour", songs which BJH had never included in the set. Lest it be thought that this was merely a retrospective show, the band also included three of the new songs from *Nexus*, plus a brand new track, yet to be recorded, with the apposite title of "New Song". The highlights of the set were many, but special mention must go to a stunning version of "River Of Dreams", slowed down and performed as a torch song, John's impassioned vocals backed only by Jeff Leach's sympathetic piano work. Suddenly the music seemed to match the sadness of the lyrics. All too soon, the set came to an end with the beautiful "Star Bright" followed, naturally, by "Hymn".

The tour was more successful than many had expected, with attendances well up on the 1997 *River Of Dreams* outing, and a number of extra shows and summer festivals were added, the latter seeing welcome returns to the live set for "Medicine Man" and "Cheap The Bullet", the latter with Craig Fletcher singing the lead vocal. It was very noticeable that after the first few concerts, the five musicians really began to gel into a unit, the rhythm section of Craig Fletcher and Kevin Whitehead gaining confidence and enjoying the music, and the set became longer as John, especially, realised that he had the luxury of being able to improvise and extend solos at will, knowing that the rest of the

Left: Hamburg Fabrik [photo by Gregor Lellek]

Opposite, top: German open air [photo: Frank Wagener]

Below: Zaphod Beeblebrox, I presume ...

band would enthusiastically join in. Such freedom had become a rare commodity on BJH's tours since the mid eighties, and whilst it inevitably led to some mistakes, it also introduced a much-needed spontaneity and freshness to the proceedings. The new *esprit de corps* was also apparent in the humorous on-stage banter and the much-improved rapport with the audience. Woolly's legendary introductions had not only the punters but also the musicians in stitches, and the band could frequently be found in the hall or a nearby bar after the shows, chatting happily with concertgoers.

At the Tollwood open-air in July, John proudly presented a special guest on stage: John Joseph Lees, playing the cornet part on "Mocking Bird".

J.J. Lees and Woolly at Tollwood [photos by Andreas Gab]

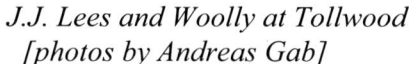

On 12th September the band (minus Jeff Leach) was in Berlin to join in the party celebrating the reinstatement of the city as the official German capital. At an open-air TV show in front of the Brandenburg Gate, they helped to launch a new broadcaster, *TV Berlin*, by miming to "Loving Is Easy", "Brave New World", "Star Bright", "Hymn" and "Mocking Bird".

1999 also saw some back catalogue releases of interest: EMI produced a lavish five CD set documenting the history of the Harvest label, contained in a beautifully produced, LP-sized book. *Harvest Festival* appeared in July, and included not only four BJH songs, but also a piece written by Woolly in which he recalled some episodes of the band's time with the label. The book was also notable for containing the first official acknowledgement, by those who were involved at the time, that the label was, in fact, named after Barclay James Harvest. In October Eagle released John's solo album, *A Major Fancy*, on CD for the first time, adding three 1974 recordings to the original LP released in 1977 but recorded in December 1972. These comprised both sides of the highly collectable Polydor single, the Eagles cover "Best Of My Love" and John's original "You Can't Get It", plus John's previously unreleased cover version of "Please Be With Me", the country rock ballad originally recorded by Duane Allman's band Cowboy, but popularised by Eric Clapton. Towards the end of the year, the fan club magazine came with the first in what was to become a series of free CD singles of rare material. With John and Woolly's blessing, *Origin Of Pieces* gave fans an insight into the genesis of two of the *Nexus* songs by including the original 1971 Abbey Road recording of "Brave New World", John's 1983 demo of "Star Bright" and an early instrumental mix of the same song from the 1999 *Nexus* sessions.

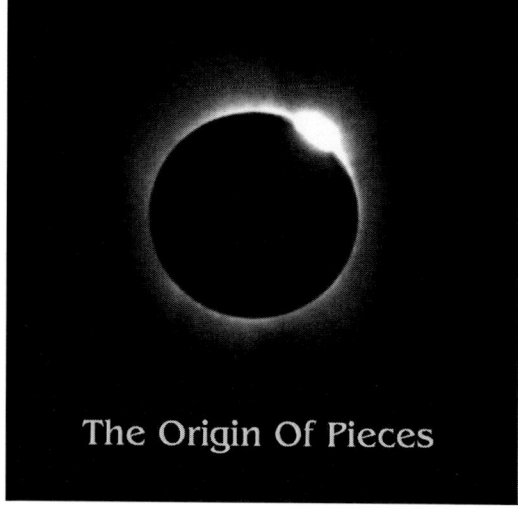

Curtain call at Hamburg [photo: Gregor Lellek]

Meanwhile, in June 1999 the first news emerged of Les's plans: he told the fan club that he had written around six or seven new songs for a solo album which could be released as early as the end of the year. Musically, the album would have more in common with recent BJH albums than the more "retrospective" sound favoured by John and Woolly, and Les was considering which old BJH songs would be suitable for re-recording. By October, Les reported that he had recorded some home demos, but was not yet ready to present them to a record company, as they didn't yet have quite the spark he was looking for. Mel had heard everything that Les had done, and would be involved in the album once recording got under way, but no firm plans had been made regarding any other musicians. On the subject of the use of the Barclay James Harvest name, Les said that in an ideal world none of the solo projects would have used the name at all, but accepted that such things might be unavoidable. Whilst he would rather not work under the "Barclay James Harvest Through The Eyes Of Les Holroyd" name, he said that he might have to in order to get a deal. He expressed concern over the apparent confusion in the media over the actual state of affairs in the band, and asked the fan club to stress that,

"Barclay James Harvest still consists of John, Mel and myself, and will continue to do so unless all three of us decide otherwise. Anything which the members of the band produce during the sabbatical should be seen as solo projects and enjoyed for what they are rather than as new Barclay James Harvest albums."

The individual band members' attitudes were becoming more difficult to reconcile: Les believed that the trio still had a future, whilst John (and David Walker) had already said that BJH should get back together as a quartet with Woolly, something which Les had totally ruled out. Unless there was a dramatic change in one or both of their viewpoints, a reunion was looking increasingly unlikely.

15

That Was Then ...

With the dawn of a new millennium (or, for the purists, the last year of the old one), although a BJH reunion looked implausible, there was still plenty to look forward to. An album from Les, including contributions from Mel, was in the pipeline, whilst Eagle had been sufficiently impressed by rough mixes of "She Said" and "Poor Man's Moody Blues" from the *Nexus* tour to give the green light to a live album. John and Woolly selected the best versions of individual songs from mixing desk recordings made by Martin Lawrence at six of the German and Swiss shows, and the live album was mixed at Friarmere with a minimum of reworking. *Revival* was issued in March 2000, complete with

fans' photos in the artwork and included the song premiered on the 1999 tour, now retitled "New Song (Old Story)". The live atmosphere and ecstatic audience reaction was rather lacking from the recordings, as the audience had not been miked up, but there's no doubting the quality of the live performances, and the album received rave reviews. It included all of the previous year's live set bar four songs, but in response to demand from fans, it was promised that these, too, would be made available in one form or another at some point.

A German promoter was approached about a possible tour to promote the live album, but unfortunately jumped the gun and began advertising gigs before any contracts had been signed. The resulting confusion didn't help when it came to trying to organise shows in other countries such as the UK, where John and Woolly were determined to play live. A great deal of effort was expended in countering all the misinformation and in trying to set up concerts for later in the year.

In July, Les responded to those who were impatiently waiting to hear his new material, revealing that he had a total of fourteen new songs at various stages of completion, but that he would not be recording demos of them until after the summer holidays. He also said that whilst certain songs would need to be recorded as a band, the majority would be true solo recordings, with himself on guitar, vocals and keyboards. His explanation for the delay was that the original concept of the sabbatical announced in March 1998 had been for the band members to take two years out, so he had simply used all of that time to compose new material. Again, the interpretation of the main protagonists seems to have been somewhat different, with John's understanding being that the band Barclay James Harvest should take two years out, not the individual members, in line with the original announcement that the band members would be using the time of the sabbatical to undertake solo projects.

John and Woolly's tour plans had to be put on hold for a short while, as Jeff was unavailable on the not unreasonable grounds that his wife Sadie was expecting their first child in September. The remainder of the band travelled to Germany for a big live TV show on October 3rd, in honour of the tenth anniversary of German reunification, and John found himself on the steps of the Reichstag once more, only alongside Woolly on this occasion, as they mimed to "Child Of The Universe" and "Hymn", twenty years after performing those same songs at BJH's biggest ever concert. October also saw the release of a CD reissue of Woolly's *Mæstoso* as the third and final release on the Brimstone label.

The tour itself began at the end of November, when Jeff, now the proud father of a baby daughter, Romy, was able to take part. At one point the German promoter had proposed a double header with Barclay James Harvest Through The Eyes Of John Lees supported by Asia, but John and Woolly vetoed the idea as they didn't consider that Asia's brand of AOR would fit well with their own style. To coincide with the tour, Eagle jumped on the contemporary music business bandwagon of reissuing an album with an added "bonus disc" of extra material, by producing a limited "Tour Edition" of *Revival* with the four missing tracks from the 1999 tour, plus a computer screensaver. Anticipating the inevitable cries of "rip off" from those who had already coughed up for the standard edition when it was first released, Woolly and John persuaded Eagle to allow the bonus disc to be sold separately, and it was made available on the tour.

Kicking off the 2000 live jaunt in Pratteln in Switzerland, Barclay James Harvest Through The Eyes Of John Lees kept things fresh and surprised their audiences by featuring not only "Medicine Man" and "Cheap The Bullet" from the previous year's summer festivals, but also the return of the classic "Child Of The Universe", and the less predictable - "In Search Of England" and a storming re-work of "Panic", never performed live before, and now sung by Woolly! The tour attracted more glowing reviews, although there still seemed to be a deal of confusion in the media about who was in the band and how it should be billed.

John and Craig at the Vacha Vachwerk, December 2000

Above: "And what would you like for Christmas?" [photo: Gregor Lellek]

Right: He's only had one drop, honest ...

At the end of November a second fan club-only CD single was produced as a Christmas gift. *Strangely Mixed* took its title from Woolly's self-deprecating introduction to a live audience recording of "American Excess", recorded in Vienna on the 1982 tour by his band Mæstoso, and the disc also offered two other pieces donated by the band. "Untitled" is a Springsteen-esque mid-eighties demo wherein John's tongue is lodged firmly in cheek, and "Poor Man's Moody Blues" is a different 1999 live recording from the one on *Nexus*. This one, recorded in Nürnberg, was actually the one sent to Eagle as a demo and on the strength of which John was offered a contract for the live album. More compilation CDs also hit the market towards the end of the year; Universal came up with *Millennium Edition*, itself merely a repackage of an earlier set called *Master Series*, while EMI offered a budget-priced compilation called *The Collection*.

John was amused at the fan club's attempt at diplomacy when describing his "Untitled" demo on the telephone: "It's full of naive charm and the lyrics are, er, er, what's the word I'm looking for?" "Crap - that's the word you're looking for ..."

At the beginning of 2001 came the news for which the band's domestic audience had waited so long - British concerts had been booked for Barclay James Harvest Through The Eyes Of John Lees. Only three, admittedly, and none outside of England, but it was a start, and the shows in Bristol, Manchester and London were described as a toe in the water with a view to undertaking a full UK tour in the autumn. The first ever shows in Greece by any members of BJH were announced at the same time, to precede the English concerts. Both sets of shows were well received, Greek fans being remarkably welcoming for a "new" territory, and English fans ecstatic to see the first live shows by John, or indeed any member of BJH, in nine years, supported by old friends To Hell With Burgundy. The Manchester show was very much a family affair for John, with son John Joseph again contributing cornet to "Mocking Bird", and daughter Esther singing lead vocals on "Galadriel"! The concert at London's Astoria was packed out, in spite of there being a tube strike on that day, and many old faces were there to welcome them back, although curiously, David Walker was absent - perhaps an indication that his interest in Barclay James Harvest was waning.

Above and right: the proud father and his daughter Esther, live in Manchester [photos: Steve Wright and Pete Noons]

Les, too, was busy, saying that he was hoping to begin recording soon and mentioning "At The End Of The Day", "Classical G Minor", "That Was Then, This Is Now", "It's My Life", "St. Petersburg" and "Missing You" as the working titles of candidates for inclusion. He was upbeat about the future, even though the demos which he had sent to Handle for submission to several record companies had met with no response, and no record deal was forthcoming. Les therefore began to explore other avenues, and contacted Andy MacPherson, the co-producer of *Welcome To The Show* with whom Les had struck up a friendship. MacPherson used his contacts with a new company called Musedia, and they were sufficiently enthusiastic to enable recording of the album to go ahead in April, partly at Les's home and partly at Andy Mac's own Revolution Studios in Cheadle Hulme.

With Andy's contacts, a new band was put together comprising Les and Mel plus guitarist/vocalist Ian Wilson and lead guitarist Mike Byron-Hehir (both erstwhile members of the excellent Mancunian band Sad Café), multi-instrumentalist Colin Browne, familiar from his work on BJH's *Turn Of The Tide* and *River Of Dreams* plus numerous BJH tours, Steve Butler (formerly lead singer with seventies rockers Monroe) and Steve Pigott, keyboard-player from Living In A Box and a programming expert. A second drummer, Roy Martin, was also engaged to play on the album, although he wasn't credited amongst the musicians on the CD, but listed instead in the "Special Thanks" section.

In June 2001, John and Woolly announced their intention to start work on a second studio album, which was likely to include "New Song (Old Story)", plus new Woolly material with titles like "Bryan MacLean" (prompted by the death of the founder member of Love and writer of the classic "Alone Again Or"), "One Drop In A Dry World", "A Stolen Life" and "Hiraeth". John, by contrast, had little new material, but was persuaded, as with *Nexus*, that there was enough in the way of his unused songs to obviate the need for much new writing. A deal was eventually struck with Eagle, although not without difficulty. Lindsay Brown found himself torn between the rock of his loyalty to the band and the hard place of economic realities at the record company which employed him, and which dictated that the advance to be handed out in advance of sales would not be as large as for *Nexus*. In an informal chat, Woolly suggested that John might be prepared to accept a more modest advance to ensure that the band could remain with Eagle, and a smaller offer was duly made. David Walker was livid at what he saw as Woolly's interference, and even John was not amused, believing that they could have held out for more, but put his signature to the deal in spite of his misgivings. The promised Autumn tour of the UK never materialised, notwithstanding the success of the three dates in March, leaving John and Woolly frustrated at the apparent lack of will to keep the momentum going. There was, however, some talk of ambitious plans for other live work in the UK and other European countries, including a number of shows in Germany complete with an orchestra, plus a Tyrolean festival in Austria for which they had been invited to write some original music.

The relentless tide of compilation CDs continued with two *Mocking Birds* - an EMI mid-price *Best Of*, and a budget Spectrum release covering the band's Polydor years, and chiefly notable for including "Back In The Game" from the Polydor Germany album *River Of Dreams* alongside earlier material. Polydor Japan got in on the act, too, issuing *Everyone Is Everybody Else* and *Time Honoured Ghosts* as remastered CDs in beautifully presented card sleeve reproductions of the original album sleeves, complete with a facsimile of the original inner sleeve in the case of *Ghosts*.

At Revolution Studios work continued on Les's new album, and it was announced that Musedia would arrange distribution with various labels; Les told the fan club that Virgin, BMG and even EMI as amongst those who were seriously interested, and mentioned that David Walker was delighted with the new deal. Two old BJH songs were now said to be possible inclusions on the album, one of which would be a revamped "Life Is For Living", based on the "unplugged" rendition played by Les on the last BJH tour.

At the end of August all of BJH's members and followers were shocked by the news that David Walker had died suddenly from a heart attack after a party to celebrate his son's eighteenth birthday, twenty-one years to the day after the Berlin Reichstag concert. For several years Walker had concentrated on managing Status Quo, who by now were the bigger attraction, but he had continued to act in a business capacity for Barclay James Harvest, including the

delicate negotiations required when the band members no longer saw eye to eye. His relationship with the band members went beyond business - he was godfather to John's son, and was not only the band's long-time manager but also frequently their confidant. With Lindsay Brown now working closely with John and Woolly in his new job at Eagle Records, David Walker was one of the few people left in the music business to whom both Les and John were speaking, and in many ways he acted as a conduit of communication between them. Now even that point of contact was gone.

David Walker

Work on both Les and Mel's and John and Woolly's projects came to a halt whilst they came to terms with David's loss and the implications for future management of the band. John and Woolly had planned to begin work on the follow up to *Nexus* in September, but that went by the wayside with John, in particular, badly hit by David's passing.

Les had been unhappy with the "Through The Eyes Of ..." tag, and with the way that it had been used not just for a one-off album title, but as the band name for John and Woolly's subsequent tours and live album. He was determined not to follow suit, and instead came up with "Barclay James Harvest Featuring Les Holroyd" as an alternative. Les explained his thinking thus:

"I thought it was a good way of doing two things – it was a good way of doing my interpretation of Barclay James Harvest, also it was leaving it open so that it could be added to, certainly in a live situation with posters or whatever saying Barclay James Harvest Featuring Les Holroyd and Mel Pritchard. I hope people will realise that it's just my interpretation, through my songs, of Barclay James Harvest."

Although it could be seen as staking a more explicit claim that his band was actually Barclay James Harvest, the name appears to have been agreed between Les and David Walker shortly before David's untimely death, although John knew nothing of this.

A number of cover versions or samples of BJH songs appeared in 2001. German rapper Samy Deluxe used a sample from "The Song (They Love To Sing)" on his eponymous album, which went to number two on the German chart in April. The song also reached number four as a single in its own right later in the year. American rappers Mobb Deep's album *Infamy* included a song called "Get Away", drawing heavily on Les's "Taking Me Higher", whilst Italian artist Graziella released a CD single of "Hymn". Perhaps the best of the bunch, though, was another version of "Hymn", recorded by an ensemble called Gregorian for an album entitled *Masters Of Chant, Chapter 2*. It's a hugely powerful reading which doesn't spare the kitchen sink, and met with John and Woolly's wholehearted approval.

There were further BJH-related releases towards the end of the year, starting in September with a Tribute CD of BJH cover versions suggested by Tim Beckwith and recorded by the band's fans. Produced on a shoe string and sold at a budget price, *Everyone By Everybody Else - Barclay James Harvest Through the Eyes Of Their Fans* contained several surprisingly good renditions of BJH favourites (together with one or two which were just surprising!), and sold remarkably well. More importantly, EMI had plans to remaster the band's Harvest label albums individually for the first time, and engaged music consultant Mark Powell to oversee the releases. Mark had previously worked on similar projects for bands such as Caravan and Camel, and was a big fan of

BJH's music. He promptly set about consulting the fan club and band members about extra material which could be added to each disc. In September, a 16mm film of the *Caught Live* documentary from 1977 came up for sale on the eBay Internet auction site, and was bought by the club. Immediately after the end of the auction, the seller apologised profusely, having just discovered that the auction description had been incorrect, since part of the film was not from *Caught Live*, but was some other, older film of the band. As this turned out to be the classic film of the band at the Drury Lane Theatre Royal in 1974, the club declined his kind offer to nullify the deal! At the end of the year the club produced its now traditional Christmas CD single, featuring live versions of "Child Of The Universe", "In Search Of England", "Panic" and "Cheap The Bullet" from the 2000 tour by Barclay James Harvest through The Eyes Of John Lees under the title *Au Naturel*.

Management of Les's solo career was taken over by Alex Rose, who had worked for Handle Artists as a temp in 1979, then on a permanent basis since 1980. Alex would also look after BJH's back catalogue, but would not be involved in John and Woolly's current activities. He had offered to represent both Les and John, but given the worsening relations between them, John refused on the grounds that it would create a conflict of interests if the same person managed both of them.

Through John and Woolly's involvement with EMI's project to remaster the band's first four albums, they had got to know Mark Powell, who co-ordinated the project. Mark had contacts with agents and promoters through his management of Caravan, and he offered to help John on an informal basis. Mark began making enquiries with concert bookers, and tentative plans were made for a tour to promote the new studio album, which was now given the working title *North*. Woolly had already designed the artwork, a grim antidote to the pastoral idylls of many BJH covers, and was raring to go with recording.

Negotiations for a tour of Germany in April 2002 were in progress with promoters Moderne Welt when the UK-based booker made the mistake of signing an agreement in principle with the German promoter, who promptly started advertising the concerts. The fact that John had not authorised anyone to sign such an agreement on his behalf was unfortunate, but the tour could perhaps have been saved if the booker hadn't then tried to coerce John into doing them by shouting at him down the telephone. John reacted by refusing absolutely to do the tour, and the situation degenerated into farce with the BJH web site telling everyone that the tour would not be happening and then being threatened (again!) with legal action by the German promoter, Henning Tögel, who insisted that the tour was going ahead! Eventually the situation was resolved, but it left a nasty aftertaste, with blame being placed at John's door for cancelling a tour to which he had never agreed, and malicious suggestions being made that the tour had been pulled because of poor ticket sales.

Whilst all this unpleasantness was going on, John and Woolly and the band had begun work at Friarmere Studios on the new studio album in the first week of December 2001, but from day one it was apparent that all was not well. Woolly and Craig launched into recording Woolly's "It's You", but John's heart wasn't in it. Still depressed following David Walker's death and smarting over the tour fiasco, he raised the objection that the smaller advance from the record company was not enough to do justice to the recording of an album. He had almost no new material of his own, and believed that the album wouldn't be up to scratch as a result. He also felt that with Les's album imminent, it would be rather confusing for the fans to have two versions of Barclay James Harvest in the market at the same time. After a few days of agonising and mood swings in the studio, he simply decided to pull the plug on the project completely and return the cheque to Eagle. The rest of the band were stunned. Although John had grumbled about the situation, they didn't believe that he was seriously thinking about abandoning the album, but there was no discussion - the gear was packed up and that was that.

By February 2002 the first fruits of Barclay James Harvest Featuring Les Holroyd's labours were made available to members of the fan club in the form of a free four-track promotional CD, financed jointly by the club and John Whitfield of Musedia. The CD featured three new tracks, "It's My Life" and "Prelude"/"January Morning", plus a re-working of the 1980 hit single "Life Is For Living", all contained in a glossy sleeve with a stlised butterfly designed by Les for the forthcoming abum.

The album *Revolution Days*, seemingly drawing its title as much from Les's view of Barclay James Harvest's current situation as from the name of the recording studios, followed on 26th February on Musedia's own imprint, M Records in the UK, and several weeks later on Koch International in Germany. First listenings confirmed the impression given by the trailer CD: rockier than expected, whilst still recognisably in Les's familiar style. Mike Byron-Hehir's guitar, which had previously been heard on *Welcome To The Show*, underpins many of the songs in a style which, whilst not totally dissimilar to John's, gives a new slant to Les's songs.

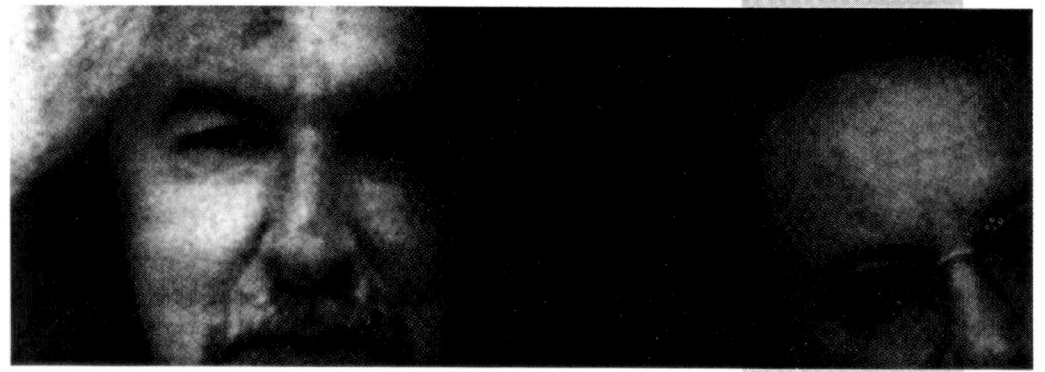

"It's My Life" gets the album underway, with a rocky style and a lyric which makes clear Les's determination to plough his own furrow without any interference. A more typical slow Les ballad, "Missing You", follows, before "That Was Then, This Is Now" comes in with a repetitive riff which works its way into the consciousness. "Prelude"/"January Morning" is perhaps the most typical BJH music on the album, with a pseudo-classical overture linked to a song inspired by a story he had heard from a friend. Les described its genesis:

"The original concept came from a friend. They spent New Year's Eve in St. Petersburg a couple of years ago. They saw these street kids, and they were actually painting pictures in the snow, with their fingers and paint, begging for money. They said that a couple of days later when they went back it had just disappeared because the sun had been out and it had just melted. I just thought about the government of those sort of places where they get in power, they promise this and nothing's actually changed. It's still the people at the top that get the money and all the corruption that goes with it. When they get in power they just melt away. These street kids are still living like that, having to beg for survival in the worst winters in the world. It just struck me that they celebrate the New Year so strongly in places like Red Square and St. Petersburg and then the following day nothing changes. It's why the Prelude is so important, because I tried to recreate a feeling of New Year's Eve in Russia, with a Russian feel to the music, and then it sort of fizzles out and comes down into the January morning, the dawn if you like. The Prelude is very important in that, to paint the picture before it starts."

"Quiero el Sol" ("I want the sun") features Les's newly acquired Rickenbacker and harmonies reminiscent of The Eagles. The remake of "Life Is For Living" is something of a hybrid between the unplugged 1997 tour reading and the original keyboard-led version, and the laid-back "Totally Cool" is a new departure, being penned not by Les but by Tim Green and Mike Byron-Hehir. The languid guitar licks on "Sleepy Sunday" (originally known as "Classical G Minor") add to the dreamy atmosphere of a song inspired by the ambience of Munich's *Englischer Garten*:

"That was inspired by just walking in one of my very, very favourite places, and that's the English Garden in Munich. I do go over there fairly regularly, me and Christopher. We just chill out in the English Garden, an incredible place to be in summer. I got back to the hotel one day and just started putting it on tape, and that's all that song is, really, just a feeling of a sleepy day, nothing to do, just wander about."

"Revolution Day" brings the tempo up again with a neat recurring guitar line and a catchy melody. Finally, a homage to the great cabaret star "Marlene" (Dietrich), in the form of a trademark Les ballad, subtitled "from the Berlin Suite". The original plan here was for a suite which would contain a reworking of "Berlin" along with some orchestral pieces and ending with "Marlene".

Les had criticised John and Woolly's *Nexus* for the inclusion of several remakes of old BJH songs, so although he had himself recorded a remake of "Love On The Line" and a German-language version of "Life Is For Living" at the album sessions, they were left off the album, as was "At The End Of the Day", one of the songs Les had mentioned as possible inclusions.

Generally the album was well-received by fans, who considered that Les's songs were stronger than many of those he had written for recent Barclay James Harvest albums. Predictably, fans of the seventies BJH sound tended to prefer John and Woolly's output, whilst those who liked the eighties or nineties material gravitated towards Les and Mel. Perhaps surprisingly, many liked both styles in spite of the time-honoured "musical differences" perhaps being more readily apparent in the solo albums. More controversial were the lyrics: some fans interpreted the lyrics of songs like "It's My Life" and "That Was Then, This Is Now" as being bitter reflections on the split in BJH, and "Quiero el Sol", with lines like:

> ... to give up your friends at the drop of a dollar
> You really were no friend at all,
> Did you think that they would still be around
> To catch you when you fall?

was seen as a direct attack on John, despite Les's protestations that it was merely a reflection on hypocrisy in the music business in general:

"It's not about me, it's not about anybody. It's just generally about a lot of people in the business. I get annoyed, you see, with people who go, 'We're in it for the art - we're not interested in the money'. The plain fact is that of course everyone likes the art side of it, that's what drives you forward, but you have to have a commercial side to it, in terms of going out there and performing and selling records. Of course you do it for the money, because otherwise you wouldn't be doing it! It's just a reflection on people that say that, no-one in particular, just a rock and roll thing, really."

Some were unconvinced, and found it a difficult pill to swallow, having been brought up on a diet of peace, love and butterflies. For the first time, even some of the band's most die-hard followers began to suspect that a reunion was extremely unlikely, as the rift appeared to widen.

Along with the Barclay James Harvest Featuring Les Holroyd sampler CD in the March issue of the fan club magazine, *Nova Lepidoptera*, came an announcement which underscored the growing importance of the Internet; the fan club would soon cease to produce quarterly printed magazines, concentrating instead on maintaining the BJH web site and associated e-mail news bulletins, whilst still producing occasional printed newsletters for those without on-line access. The industry as a whole was rushing to get on the Web, and with BJH in the vanguard in terms of having an online presence since the pioneering days of 1995, their online fans were now in a big majority.

With the fan club in possession of the *Caught Live* and Drury Lane film footage, Mark Powell had offered to check out the rights situation regarding ownership of the film, and when Polydor confirmed that it did not belong to them, a deal was negotiated with Classic Pictures whereby the historic footage could be made available on DVD. Although a great deal of effort went into digital restoration of the film, the final results were disappointing: although the picture quality was good, the sound was poor on *Caught Live*, and on the 1974 material one of the two stereo channels seemed to have been lost altogether. The DVD went ahead anyway, as this was the only known copy of the precious footage, and fans were prepared to tolerate the sound quality for a chance to see the 1977 documentary film and the pictures which went with the band's first live album.

In April and May 2002 two announcements were made of the first ever concerts by Barclay James Harvest Featuring Les Holroyd, comprising one open-air festival in Colmar, France in August, followed by a French indoor tour in October. Just days after the announcements, the shocking news came through that Les's wife, Christine Roberts-Holroyd, had been killed. Details were hard to come by, but it seemed that she had been kicked by one of their horses, and although airlifted to hospital, died of her injuries on May 21st, aged 52. Les and their son Christopher were overwhelmed with messages of support and condolence, including one from John and Olwen, and many through the BJH web site which broke the news. Les later announced that,

"Christopher and myself decided that the concerts for this year should go ahead as planned, as a mark of respect and the much love that we both have for a very special lady."

The eagerly awaited EMI remasters were released at the end of May, and were an absolute treasure trove; in addition to much-improved sound quality (the remastering having been carried out by original Abbey Road engineer Peter Mew and overseen by Woolly), authoritative sleeve notes and rare photos, the packages included a cornucopia of bonus material. Of course the non-album and single B-sides were there, but so too were previously unheard gems from BBC sessions and the EMI archives - the first album alone boasted no less than thirteen extra tracks, amongst them "So Tomorrow", "Night", "Need You Oh So Bad" and "Small Time Town" which had never been released in any form before. The icing on the cake was a fifth CD, *BBC In Concert 1972*. Off-air tapes of this performance and a BBC transcription disc had been in limited circulation for some time, with the show achieving legendary status as a result. Now the only known recording of the band performing live with the orchestra was available to a wider public, who could finally appreciate this wonderfully exuberant performance. There was even a choice of mono or stereo versions in the double disc package, completely different mixes recorded by the BBC's engineers for domestic and overseas use and each of which had its own charm.

Having never been happy with the Baby James Harvest version of "Moonwater", Woolly decided to check the multi-tracks to see whether the noise which had spoilt the original when the tapes were played back at Strawberry Studios could be removed. To his astonishment, there was no trace of the noise, and he and Peter Mew completed the 2002 remix with all of Woolly's original arrangement intact before the likely explanation dawned: the machine they were using at Abbey Road was, in all likelihood, the very same one on which the original recording had been made thirty years before ...

Barclay James Harvest Featuring Les Holroyd hit the road in the summer and autumn of 2002 with an extensive itinerary taking in France, Germany and Switzerland. The tour was booked by the same promoter used for the Barclay James Harvest Through The Eyes Of John Lees, Moderne Welt, and the same problems were apparent yet again. Many gigs were advertised purely as Barclay James Harvest, often with a photo of John, Les and Mel (or even John and Woolly!), and there was a degree of confusion amongst concert-goers who were expecting to hear songs like "Mockingbird" and "Hymn" - one or two even approached manager Alex Rose with a request for John's autograph! However, the gigs generally went off well, with the set concentrating in the main on the new album and Les's songs from the post-Woolly BJH catalogue, although there was still room for "Rock 'N' Roll Star" and "Berlin" and Les surprised German audiences by singing "Life Is For Living" in German. The on-stage line-up numbered seven, with Les and Mel augmented by Mike Byron-Hehir, Ian Wilson, Colin Browne, Steve Butler and drummer Chris Jago.

Barclay James Harvest Featuring Les Holroyd - Ian Wilson, Chris Jago, Les, Mike Byron-Hehir, Mel, Colin Browne and Steve Butler in Magdeburg [photo: Gregor Lellek]

Mike Byron-Hehir and Ian Wilson by Stéphan Hill. Mel by Olivier Gille

Eyebrows were raised at the inclusion of a second drummer, especially when Chris's acoustic drums were prominent both on-stage and in the mix, whilst one or two fans complained that Mel's electronic kit could barely be heard. Rumours circulated that Mel was unwell, and not playing at all during some songs, but backstage Mel was the life and soul of the party, keeping everyone entertained with his acerbic wit. Attendances at the shows were similar to those for the Barclay James Harvest Through The Eyes Of John Lees tours, so it seemed that the market was big enough to support both bands - if not to the degree of success that they had known in the past, then at least to provide them with a living. One of the concerts on the tour was originally scheduled to take place at the

Les sees the funny side in Hamburg [photo: Peter Pforr]

Brückenforum in Bonn, but after the venue was severely damaged by fire, the show was moved to the Stadthalle in the nearby town of Bad Godesburg. This gig was professionally recorded for possible release as a live CD, whilst manager Alex Rose also took a broadcast quality Sony PD150 video camera on tour with a view to producing a DVD. During the tour, there was another body blow when news came through that the UK record company, M Records, had gone into liquidation, taking with it any profits which Les and Mel could expect to see from *Revolution Days*.

On September 27th, Woolly's father, John James Wolstenholme, died at the age of seventy-nine after a protracted illness. Although the bereavement was not unexpected, it affected Woolly badly, particularly since he had to divide his time between Oldham, overseeing funeral arrangements and looking after his mother, and North London, where he was now living with girlfriend Sue Foulston, an old friend of the band's from the Preston House days and now a leading light in the fashion industry. Woolly had been particularly upset by the abrupt cancellation of *North*, as he had been the main driving force behind the project, and felt that he should have been consulted even though the Eagle contract was only with John. However, he and John had remained in touch, keeping open the possibility of a further collaboration in the future. This latest blow, though, saw the strain begin to tell on him: always prone to depression, Woolly began to slide into his blackest spell yet, and on another trip up north at the beginning of 2003, armed with sleeping tablets, he came perilously close to ending his own life. Regaining consciousness in hospital, Woolly voluntarily checked into Bootham Park Hospital in York in the middle of February to begin the slow and painful process of rediscovering his self-belief.

For a long time Woolly couldn't even listen to music, let alone play or compose. His muse had deserted him, together with the ability to perform even the most mundane actions which most of us take for granted - tasting food, going shopping, writing letters. However, with the help of his loved ones, especially Sue, who spent months travelling up and down from London, and an army of well-wishers who sent him get well cards and presents, flashes of the old Woolly began to reappear. He was delighted the day that he managed to go out to a shop and buy a yoghurt on his own, and before long was even listening to music on a portable CD player, then going out at weekends. More than two months of his life had elapsed since his admission to hospital when he was finally well enough to be discharged on April 26th. On his return home, he almost immediately began to pour his heart and soul into a torrent of new songs - the muse was back with a vengeance.

A second archive DVD appeared without warning in February on the Classic Rock Productions label, under the name *25th Anniversary Concert*. This turned out to consist of the Central TV edited broadcast of the 1992 Town And Country Club concert, plus some footage of other artists. Neither Alex Rose nor Mark Powell had been consulted about the release, and there is some doubt as to whether the original deal between BJH, Polydor, Virgin and Central allowed for sub-licensing to a fifth party! Les and Alex were becoming increasingly unhappy at what they saw as a flood of substandard reissues on the market over which they had no control.

As far back as January 2002, it had been announced that remasters of the Polydor CDs were on their way. In May 2003 the first batch finally appeared, covering the studio albums from *Everyone Is Everybody Else* to *XII*. Like the EMI issues, they were co-ordinated by Mark Powell, and featured superb sound courtesy of Paschal Byrne's excellent remastering, extra material, rare photographs and Mark's own sleeve notes. The added tracks ranged from well-known songs such as B-sides or the 1974 band version of "Mæstoso" which had already appeared on *Endless Dream* to previously unreleased mixes, different recordings of "Child Of The Universe" and, best of all, a completely unknown song called "Lied", recorded by the band during the sessions for their most successful album ever, *Gone To Earth*.

The fans were delighted with the remasters, which also received very favourable reviews in the press, and there was eager anticipation for the next batch. Not everyone shared this enthusiasm, though. Alex Rose was deeply unhappy, and wrote on Les's behalf to Universal, Mark Powell and to the fan club to express his concerns. Amongst the objections raised were that Alex and Les had not been consulted about the remasters and that there was therefore a bias towards John and Woolly. Universal rebutted the claims, but their enthusiasm for marketing the CDs showed a marked decline, and plans for further BJH releases were shelved. Alex later admitted that Les had been asked if he would approve the use of alternative versions of some of his songs, but had declined, as he felt that the quality was not sufficient to include for sale to the public. The spat, much of it carried out in public, dismayed fans and did nothing to improve the worsening relations between John and Les.

From May 2003, both Alex and Les began saying publicly that John had actually left Barclay James Harvest in 1998, basing their argument, at least in part, on Mark Powell's sleeve notes for the remastered CDs, which refer to "Woolly ... teaming up with John Lees in 1998 following the demise of Barclay James Harvest the previous year." Alex asserted in July 2003 on an online discussion forum that,

"At the time the reissued albums were released, Les and Mel (as well as the fans?) believed that BJH was alive and as well as could be expected in a state of limbo."

Unfortunately, this didn't square with what most fans believed, or, indeed, with what Les himself had said in an interview more than a year earlier, which had even been reproduced in his official tour programme: when asked whether he thought that we've seen the last of the old line up of BJH, Les replied,

"In this business you never say never, but I think it's increasingly looking like it's not on the cards, to be honest. If only from the fact that we're not young men any more, and I still think that I have got a lot to do individually, with this project that I'm doing now ... I think the old Barclay James Harvest has run its course, to be honest."

Interviewed in the July 2003 edition of German magazine *Feedback*, Les was quoted as saying that his band was now Barclay James Harvest. When asked who was actually the real BJH line-up, Les's answer was,

"That is quite clearly Mel Pritchard and me, plus our new guest musicians. The reason for that is simply that Woolly left the band already in 1978 *[sic]* and John left in 1998, because he didn't agree with the musical direction. Mel and I have kept the original band going, so we are Barclay James Harvest. I also think that John and Woolly's band doesn't exist any more anyway."

Controversial stuff, although Les's actual words could have lost something in translation. In any case the claims and counter-claims were becoming more emotive, and upsetting many fans who wanted to see a reconciliation, or at the very least an amicable agreement. Clearly, the real issues were about John and Les and their managers, and who had control over the band's legacy and name, but others were caught in the crossfire. Battle lines were being drawn, and it would no longer be possible for anyone, even the fan club which had bent over backwards to remain neutral, to please everyone.

The web site became one battleground, with many words expended over whether it had official status, and if so, why views with which Les disagreed were not censored. The upshot was that the site simply replaced the word "Official" with "Original", even though it was still the official site so far as John and Woolly were concerned, and continued to cover all of the members' (or ex-members'!) activities as a service to fans without fear or favour. This resolved the immediate issues, and an uneasy truce prevailed, with Alex and Les continuing to use the existing site and news bulletins to promote their work, but also announcing their intention to set up an official Barclay James Harvest Featuring Les Holroyd site in due course. The unanswered question, though, was whether two versions of Barclay James Harvest could continue to co-exist, if not in perfect harmony, then at least without major discord.

16

The End Of The Road?

In August 2003 a new version of *Revolution Days* appeared. With M Records having gone into liquidation, Alex Rose understood that the rights reverted to Les, but the situation in Germany, where there was a pressing and distribution deal with Koch International, was less clear cut. The original version was still in the shops, although Les was not receiving the royalties due to him. Alex therefore reissued the album on his own record label, Pure Music, with new artwork and an extra song, the remake of "Love On The Line" which had been recorded at the *Revolution Days* sessions but not included on the original release.

More Barclay James Harvest Featuring Les Holroyd dates were set up for the summer and late autumn of 2003, taking in festivals in The Netherlands, Germany and Belgium, followed by October and December tours through

Les and Ian in Nümbrecht [photo: Philippe Plazenet]

Germany, Switzerland and France again. The only change to the live line-up was Roy Martin coming in as replacement drummer for Chris Jago, who was unavailable due to other commitments. The live set was very similar to that of the 2002 tour, the only addition being "Play To The World", at the expense of the German-language "Life Is For Living". To coincide with the live shows, Pure Music issued a live CD from the concert recorded during the German tour in October 2002. Unfortunately, in the ensuing period it had been forgotten that the Bonn show was cancelled and moved to the Bad Godesberg Stadthalle, so the CD was issued under the title *Live In Bonn, 30th October 2002*.

Notwithstanding this minor error, the album, which was mixed at Revolution Studios, is a reasonable representation of the live show, but with four BJH live albums already on the market, plus John and Woolly's *Revival* and assorted live videos and DVDs, interest was bound to be confined to the band's loyal fanbase. Attendances on the tour were rather smaller in some places than those from the previous year, and some shows in France were cancelled due to flooding, but the audiences were no less enthusiastic.

Roy Martin (left), Mike Byron-Hehir and Steve Butler, German radio recording, November 2003

The band played to a much bigger crowd, including a TV audience of millions, when they performed at five shows as part of *Art On Ice*, an annual ice-skating spectacular. Set to live music, the show was staged over four days in January 2004 at the Hallenstadion in Zürich, scene of many sell-out BJH gigs in the seventies and eighties. Sharing the billing with Roger Hodgson and John Helliwell of Supertramp, Justin Hayward from the Moody Blues and Jeremy Spencer of Fleetwood Mac fame, the band played "Life Is For Living", "Love On The Line" and "Berlin" live on the stage at one end of the cavernous hall, punctuated by applause for the skaters leaping and twirling on the ice! The band thoroughly enjoyed the event, including the aftershow party, and returned home in good spirits after the last show, waving goodbye to Mel as they left Manchester's Ringway Airport. It was the last time that they would see him alive.

Just a day later, during the night of 27th/28th January 2004, Mel complained to his girlfriend, Debbie, of chest pains, and she went to fetch him a glass of water and to call a doctor. By the time she returned, he was gone, the victim of a massive heart attack brought on by a blood clot. An inveterate smoker and drinker, Mel had always taken full advantage of all the benefits of success, describing life in a rock band as "a one-way ticket to paradise". The journey may have been shorter than expected, but Mel would have been the last one to change his lifestyle.

Mel jamming with the Gaïa Band at Art on Ice [photo: Steve Butler]

Art On Ice, 25th January, 2004 - Mel's last appearance on stage

Mel's funeral, on 9th February, was attended not only by Les, Alex Rose, Ian Wilson, Mike Byron-Hehir, Steve Butler and Colin Browne, but also by John and Woolly, Craig Fletcher and Kevin Whitehead, Ian Southerington, members of the road crew such as Charlie Kidd, Robbie Kwik and Nigel and Dawn Banks, plus fans from the UK and Germany. A friend of Mel's, Alex Flannagan, gave the oration in the chapel, and it was evident that Mel would be much missed, not just by his family and musical colleagues, but by his many friends. He was described as a generous man, but one who did not suffer fools gladly. One anecdote related how, when stuck in a group of people comparing notes on their various models of top of the range cars, Mel chipped in:

"I prefer the 180 meself"

Puzzled looks.

"Er, I don't think I'm familiar with that one".

"It's a diesel".

"No, don't think I know it".

"It's a double decker, runs from Greenfield to Oldham every hour"!

Although there was no BJH music during the service, it ended with one of Mel's all-time favourites, Steely Dan's "Deacon Blue". Afterwards, many of the mourners repaired to The Commercial pub in Uppermill, one of Mel's favourite pubs, to drink one last toast to a unique talent and one of the finest drummers of his generation.

Whilst Les and Mel had been touring, Woolly had not been idle. With a dozen songs written for the aborted *North* album plus the large number written since he had come out of hospital, he began to think about ways of getting them to a wider public. John felt that the Barclay James Harvest name had been devalued by the schism in the band and the confusion surrounding the band name, and that as a result there wasn't sufficient demand to justify releasing a new album at that time. It was evident to Woolly that if he wanted to continue making music, he would have to go it alone, at least for a while. Plans for a new CD of the *Black Box* sessions gave him the perfect opportunity to put a toe in the water of the music business again without too great a personal risk, but weren't sufficient to satisfy his creative urge, so the idea of recording new material without John's input began to take shape. Woolly signed a management contract with Mark Powell, and began work on a new solo album, his first since *Mæstoso*, twenty-four years earlier!

Woolly had stayed in contact with all of the members of the Barclay James Harvest Through The Eyes Of John Lees touring band, so they were the obvious candidates to play on the album. Only the lead guitarist was missing. As luck would have it, amongst those who had read the news about Woolly's illness on the web was Steve Broomhead, original guitarist with the Mæstoso band. Steve got in touch with Woolly at Bootham Park, and told Woolly that he was keen to get back into playing music professionally again. Some impromptu rehearsal sessions after Woolly returned home demonstrated that the old chemistry was still there and the line-up for the album was complete. Mark Powell booked the band into Chapel Studios in Norfolk, where The Darkness had recently recorded their multi-platinum debut album, and in December 2003 the band got down to work. Time was tight - the actual recording sessions lasted a mere thirteen days - but everyone set to with a will, and the album was completed on time. The first monitor mixes were compelling: the band crackled with energy and there was a depth to the material which had been absent from much of the recent BJH output. Some polishing was done during the mixing stage first at Chapel and then by Julian Hastings, son of Caravan's frontman, Pye Hastings, at Delta Studios in Canterbury.

Pending the release of the new album, Mark Powell's recently launched Eclectic Discs label issued two related CDs in February - Woolly's *Black Box Recovered* collection and a reissue of Mandalaband's *Eye Of Wendor*, with original artwork restored and an extra track in the form of an alternative take of Justin Hayward singing "Dawn Of A New Day". *Black Box Recovered* comprised many of the 1982 recordings which had appeared on the 1994 *Songs From The Black Box* set, plus an unreleased song and alternative versions from the same period, together with unheard demos from the *Maestoso* album. Crucially, though, *Black Box Recovered* also contained a brand new song, a home demo about Woolly's recent experiences called "Bootham Park Elegy".

On 19th April yet another DVD arrived unheralded, with the grandiose title of *The Ultimate Anthology*. Although this proved to be something of a misnomer, the bulk of the new release being simply a repackage of the 1992 live show already released as *25th Anniversary Concert*, there was much excitement amongst the cognoscenti when it was discovered that the "archive footage from the early years" advertised on the packaging was actually the incredibly rare 15 minute archive film of the band at Preston House in 1968, filmed for Granada TV by Lawrence Moore. This included early takes of "Early Morning" and "Mr. Sunshine", plus the otherwise unavailable "Washing Up Dishes", together with John's Dad's priceless comments on his son forming a rock band!

Rather than release the new studio album under his own name, Woolly opted to emphasise the collaborative nature of the work by resurrecting the Mæstoso moniker for the new band, and it was under this name that *One Drop In A Dry World* hit the racks on May 17th, 2004. The album was immediately hailed as a triumphant return for Woolly. Whilst the performances were less than perfect in places, due to the rushed recording on a very limited budget, Woolly had poured his soul into them, and they were full of passion and musicality.

The typically dramatic instrumental prelude, "The Bells, THE BELLS!", constructed around retro sounds from a Roland D50 keyboard and a hint of "Ra", leads straight into one of the highlights of the album, "Blood And Bones". The original idea was inspired by *Bodyworlds (Körperwelten),* the hugely successful exhibition wherein human bodies were subjected to a process called plastination and posed to allowing the viewer to observe three-dimensional human anatomy. Also drawing on Thomas Mann's *Death In Venice* (hence the sub-title of the first part, "Tod in Venedig") and Nicolas Roeg's film *Don't Look Now*, the piece highlights all of Woolly's strengths in the twists and turns from the welcome return of the Mellotron to the delicate solo violin in the "Requiem" and the inspirational "Reprise". "A Waiting Game" takes a gentle poke at the over-commercialisation of Christmas, and "It's U", originally written for the TV teen drama *S.W.A.L.K.* in the early eighties, is presented as a sixties mix complete with thrashing drums and weird stereo separation.

In "Souk", based on a Steve Broomhead instrumental called "Miró", East meets West in a sensual feast which somehow combines Led Zeppelin, the Arabian Nights, belly dancing and Tikka Massala! The huge seven-minute title track examines alcoholism from close to home, mixed with gallows humour in an irresistible cocktail. There's more wit as "A.N.S.S." ("A Nothing Summer Song") neatly skewers the stereotypical bad behaviour of Brits on holiday, contrasting with "The End Of The Road", with Woolly reflecting poignantly on his own experiences and inescapable destiny. "Explorers" uses a tale of 15th

century mariners to comment on human endeavour and fate, whilst "2 a.m." combines an unanswered question about the Iraq war with a very personal story of insomnia and depression. "The Starving People Of The World All Thank You For Your Time" (the longest ever song title by a BJH member, music-lovers!) makes an ironic point with relentless repetition, and the album proper closes with a bang (or four) in the form of "Carpet", whose lyrics are clearly about the history of Barclay James Harvest, and can be read as referring to a number of the people associated with the band over the years.

Early purchasers of *One Drop In A Dry World* were rewarded with a limited edition including a bonus CD with alternative versions of "It's U" (an eighties demo and an over-sixties mix!), "A Waiting Game" with Craig Fletcher singing the lead vocal, "The Starving People" and "Requiem", plus unreleased material including some unadopted soundtrack music written in the eighties for *The Wind In The Willows*; an instrumental piece entitled "Flip!", the distinctly weird "Camelherd Hit By Falling Building" and a sublime demo of another new song, "The Angelus". Even the CD booklet had clearly been put together with more than the usual degree of care, with visual gags scattered throughout.

Fans of the earlier BJH sound were transported back to their youth in a wash of Mellotron, and the limited edition of a thousand copies was largely sold out before the release date. The euphoria proved a little premature, though, as news filtered through that five UK live shows which had been booked to promote the album were selling very poorly. After a gap of more than twenty years since his last solo gigs, and without new material by which to judge his music, punters were playing their own waiting game. To make matters worse, drummer Kevin Whitehead pulled out when he got an offer he couldn't refuse to join a band called Proud Mary, protégés of Oasis, but the day was saved when he was replaced by another familiar face from the Mæstoso band, Kim Turner, the live line-up being completed by Jeff Leach, moonlighting from his other job as a member of the *We Will Rock You* house band. Woolly's loyal fan base rallied round to try to save at least one concert, concentrating on a showcase at the Mean Fiddler in London's Charing Cross Road.

Mæstoso live at the Mean Fiddler, May 2004 [photo: Rob Price]

It worked - whilst the provincial shows all had to be cancelled, London went ahead on May 12th, and Woolly Wolstenholme's Mæstoso took to the stage to a rapturous reception from a small but vociferous crowd of a couple of hundred which was in party mood from the off. Not above joking at his own expense, Woolly welcomed everyone to the first - and last - night of the tour, and after "Blood And Bones" went somewhat awry in the middle, commented wryly, "Don't worry, we'll get that one right tomorrow night"! The band had concentrated on rehearsing the older material with which some of the musicians were unfamiliar, and it showed - a new arrangement of "Poor Wages" with a stonking guitar solo at the end got the crowd rocking, and there was a murmur in the crowd as the opening strains of "The Poet" were heard - did that mean that ... yes, a thunderous version of "After The Day" followed. By the end of the show, there wasn't a dry eye in the house when, over the opening chords of "Early Morning", Woolly announced, "This is for Mel". It was a magnificent return, but the fact that it had been witnessed only by a select few meant that there was a lot of promotional work still to do.

On the day of Woolly's Mean Fiddler show, it was announced that Les and his band had decided to carry on making music as Barclay James Harvest Featuring Les Holroyd, following Mel's death, and would not be hiring a replacement electric kit drummer but touring instead as a six piece band, starting with a festival in Switzerland at the end of July, with a second show soon added for September.

There was more sad news when the Oldham Evening Chronicle announced the death of Mel's father, Norman, on June 9, 2004, aged 79 years, "Beloved husband of the late Fanny and dear father of the late Melvyn."

In July a second fans' tribute CD, a more ambitious double disc set, made its appearance under the title *Their Light Still Remains, Tribute 2 Barclay James Harvest*, dedicated to the memory of Mel. In the same month came news of a second Mæstoso concert, with Woolly and the band supporting Caravan at the Bloomsbury Theatre in London. Plans were also in hand for a live "official bootleg" CD of the Mean Fiddler concert from the previous May, to be taken directly from a stereo tape recorded straight off the mixing desk on the night.

In spite of the difficulties which Barclay James Harvest Featuring Les Holroyd faced in carrying on without Mel, the shows in Switzerland went off well, with "A Matter Of Time" and "Ring Of Changes" added to the live set. "Life Is For Living" was absent, though, dropped by Les for the first time since the Berlin concert in 1980. Between the two festivals, a new compilation of Barclay James Harvest material was issued on Les and Alex's Pure Music label, entitled *Evolution Years - The Best of Barclay James Harvest, featuring the songs of Les Holroyd*. As the title implies, the CD was different from any previous collection of BJH material in that it contained only songs written by Les. The carrot for existing fans was that two previously unreleased recordings

*Mike in Switzerland,
summer 2004 [photo:
Sabine Küssner]*

were included: an unplugged German radio recording of "Berlin" from 2003, and "Lebe Fur's Leben", the German language studio version of "Life Is For Living" which had been recorded at the *Revolution Days* sessions. By October 2004 more shows in Germany had been announced for Les and his band, this time a double-header with Asia for early 2005, together with a release for a long-awaited live DVD, filmed by Alex Rose at a number of German shows on the 2002 tour and set to the soundtrack used for the earlier *Live In Bonn* CD.

Back in the UK, Woolly was busy again, starting work on October 20th on a follow-up album to *One Drop In A Dry World*. Rather than spend a frenetic fortnight (not to mention large amounts of money!) in a commercial studio, the band decided to record the album as far as possible at Steve Broomhead's home studio, taking more time over it and hiring another studio only if it was absolutely necessary, for example to record the live drums. Kim Turner would be the "new" face, re-joining Woolly, Craig and Steve as a full-time member of Mæstoso. Amongst the songs being lined up for possible inclusion on the album, now entitled *Grim*, were "Love Is ..", "A Lark", "Harp And Carp", Steve Broomhead's "Hebden Bridge", "Musical? The Musical" (incorporating "Marsch Burleske" - a Mahlerian overture - and "Scene From A London Flat"), "Storm", "That's The Price You Pay" (written by Kim Turner) and "Birds". Early listenings promised that *Grim* would be even stronger than *One Drop*, with "Storm" and "Harp And Carp" outstanding examples of Woolly's epic vision, and variety once again being a hallmark.

Woolly starts work on "Grim"

Meanwhile, the Bloomsbury concert had virtually sold out, setting the scene for the second night in Mæstoso's world tour! The sound balance was poor when the band took to the stage, but they soon won over a lot of the neutral Caravan fans, not to mention those in the audience who were only there for Mæstoso. Half way through the set, Woolly moved to scotch the rumours which he said had been circulating about the appearance of a special guest:

"It's not true!"

At that moment, on walked a familiar figure carrying a guitar, beaming all over his face, as Craig joked,

"Tonight, Matthew, I'm going to be John Lees from Barclay James Harvest".

John and the band (minus Steve Broomhead, who gracefully gave way for ten minutes), then launched into a flawless rendition of "Galadriel", before John sang an affectingly beautiful version of "River Of Dreams" accompanied by Jeff Leach at the piano. It was a significant moment, proving as it did that not only were the rumours of John's retirement somewhat premature, but also that he and Woolly were still good friends and had every intention of continuing their working relationship as well.

All too soon the cameo was over, and Steve resumed his place on stage for the remainder of the set, finishing to tumultuous applause after fine versions of "Early Morning" and "The Poet"/"After The Day". Most of the band and a sizeable number of BJH fans then repaired to a local hostelry to celebrate and discuss future plans - John Lees was most definitely back in business!

With sound engineer Tom Tough backstage at the Bloomsbury [photo: Paula Southern]

2005 showed every sign of being a busy year for all of the original founder members of Barclay James Harvest. On January 5th, the first UK dates for Barclay James Harvest Featuring Les Holroyd were revealed - three shows in Nottingham, Wolverhampton and London where they would again share the bill with Asia. In Germany, where BJH music was still the bigger draw, Asia would go on first, but in England Les's band would play for only an hour and be followed by Asia. Still, this was the first time that Les had set foot on an English stage for more than thirteen years, and the gigs were eagerly awaited. A Manchester show was added soon afterwards, and the live DVD, *On The Road*, finally appeared on January 24th. The DVD offered five extra songs over the *Live In Bonn* CD plus text-only reproductions of fan club interviews with Les and Mel and band member biographies. Also in January, Alex, with much assistance from Mike Byron-Hehir, launched the new official site which would cover only Barclay James Harvest Featuring Les Holroyd.

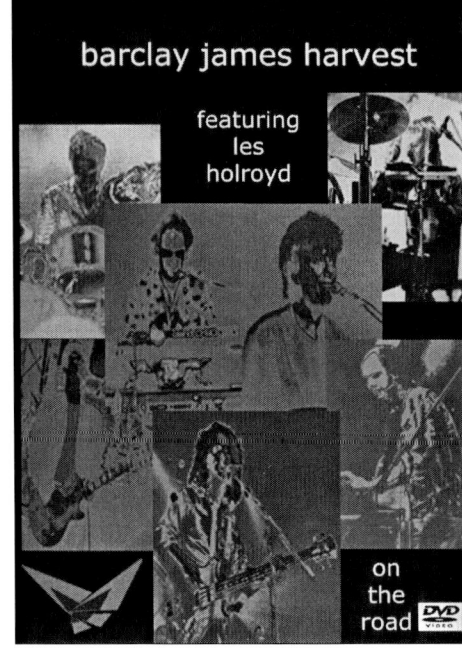

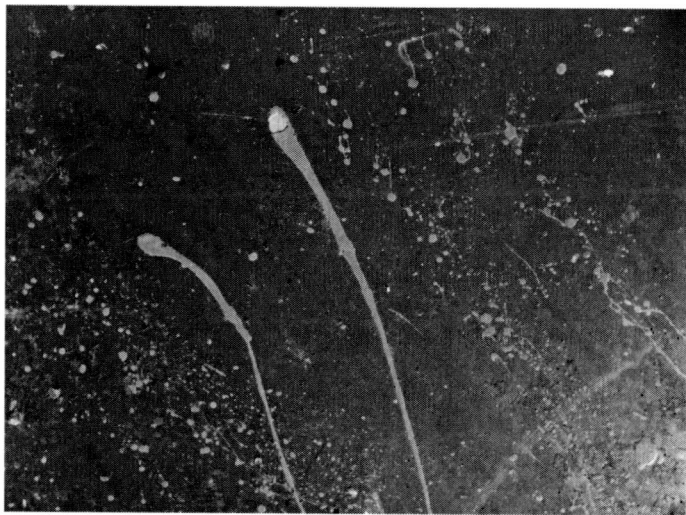

The Maestoso live CD, *Fiddling Meanly,* was officially made available on February 21st, and was surprisingly successful; initially intended to be a private pressing available only through the web site, it became an official release when Eclectic found that there was a lot of interest from distributors, and issued it under their own imprint.

A day later, Barclay James Harvest Featuring Les Holroyd kicked off their tour with Asia in Munich. With fresher material such as "Back In The Game" and "Victims Of Circumstance" returning, the German "Lebe Fur's Leben" brought back into the set (for the last two nights, at least) and "The Time Of

Our Lives" from *River Of Dreams* making its first ever concert appearance, the band was on good form and enjoying the live shows. However, although the band adjudged the shows a success, some of the reviews, both from the press and concertgoers, were less than complimentary. Although every effort had been made by those around the band to ensure that everyone was aware of the band line-up and the recent history of Barclay James Harvest, it seemed that many of the shows had been advertised locally simply as Barclay James Harvest, and a minority of fans was aggrieved when the band not only didn't sound much like the old BJH, but also didn't play some of the best-known BJH songs such as "Mockingbird", "Poor Man's Moody Blues", "Child Of The Universe" and, of course, "Hymn". The band tried to counter the backlash in Germany and back home in the UK, with Mike Byron-Hehir posting his responses to individual criticisms online, and Les giving interviews to put over his own viewpoint, and saying that it was now "a matter of principle" that he would only play his own back-catalogue songs. On several occasions in the course of these interviews he restated his position that John had left the band in 1998, something which was also bound to provoke a reaction.

Hamburg, 2005 [photo: Ueli Frey]

Ian and Mike in München [photos by Christian Reiter]. Below - Mannheim [photo: Georgie Wisniewski]

In March 2005 the reaction came. John had consistently corroborated the version of events given out by David Walker, and felt that Les had failed to adhere to the agreement by using a different form of the BJH name without consulting John. Until now he had kept his silence about the new stories which were being aired, but he was aware that if he failed to rebut these assertions, it could be seen as a tacit acceptance of Les's interpretation of the facts. John decided to formalise his relationship with Mark Powell and take him on as his manager, a role which Mark was already fulfilling for Woolly. On March 3rd, Mark issued the following statement on John's behalf:

JOHN LEES' BARCLAY JAMES HARVEST

In a statement today, John Lees has announced his plans for 2005/2006 with Woolly Wolstenholme to record a new album and to tour.

"As was well documented a few years ago, following the release of the albums *Nexus* and *Revival* on which I worked with Woolly Wolstenholme, I had planned to collaborate with Woolly on a second studio album, with the working title *North*. We began work at my studio in Saddleworth, but I reflected on my inspirational muse and didn't feel ready to make an album that was worthy of what I felt Woolly and I could deliver. Woolly embarked on his solo album project and kindly invited me to join him at Mæstoso's concert opening for Caravan at the Bloomsbury Theatre in London last year. I thoroughly enjoyed the experience and now feel that the time is right for me to make plans for the next year. I intend to concentrate on completing some new songs in April and plan to go into the studio with Woolly soon after to record a new album. The album will be followed by a tour of the UK at the very end of 2005 with the possibility of concerts in Europe being investigated soon after".

On the timing of this announcement John states; "I think the time is now right to work once more and I feel more inspiration to make music now than I have done for the past few years. I want to make an album that draws on the best music Woolly and I created in the past, but music that is also relevant in 2005".

On the recent claims in some quarters that John left Barclay James Harvest in 1998, John states; "I can only say that this is totally untrue. I felt that I could no longer go on working with Les in the way that we had been and I wasn't happy about our moving so far away from what I saw as the original musical ideals of Barclay James Harvest. Our manager at the time, David Walker, suggested that both Les and I record and tour with our own visions of Barclay James Harvest and the 'Through the Eyes of…' moniker was a way of doing that. David's statements to the press at the time clearly stated this. It wasn't a case of me 'leaving' Barclay James Harvest or trying to 'oust' Les from the proceedings, it was simply an equal parting of the ways due mainly to an increasing gulf in the way the three of us were making music. When sessions began for *Nexus*, Woolly and I invited Mel Pritchard to participate, but on reflection, he felt less sympathy for our musical direction and decided to work with Les. As far as I'm concerned all that is in the past and I am only looking forward to concentrating on the positive, making some new music and performing concerts once more".

Over recent confusion over the billing of concerts by Barclay James Harvest featuring Les Holroyd, John commented; "Woolly and I have been aware that some fans have attended concerts in Germany recently and were unhappy about the shows not featuring any songs that I had written such as 'Hymn', 'Child Of The Universe' or 'Poor Man's Moody Blues'. In order to avoid any such confusion, future work will be billed as *John Lees' Barclay James Harvest*. I think that states quite clearly the sort of music people can expect to hear, both on record and in concert". Further announcements will be made once the new album is nearing completion and tour plans are confirmed.

John and Craig hard at work on the new studio complex

The response from the other "camp" to this statement was to announce more live concerts from June to October in Germany, Austria and France, still using the Barclay James Harvest Featuring Les Holroyd banner, and to unveil a new live set at those shows, including both "Mockingbird" and "Hymn"! Concertgoers were delighted at Les's change of heart, and the shows were very well received. One of the concerts saw Les returning to the beautiful surroundings of the Loreley Amphitheater, high above the River Rhine and scene of one of the earlier band's most memorable shows in 1979, just before Woolly left the band. "Some things change, some stay the same" - or "that was then, this is now"?

In July Mark Powell's Eclectic Discs released a remastered CD of *Barclay James Harvest Live*, with a limited edition boasting a card slipcase and an insert autographed by John, Woolly and Les. The same label's release plans also included not only Mæstoso's *Grim* but also a five-CD box set and book entitles *All Is Safely Gathered In*, covering Barclay James Harvest's entire output from 1968 to 1997 - the first BJH collection ever to include material from both the EMI and Polydor catalogues.

At the time of writing the Barclay James Harvest which we knew and loved as a quartet and as a trio for three decades has reached the end of the road. With Mel's passing any faint glimmer of hope that the original quartet would reunite was extinguished. The musical and personal differences between the surviving members seem insurmountable, and yet some observers interpreted the joint endorsement of the *Barclay James Harvest Live* CD as a sign that relations between the ex-band members might be thawing.

BJH's music lives on regardless - not only in the catalogue of memorable music which is treasured by fans young and old, but also in their solo output which continues to delight their loyal followers, and will hopefully do so for years to come. The next year or two should see brand new studio albums from Mæstoso, Barclay James Harvest Featuring Les Holroyd and John Lees' Barclay James Harvest, so there is plenty to which we can look forward as well as the many memories upon which we can look back. With apologies to *This Is Spinal Tap*, their appeal may have become more selective than in the heady days of the late seventies and early eighties when they sold millions of albums, but thirty years is a ripe old age for an ephemeral entity like a rock band. It was indeed a magic carpet ride, and we were privileged to be along for the ride on much of that journey, and to have experienced at first hand the magic of Barclay James Harvest.

Appendix A: Discography

UK Singles

04-68 Early Morning/Mr.Sunshine   Parlophone
06-69 Brother Thrush/Poor Wages   Harvest
08-70 Taking Some Time On/The Iron Maiden   Harvest
03-71 Mocking Bird/Vanessa Simmons   Harvest
04-72 I'm Over You/Child Of Man   Harvest
09-72 Breathless/When The City Sleeps (as "BOMBADIL")   Harvest
10-72 Thank You/Medicine Man   Harvest
05-73 Rock And Roll Woman/The Joker (BJH logo sleeve)   Harvest
05-74 Poor Boy Blues/Crazy City Polydor
03-75 Mocking Bird/Galadriel   Harvest
03-75 Breathless/When The City Sleeps (as "BOMBADIL")   Harvest
11-75 Titles/Song For You   Polydor
03-77 Live EP [Rock 'N' Roll Star/Medicine Man pt.1/pt.2] PC   Polydor
07-77 Hymn/Our Kid's Kid PC   Polydor
03-78 Friend Of Mine/Suicide? [live] Polydor
12-78 Loving Is Easy/Polk Street Rag (live) [20,000 in blue vinyl] Polydor
12-78 Loving Is Easy/Polk Street Rag (live) [black vinyl]   Polydor
12-79 Love On The Line/Alright Down Get Boogie (Mu Ala Rusic) PC   Polydor
03-80 Capricorn/Berlin   Polydor
11-80 Life Is For Living/Shades Of B Hill PC Polydor
05-83 Just A Day Away/Rock 'N' Roll Lady (live Berlin) PC   Polydor
05-83 Just A Day Away/Looking From The Outside [butterfly picdisc] Polydor
05-83 Just A Day Away/Rock 'N' Roll Lady (live Berlin) [mispress pd]   Polydor
11-83 Waiting For The Right Time/Blow Me Down PC   Polydor
11-83 Waiting For The Right Time LP/edit/Blow Me Down 12" PC   Polydor
03-84 Victims Of Circumstance/Victims Of Circumstance (instr.) PC   Polydor
03-84 Victims Of Circumstance/Victims .. (instr.) [clown pic disc] Polydor
03-84 Victims Of Circumstance/Victims .. (instr.)/Love On The Line (live) 12" PC   Polydor
09-84 I've Got A Feeling (new version)/Rebel Woman PC Polydor
11-86 He Said Love/On The Wings Of Love PC   Polydor
11-86 He Said Love/Hymn (live Berlin)/On The Wings Of Love 12" PC   Polydor
02-90 Cheap The Bullet/Shadows On The Sky PC Polydor
02-90 Cheap The Bullet/Shadows On The Sky/Berlin (live) 12" PC   Polydor
02-90 Cheap The Bullet/Shadows .../Alone In The Night (live)/Hold On (live) CD Polydor
05-92 Stand Up/Life Is For Living (live at the T&C)   Polydor
05-92 Stand Up/Life Is For Living (live at the T&C) MC   Polydor
05-92 Stand Up/John Lennon's Guitar (live)/Play To ... (live)/Stand Up (ext) CD   Polydor
05-92 Stand Up/Alone ... (live)/Life Is ... (live)/Poor Man's ... (live) [ltd. CD] Polydor

UK Solo Singles

09-74 JOHN LEES - Best Of My Love/You Can't Get It   Polydor
07-77 JOHN LEES - Child Of The Universe/Kes (A Major Fancy) Harvest

Selected Non-UK Singles

1983   Ring Of Changes (remix)/Blow Me Down [Germany]   Polydor
1987   Panic (edited remix)/All My Life [Germany]   Polydor
1987   Panic (extended remix)/All My Life [12", Germany] Polydor
1987   Panic (extended remix)/All My Life [CD, Germany] Polydor
1992   Stand Up/Rob Bolland: Is It Really True [Germany, Netherlands]   Dino
1992   Stand Up/Is It../Stand Up (Power Version) [CD, Germany, Netherlands] Dino
1982   Mockingbird (live Berlin, edit)/Rock 'N' Roll Lady (live) [Ireland]   Polydor
1974   Child Of The Universe (different recording)/Crazy City [USA, France]   Polydor
1984   I've Got A Feeling (new version)/Rebel Woman/I've Got..(edit) [12", France]   Polydor

Selected Promotional Releases

1980   Life Is For Living [1-sided in-store promo with Alan Freeman voiceover]   Polydor
1984   *The Interview Album* [spoken answers plus cue sheets] Polydor
1984   I've Got A Feeling (full new version)//Rebel Woman/I've Got.. (7" edit)   Polydor
1990   *Welcome To The Show* CD sampler [with early mix of Halfway To Freedom]   Polydor
1991   Too Much On Your Plate [fan club flexi of unreleased song from 1970] Swallowtail
1999   The Origin Of Pieces CD [fan club Christmas CD, unreleased versions] Swallowtail
2000   Strangely Mixed CD [fan club Christmas CD, unreleased song/versions] Swallowtail
2001   Au Naturel CD [fan club Christmas CD, unreleased live versions]   Swallowtail
1993   *Coca-Cola Is The Music - Live Collection 1* [with Hymn live at the T & C] PolyGram
2004   *A History Of Progressive Rock* [Mockingbird, Poor Man's .., live at T & C] Retro

Albums

BARCLAY JAMES HARVEST [Harvest, June 1970]
Taking Some Time On; Mother Dear; The Sun Will Never Shine; When The World Was Woken; Good Love Child; The Iron Maiden; Dark Now My Sky

[plus Early Morning, Mister Sunshine, So Tomorrow (BBC session), Eden Unobtainable (BBC session), Night (BBC session), Pools of Blue (BBC session), Need You Oh So Bad (BBC session), Small Time Town (BBC session), Dark Now My Sky (BBC session), I Can't Go On Without You, Eden Unobtainable, Poor Wages, Brother Thrush on remastered CD]

ONCE AGAIN [Harvest, February 1971]
She Said; Happy Old World; Song For Dying; Galadriel; Mocking Bird; Vanessa Simmons; Ball And Chain; Lady Loves

[plus Introduction - White Sails (A Seascape), Too Much On Your Plate, Happy Old World (quadraphonic mix), Vanessa Simmons (quadraphonic mix), Ball And Chain (quadraphonic mix) on remastered CD]

AND OTHER SHORT STORIES [Harvest, November 1971]
Medicine Man; Blue John's Blues; Ursula (The Swansea Song); Little Lapwing; Song With No Meaning; Harry's Song; Someone There You Know; The Poet; After The Day

[plus Brave New World (demo version), She Said (BBC session), Galadriel (BBC session), Ursula (The Swansea Song) (BBC session), Someone There You Know (BBC session), Medicine Man (BBC session) on remastered CD]

BABY JAMES HARVEST [Harvest, November 1972]
Crazy (Over You); Delph Town Morn; Summer Soldier; Thank You; One Hundred Thousand Smiles Out; Moonwater

[plus Child Of Man, I'm Over You, When The City Sleeps, Breathless, Thank You (Old Grey Whistle Test version), Medicine Man (single version), Rock And Roll Woman, The Joker, Child of Man (BBC session), Moonwater (2002 remix) on remastered CD]

EVERYONE IS EVERYBODY ELSE [Polydor, June 1974]
Child Of The Universe; Negative Earth; Paper Wings; The Great 1974 Mining Disaster; Crazy City; See Me See You; Poor Boy Blues; Mill Boys; For No One

[plus Child Of the Universe (US single version), The Great 1974 Mining Disaster (original mix), Maestoso - A Hymn In The Roof Of The World (1974 BJH recording), Negative Earth (original mix), Child Of The Universe (21st February, 1975 recording) on remastered CD]

BARCLAY JAMES HARVEST LIVE [Polydor, November 1974]
Summer Soldier; Medicine Man; Crazy City; After The Day; The Great 1974 Mining Disaster; Galadriel; Negative Earth; She Said; Paper Wings; For No One; Mockingbird

TIME HONOURED GHOSTS [Polydor, October 1975]
In My Life; Sweet Jesus; Titles; Jonathan; Beyond The Grave; Song for You; Hymn For The Children; Moongirl; One Night

[plus Child Of The Universe (13th January, 1975 recording) on remastered CD]

325

OCTOBERON [Polydor, October 1976]
The World Goes On; May Day; Ra; Rock 'N' Roll Star; Polk Street Rag; Believe In Me; Suicide?

[plus Rock 'N' Roll Star (early mix), Polk Street Rag (first mix), Ra (first mix), Rock 'N' Roll Star (Top Of The Pops recording), Suicide? (first mix) on remastered CD]

GONE TO EARTH [Polydor, September 1977]
Hymn; Love Is Like A Violin; Friend Of Mine; Poor Man's Moody Blues; Hard Hearted Woman; Sea Of Tranquility; Spirit On The Water; Leper's Song; Taking Me Higher

[plus Lied (previously unreleased), Our Kid's Kid, Hymn (single edit), Friend Of Mine (single version), Medicine Man (Live EP version) on remastered CD]

LIVE TAPES [Polydor, June 1978]
Child Of The Universe; Rock 'N' Roll Star; Poor Man's Moody Blues; Mockingbird; Hard Hearted Woman; One Night; Taking Me Higher; Suicide?; Crazy City; Jonathan; For No One; Polk Street Rag; Hymn

XII [Polydor, September 1978]
Fantasy: Loving Is Easy; Berlin; Classics: A Tale Of Two Sixties; Turning In Circles; Fact: The Closed Shop; In Search Of England; Sip Of Wine; Harbour; Science Fiction: Nova Lepidoptera; Giving It Up; Fiction: The Streets Of San Francisco

[plus Berlin (single edit), Loving Is Easy (single version), Turning In Circles (first mix), Fact: The Closed Shop (first mix), Nova Lepidoptera (ambient instrumental mix) on remastered CD]

EYES OF THE UNIVERSE [Polydor, November 1979]
Love On The Line; Alright Down Get Boogie (Mu Ala Rusic); The Song (They Love To Sing); Skin Flicks; Sperratus; Rock And Roll Lady; Capricorn; Play To The World

TURN OF THE TIDE [Polydor, May 1981]
Waiting On The Borderline; How Do You Feel Now; Back To The Wall; Highway For Fools; Echoes And Shadows; Death Of A City; I'm Like A Train; Doctor Doctor; Life Is For Living; In Memory Of The Martyrs

BERLIN - A CONCERT FOR THE PEOPLE [Polystar German ltd. ed., January 1982]
Love On the Line; Mockingbird; Rock 'N' Roll Lady; Nova Lepidoptera; Sip Of Wine; In Memory Of The Martyrs; Life Is For Living; Child Of The Universe; Berlin; Loving Is Easy; Hymn

[later released as unlimited 9-track LP with following tracks:
Berlin; Loving Is Easy; Mockingbird; Sip Of Wine; Nova Lepidoptera; In Memory Of The Martyrs; Life Is For Living; Child Of The Universe; Hymn]

RING OF CHANGES [Polydor, May 1983]
Fifties Child; Looking From The Outside; Teenage Heart; High Wire; Midnight Drug; Waiting For The Right Time; Just A Day Away (Forever Tomorrow); Paraiso Dos Cavalos; Ring Of Changes

VICTIMS OF CIRCUMSTANCE [Polydor, April 1984]
Sideshow; Hold On; Rebel Woman; Say You'll Stay; For Your Love; Victims Of Circumstance; Inside My Nightmare; Watching You; I've Got A Feeling

FACE TO FACE [Polydor, January 1987]
Prisoner Of Your Love; He Said Love; Alone In The Night; Turn The Key; Guitar Blues; African; Following Me; All My Life; Panic; Kiev [plus You Need Love on CD/MC, On The Wings Of Love on CD only]

GLASNOST [Polydor, April 1988]
Berlin; Alone In The Night; Hold On; African; On The Wings Of Love; Poor Man's Moody Blues; Love On The Line; Medicine Man; Kiev; Hymn [plus Turn The Key and He Said Love on CD and MC only]

WELCOME TO THE SHOW [Polydor, March 1990]
The Life You Lead; Lady Macbeth; Cheap The Bullet; Welcome To The Show; John Lennon's Guitar; Halfway To Freedom; African Nights; Psychedelic Child; Where Do We Go; If Love Is King [plus Origin Earth and Shadows On The Sky on CD and MC only]

CAUGHT IN THE LIGHT [Polydor, June 1993]
Who Do We Think We Are; Knoydart; Copii Romania; Back To Earth; Cold War; Forever Yesterday (longer version on MC); The Great Unknown; Spud-U-Like; Silver Wings; Once More; A Matter Of Time; Ballad Of Denshaw Mill

RIVER OF DREAMS [Polydor Germany, May 1997]
Back In The Game; River Of Dreams; Yesterday's Heroes; Children Of The Disappeared; Pool Of Tears; Do You Believe In Dreams (Same Chance For Everyone); (Took Me) So Long; Mr. E; Three Weeks To Despair; The Time Of Our Lives

BBC IN CONCERT 1972 [EMI 2CD, May 2002]
CD 1 (mono): Mocking Bird; Medicine Man; Galadriel; Summer Soldier; The Poet; After The Day; Moonwater; Dark Now My Sky
CD 2 (stereo): Mocking Bird; Medicine Man; Moonwater; Summer Soldier; The Poet; After The Day; Galadriel; Dark Now My Sky

Barclay James Harvest Through The Eyes Of John Lees Albums

NEXUS [Eagle, February 1999]
Festival!; The Iron Maiden; Brave New World; Hors d'Oeuvre; Mocking Bird; Sitting Upon A Shelf; Hymn; The Devils That I Keep; Titles; Float; Loving Is Easy; Star Bright

REVIVAL - LIVE 1999 [Eagle, March 2000]
A Devilish Intro; She Said; Festival!; For No One; The Iron Maiden; Hors d'Oeuvre; Mocking Bird; Harbour; River Of Dreams; Poor Man's Moody Blues; New Song (Old Story); Brave New World; Galadriel; Loving Is Easy; Star Bright

[reissued as limited 2CD Tour Edition in November 2000 with bonus disc containing: Suicide?; Brother Thrush; Mr. E; Hymn plus screensaver]

Barclay James Harvest Featuring Les Holroyd Albums

REVOLUTION DAYS [M Records, February 2002]
It's My Life; Missing You; That Was Then... This Is Now; Prelude; January Morning; Quiero El Sol; Totally Cool; Life Is For Living; Sleepy Sunday; Revolution Day; Marlene (from the Berlin Suite)

[reissued in August 2003 by Pure Music with extra track "Love On The Line"]

LIVE IN BONN, 30th OCTOBER 2002 [Pure Music, October 2003]
It's My Life; Revolution Day; Yesterday's Heroes; Prelude; January Morning; Rock 'N' Roll Star; The Song (They Love To Sing); Life Is For Living; Marlene

Solo Albums

JOHN LEES - A MAJOR FANCY [Harvest, July 1977]
Untitled No.1 - Heritage; Child Of the Universe; Kes (A Major Fancy); Untitled No.2; Sweet Faced Jane; Witburg Night; Long Ships; Untitled No.3

[remastered CD issued in October 1999 by Eagle Records with extra tracks:
Please Be With Me; Best Of My Love; You Can't Get It]

WOOLLY WOLSTENHOLME - MÆSTOSO [Polydor, October 1980]
Sail Away; Quiet Islands; A Prospect Of Whitby; Lives On The Line; Patriots; Gates Of Heaven (14/18); American Excess; Mæstoso - A Hymn In The Roof Of The World; Waveform

WOOLLY WOLSTENHOLME - TOO LATE... [Swallowtail, October 1989, ltd. MC]
Too Much, Too Loud, Too Late; Deceivers All
Has To Be A Reason; Down The Line; All Get Burned

MÆSTOSO - ONE DROP IN A DRY WORLD [Eclectic, May 2004]
The Bells, THE BELLS!; Blood And Bones; A Waiting Game; It's U (Sixties mix); Souk; One Drop In A Dry World; A.N.S.S.; The End Of The Road; Explorers; 2 a.m.; The Starving People of the World All Thank You for your Time; Carpet

[First 1,000 copies include bonus disc ("Second Splash"), with:
It's U (the over-sixties mix); Flip; Music for The Wind In The Willows; The Starving People... (short version); Requiem from Blood And Bones; It's U (Eighties demo); A Waiting Game (version with Craig Fletcher on vocals); The Angelus; Camelherd Hit By Falling Building]

MÆSTOSO - FIDDLING MEANLY [Eclectic, February 2005]
Abendrot; The Bells, THE BELLS!; Deceivers All; Has To Be A Reason; In Search Of England; The Iron Maiden; Sunday Bells; Poor Wages; The Poet/After The Day; The Will To Fly; A Prospect Of Whitby; Harbour; Early Morning; Big Organ End

MÆSTOSO - GRIM [Eclectic, September 2005]
Coming Soon To A Cinema Near You; Through A Storm; Love Is ... ; A Lark; That's The Price You Pay; The Iceman Cometh; Hebden Bridge; Loot; Harp + Carp; Birds; Location, Location, Location; Abendrot; Overture: Marsch Burleske; *Pas* de Deux; Scene From A London Flat

Selected Compilations

EARLY MORNING ONWARDS [EMI/Starline, September 1972]
Early Morning; Poor Wages; Brother Thrush; Mr.Sunshine; Taking Some Time On; Mother Dear; Mocking Bird; Song With No Meaning; I'm Over You; Child Of Man; After The Day

THE COMPACT STORY OF BARCLAY JAMES HARVEST [Polydor, November 1985]
Ring Of Changes (single edit); Child Of The Universe; Jonathan; Suicide?; Berlin; Life Is For Living; Paraiso Dos Cavalos; Victims Of Circumstance (single edit); I've Got A Feeling (12" version); Mockingbird (live Berlin); Poor Man's Moody Blues (live Wembley); Hymn (live Berlin)

ANOTHER ARABLE PARABLE [EMI, October 1987]
Song With No Meaning; Mocking Bird; Rock And Roll Woman; Galadriel; Child Of Man; She Said; Ball And Chain; Summer Soldier; Vanessa Simmons; Child Of The Universe (John Lees solo); Medicine Man (single version); Mother Dear; The Poet; After The Day

ALONE WE FLY [Connoisseur, October 1990]
Poor Boy Blues*; Crazy City (live '74); For No One (live '74); Mockingbird (live '74); Rock 'N' Roll Star*; Hymn; Our Kid's Kid; Berlin; Loving Is Easy; Love On The LIne (live Berlin); Rock 'N' Roll Lady (live Berlin); Shades Of B Hill; Fifties Child; Waiting For The RIght Time (edit); Blow Me Down; Sideshow; He Said Love (edit); On The Wings Of Love*; You Need Love*
*[tracks marked * not on CD version]*

THE HARVEST YEARS [EMI, May 1991]
Early Morning; Mr.Sunshine; Pools Of Blue; I Can't Go On Without You; Eden Unobtainable; Brother Thrush; Poor Wages; Taking Some Time On; When The World Was Woken; Good Love Child; The Iron Maiden; Dark Now My Sky; She Said; Song For Dying; Galadriel; Mocking Bird; Vanessa Simmons; Happy Old World (quadraphonic mix); Ball And Chain (quadraphonic mix); Medicine Man; Ursula (The Swansea Song); Someone There You Know; The Poet; After The Day; I'm Over You; Child Of Man; Breathless; When The City Sleeps; Summer Soldier; One Hundred Thousand Smiles Out; Moonwater; The Joker

THE BEST OF BARCLAY JAMES HARVEST [Polystar, 1991]
Hymn; Loving Is Easy (Fantasy); Berlin; Child Of The Universe; Victims Of Circumstance; Poor Man's Moody Blues; Mockingbird (live at Treptower Park, 1987); Life Is For Living; Ring Of Changes; Titles; Welcome To The Show; Sip Of Wine; John Lennon's Guitar; Rock 'N' Roll Star; Love On The Line

THE BEST OF BARCLAY JAMES HARVEST [Polydor UK, June 1992]
Hymn; Loving Is Easy (Fantasy); Berlin; Child Of The Universe; Victims Of Circumstance; Poor Man's Moody Blues; Mockingbird (live at Treptower Park, 1987); Life Is For Living; Ring Of Changes; Titles; Welcome To The Show; Stand Up; Cheap The Bullet; Rock 'N' Roll Star; Love On The Line

ENDLESS DREAM [Connoisseur, July 1996]
Child Of The Universe (unreleased version); Medicine Man pt. 1 & 2 (Live EP version); Friend Of Mine (single); Loving Is Easy (single); Life Is For Living (single); Ring Of Changes (single); Mæstoso - A Hymn In The Roof Of The World (1974 BJH version); Victims Of Circumstance (instrumental); I've Got A Feeling (7" single); Panic (extended German remix); John Lennon's Guitar (live); Play To The World (live); Forever Yesterday (full version)

EVOLUTION YEARS - THE BEST OF BARCLAY JAMES HARVEST FEATURING THE SONGS OF LES HOLROYD [Pure Music, August 2004]
Berlin (single version); Kiev; Back In the Game; Halfway To Freedom; Rock 'N' Roll Star; Cold War; The Song (They Love To Sing); Ring of Changes (single version); Friend of Mine; Victims Of Circumstance (single version); Crazy City; Moongirl; Life Is For Living; That Was Then ... This Is Now; Berlin (unplugged SWR radio recording 2003); Lebe Furs Leben (German language version of "Life Is For Living")

WOOLLY WOLSTENHOLME - SONGS FROM THE BLACK BOX [Voiceprint, June '94]
Has To Be A Reason; Down The Line; All Get Burned; Too Much, Too Loud, Too Late; Even The Night; Deceivers All; The Will To Fly; Sunday Bells; Open; Sail Away; Quiet Islands; A Prospect Of Whitby; Lives On The Line; Patriots; Gates Of Heaven (14/18); American Excess; Mæstoso - A Hymn In The Roof Of The World; Waveform

WOOLLY WOLSTENHOLME - BLACK BOX RECOVERED [Eclectic, February 2004]
Deceivers All (different mix); Has To Be A Reason; Down The Line; All Get Burned; Too Much, Too Loud, Too Late; Even The Night; The Will To Fly; Sunday Bells; Open; Why Remain; Sail Away - Demo; A Prospect Of Whitby - Demo; Patriots - Demo; Quiet Islands - Demo; American Excess - Live; Lives On The Line - Live; Deceivers All - Live; Bootham Park Elegy

Appendix B: Videos and DVDs

A CONCERT FOR THE PEOPLE - BERLIN [Polygram, 1983]
Berlin; Loving Is Easy; Mockingbird; Sip Of Wine; Nova Lepidoptera; In Memory Of The
Martyrs; Life Is For Living; Child Of The Universe; Hymn
   [recorded live at the Berlin Reichstag, 30th August, 1980]

VICTIMS OF CIRCUMSTANCE [Polygram, 1985]
Life Is For Living; Rebel Woman; Waiting For The Right Time; I've Got A Feeling; Rock 'N'
Roll Lady; Paraiso Dos Cavalos; Poor Man's Moody Blues; Victims Of Circumstance; For Your
Love; Child Of The Universe; Hymn
   [recorded live at Wembley Arena, 13th October, 1984]

GLASNOST [Channel 5, 1988]
Poor Man's Moody Blues; Alone In The Night; On The Wings Of Love; African; Love On The
Line; Berlin; Medicine Man; Kiev; Life Is For Living*; Hymn
   [recorded live in Treptower Park East Berlin, 14th July 1987]

THE BEST OF BARCLAY JAMES HARVEST - X LIVE VIDEOS [Polygram, 1991]
Loving Is Easy; Mocking Bird; Sip Of Wine; Child Of The Universe; Poor Man's Moody Blues;
Victims Of Circumstance; Love On The Line; Berlin; Life Is For Living; Hymn
   [German compilation from the above three videos]

THE BEST OF BARCLAY JAMES HARVEST LIVE [Virgin, 1992]
Mockingbird; Cheap The Bullet; Medicine Man; Play To The World; Child Of The Universe;
Life Is For Living; John Lennon's Guitar; Suicide; Rock 'N' Roll Lady; Berlin; Poor Man's
Moody Blues; Stand Up; Shadows On The Sky; Hymn
   [recorded live at the London Town & Country Club, 16th February, 1992]

CAUGHT LIVE [DVD, Classic Pictures, March 2002]
   *[50 minute documentary film of the band's 1977 tour plus 30 minutes recorded live at
   the Theatre Royal, Drury Lane, London, on 30th June, 1974]*

25th ANNIVERSARY CONCERT [DVD, Classic Rock Productions, February 2003]
Mockingbird; Medicine Man; Play To The World; Life Is For Living; Rock 'N' Roll Lady; Poor
Man's Moody Blues; Stand Up; Hymn
   [edited version of the *Best Of BJH Live* video above]

THE ULTIMATE ANTHOLOGY [DVD, Ragnarock, April 2004]
Mockingbird; Medicine Man; Play To The World; Life Is For Living; Rock 'N' Roll Lady; Poor
Man's Moody Blues; Stand Up; Hymn; Early Morning (early version); Washing Up Dishes; Mr.
Sunshine (early version)
   [as above plus 15 minute Granada TV film of the band at Preston House from 1968]

BJH FEATURING LES HOLROYD - ON THE ROAD [DVD, Pure Music, January 2005]
It's My Life; Revolution Day; Yesterday's Heroes; Prelude; January Morning; Rock 'N' Roll
Star; The Song (They Love To Sing); That Was Then...This Is Now; Berlin; Life Is For Living;
Marlene (from The Berlin Suite); Love On The Line; Shadows On The Sky; Lebe Für's Leben
   [recorded live in Germany, October/November 2002]

Credits

Our grateful thanks go to the following for supplying moral support, photographs and other material used in the book:-

Mike Adams, Kari Ahtiala; Ian Alexander; Ana Azevedo, Paul Baker and Lisa Bowles; Lothar Balke; James Barry; Gabi Bauer; Tim Beckwith, Stuart Berry; Bill Bisch; Damian Blakemore; Sam Bogner; Stefan Bouton; David Bradbury, Dara Brady; Jean Brenas; Peter Brooks; Eddie and Cath Bust; Ian Chennell; Philippe Claerhout; Paul Connell; Wiebke Conrad; Paul Cox; Patrick Cross, Kev Crossley; Sue Curtis; Henk de Jonge, Marco de Niet; Johan Drejenstam, Julie Dyson; Martin Ellis; Barry Falselager; Gary Faulkner, Jürgen Fegers, Paul Ferris; Ueli Frey; Urs Freytag; Andreas Gab; Steve Gearing; Olivier Gille; Helen Goodman; Mark Gregson; Gary and Steve Heap; Jouko Heikkala, Joanne Hensman; Alan and Colin Hesketh; Steve Hibbard; Alister Hill; Stéphan Hill; Steve Hillyard; Steve Hingley; Gordon Hudson; Volker Ide; Geoff and Janet Iles; Yuko Imamura; Rob Ironmonger; David Jeffery; Peter Jung; Stefan Kaldi; Richard Kierton; Robert Kooijman; Evelyn Krause; Andreas Kubik, Inny Kuhlmann; Rick Kulik; Sabine Küssner; Jürgen Langanki; Stefan Lauer; Paul Leader, Gregor Lellek; Marina Lenti; Rupert Lenz; Lyell Loyd; Terry Luck; Grant Mason, Malcolm McInnes; Mike Melnyk; Kevin Metchear; Andrew Môn Hughes; Bjørn Åge Mossin, Toshi Motoki; Mike Muller; Dagmar Müller; Willi Murray, Michael Neumeister; Pete Noons, Matthias Oeschger; Paul Ogden; *The Oldham Evening Chronicle,* Johnny Olsen, Ana Paula Paiva, Peter Pforr; Pigeon, Roger Pilling; Philippe Plazenet; Claire Powell; Rob Price; Andreas Raschke; Angel Reichert; Christian Reiter, Stewart Renwick; Janet Richardson; Stephen Roberts; Andreas Rohde; Kate Russell; Frank Rybinski, David Saingery; Birgit, Micki and Siggi Scherrer; Jon Schick; Uwe Schuster; Dominic Scott; Albert Siebenlist; Martin Smith; Tina Smith; Paula Southern, Christian Stahl, Rodger Stankey, Robin and Barbara Stapleford; Kevin Sterry; Uwe Strubbe; Chris Symank, Ryszard Szafranski; Brian Taylor; Ann Thiry; Rolf Tombült; Richard Tucker, Reza Vakil, Henning Volb, Thomas Vollmer; René Vucko, Peter Wadsworth, Frank Wagener; Kev Walker, Karl Walsh; Heather Went; Graham Wheelwright; Mike Whitehead; Birgit Wiggermann; Dennis Wilkinson; Georgie Wisniewski, David Witts, Bridget Wright; Hans-Jürgen Zahner

Whilst every effort has been made to trace photographers and copyright owners of the pictures used in this book, in some cases it has not been possible to establish the identity of the people concerned. If you believe that your work has been used without credit, please let us know and we will give due credit on the Barclay James Harvest web site and in any future editions of the book.

Index

Updates

Corrections and updates for this book will be published online by the International BJH Fan Club at

www.bjharvest.co.uk/updates.htm

If you have any corrections, please send them to us at ibjhfc@bjharvest.co.uk or by post to the address below:

International BJH Fan Club
Hamble Reach
Oslands Lane
Lower Swanwick
SO31 7EG
UK